Hūlili

Multidisciplinary Research
on Hawaiian Well-Being

Volume 11, Number 1

Special Issue:
No ka Pono o ka Lāhui

KAMEHAMEHA PUBLISHING
KAMEHAMEHA SCHOOLS
HONOLULU, HAWAIʻI

COVER ART AND ILLUSTRATIONS: Naiʻa Lewis

DESIGN: Naiʻa Lewis, Salted Logic

The cover illustration is a visual narrative of the themes within this special edition. Each section illustration then pulls elements from the cover that are relevant and folds them into a more expansive expression of the issues addressed by the authors. The imagery–from birth and death, intergenerational trauma, aloha ʻāina, and political independence to gender identity, perpetuating indigenous knowledge, and decolonizing our minds–seeks to showcase our eternal connection to the land, and each other, despite the wholesale shift in power that has been witnessed in the Hawaiian Islands across the last two hundred years.

Hūlili: Multidisciplinary Research on Hawaiian Well-Being
Vol. 11, No. 1
Special Issue: No ka Pono o ka Lāhui

Printed in Auburn Hills, Michigan.
ISSN 1547-4526
ISBN 978-0-87336-463-8

MIX
From responsible sources
FSC® C099992
FSC
www.fsc.org

CONTENTS

No ka pono o ka lāhui

In the title of her 1992 landmark book, *Native Land and Foreign Desires*, Dr. Lilikalā Kameʻeleihiwa posed a pointed question that has motivated much of the research on Hawaiian well-being over the past two decades: "Pehea lā e pono ai?" This concise but profound question is essentially asking, how can we restore balance and maintain our ancestral relationships with our ʻāina, against rapacious and historically rooted forces of dispossession? Implicit in this question is an acknowledgment that healthy relationships with our lands and waters are foundational to healthy Hawaiian communities and individuals—which invites us to contemplate how we protect, nurture, and live such relationships in the contexts of our times.

Today, more than twenty-five years after Kameʻeleihiwa first posed this question, we have made tremendous gains on many fronts. Still, our lāhui continues to face significant political and economic barriers that keep us from full health and pono. Studies completed in the early 1980s, such as the *Native Hawaiian Educational Assessment* project and the *Native Hawaiians Study Commission* report, showed that Kānaka Maoli had the highest rates of family poverty, incarceration, school absentee rates, and various negative health indicators, including suicide and depression.[1] Both the 2014 edition of *Ka Huakaʻi: Native Hawaiian Educational Assessment* and the *2015 Native Hawaiian Data Book* show that, for our people as a whole, many social and economic trends remain seriously inequitable and have not changed much since the early 1980s. Moving from statistical to experiential data, one only has to look around to see that the number of houseless or near-houseless Kānaka has dramatically increased in the last generation. Many Hawaiian scholars and community leaders describe these conditions as part of an ongoing and multifaceted US occupation.

Despite these injustices and complex challenges, our lāhui has enacted massive resurgences, such as mobilizing to protect Mauna a Wākea, restoring fishponds and loʻi, articulating ʻāina-based EAducation, and initiating self-governance efforts at neighborhood, ahupuaʻa, moku, and national levels. All of these issues are taken up in this special issue of *Hūlili*.

This volume highlights how Kānaka Maoli and our allies are striving, across disciplines and our pae ʻāina, for justice and balance for our lāhui. The theme of this special issue, "No ka pono o ka lāhui," foregrounds this work in our communities to restore pono to our people and ʻāina. Conventional academic articles and creative nonfiction pieces reveal ways that Kānaka struggle with and build alternatives to historically rooted systems of power—whether in research practices, environmental regulatory frameworks, or refusals of structures that harm ancestral relationships.

In the initial call for papers, we encouraged submissions that draw on community-based research. This resulted in a range of topics such as urban planning, fisheries, houseless community organizing, and constitution writing. A common theme emerged from these submissions: Authors are engaging with Hawaiian communities and are working on specific, real-world issues that matter to the lives of everyday Kānaka. As guest editors for this special issue, we also made a specific call for articles on tough, contentious issues, such as natural resource management in a time of climate change, the proposed construction of the Thirty Meter Telescope (TMT) on Mauna a Wākea, and the Naʻi Aupuni-hosted ʻAha of 2016. This volume provides much-needed perspectives on these and other issues and offers guidance for moving forward as a lāhui.

Additionally, this special issue introduces frameworks that are not yet common in existing scholarship but are critical to envisioning the ways we restore pono in our lives as individuals, families, and lāhui. For instance, articles by Kauanui, Maile, and Young use anarchism and queer theory as tools for understanding contemporary Hawaiian life and Hawai'i's nuanced political context. Other articles in this volume build new/old lexicons that bridge ancestral knowledge with disciplinary traditions that developed outside of Hawai'i, such as urban planning and marine biology. The contributions of Freitas and La Valle et al. are examples of this syncretic work.

Woven throughout the volume are short stories about realities faced by everyday Kānaka: Caregiving. Trying to make ends meet. Suffering various forms of violence. But, most of all, living with dignity. We include these stories to ground our discussions about Hawaiian well-being and pono in the diverse, lived experiences of Hawaiian people. These creative nonfiction pieces were written by University of Hawai'i students in Noelani's Contemporary Native Hawaiian Politics course. The authors, of varying ages and backgrounds, wrote these accounts in response to the book, *Big Happiness: The Life and Death of a Modern Hawaiian Warrior*.

In *Big Happiness,* Mark Panek tells the story of his friend, Percy Kipapa, a young man from Waikāne, who was a professional sumo wrestler in Japan from 1991–97. Percy's life came to a tragic end when he was murdered, after returning home at the conclusion of his sumo career. The book unravels the story of Percy's death and related addictions, connecting these events to a long history of violence stemming from the US occupation, settler colonization, and capitalist exploitation of Hawaiian lands and bodies. In a dialogue with Noe's students, Mark told us about how and why he wrote the book:

> I started writing about Percy to honor his memory for his parents, but all of my research revealed his position in the middle of land-use issues that

have been ruining Hawai'i since at least statehood. . . . Percy had grown up on kuleana land that should have included the 59 acres stolen during my own lifetime. After you absorb the pain of this knowledge . . . words like "historical trauma" and "colonization" are far too abstract. But Percy's story is as compelling as stories get, and it makes us pay attention to all of these abstractions and hopefully do something about them rather than dismiss them as "politics" and move on. . . . We all know a Percy.[2]

Based on the premise that "we all know a Percy," students wrote stories about a Kanaka whom they knew well and whose individual life could be connected to larger structures of power. Some of the stories, like Percy's, are tragic, and others are hopeful.

We hope this special issue of *Hūlili* will provoke readers to think about how macro-level social and historical forces impact the individual lives of everyday Hawaiian people. We also hope this volume will add to the toolbox of ways to uplift the collective lāhui Hawai'i and the 'āina that gives us life. In the end, we hope the articles and stories gathered here contribute to the stirring of more efforts no ka pono o ka lāhui.

Noelani Goodyear-Ka'ōpua
Erin Kahunawaika'ala Wright

---

1. Kamehameha Schools Bishop Estate. (1983). *Native Hawaiian educational assessment project report.* Honolulu, Hawai'i: Author; Native Hawaiians Study Commission. (1983). *Native Hawaiians study commission: Report on the culture, needs and concerns of Native Hawaiians, persuant to public law 96-565, title III.* Final report, Vol. 1. Washington, DC: Author.

2. Mark Panek, personal communication, September 17, 2015.

Aloha ʻĀina COSMOLOGIES

Home-Free and Nothing (...)-Less: A Queer Cosmology of Aloha ʻĀina

KALANIOPUA YOUNG

Violence is what we're used to. . . .
We are no longer shocked
by raids on what is left
in the pitched tents and tarps,
our evictions from beach to beach
and park to park, the poverty
of unfurling fists open only
to the smallest of handouts.

(Brandy Nālani McDougall, "The Second Gift")

CORRESPONDENCE MAY BE SENT TO:
Kalaniopua Young
84-965 Farrington Highway, B212
Waiʻanae, Hawaiʻi 96792
Email: youngtk@hawaii.edu

Hūlili: Multidisciplinary Research on Hawaiian Well-Being, Vol. 11, No. 1

As a (qu)id,[1] I learned that Kānaka Maoli were not homeless, because Hawai'i *is* our home. I learned this from my mom's sister, Aunty Nalu,[2] who told me that I had kuleana for the land and people of Hawai'i and that such a responsibility was to be taken seriously.

It was 1993, around the time of the centennial that marked one hundred years of the illegal US invasion of our islands. Aunty Nalu had left the service industry as a cook to support land-based reclamations in Wai'anae, a ten-mile leeward coastal region on O'ahu known for Hawaiian sovereignty, indigenous resistance, and environmental justice activism. These social movements had a profound impact on the people of Wai'anae, especially Aunty Nalu, who lived by the motto, "If I don't grow it, I don't know it." Aunty Nalu is not well known in the mainstream Hawaiian movement. She is that kolohe aunty from Nānākuli Hawaiian Homestead who rarely traveled outside her comfort zone of Wai'anae, turning to hotwiring and stealing cars to make money and, on occasion, enjoying a good police chase up Wai'anae Valley for fun. I remember how some of us kids would be screaming "cheeeehooo!" all the way up the mountain road, police sirens blaring behind us, pakalolo in the air, with Aunty Nalu cackling at the helm of yet another stolen land yacht. Somehow, Aunty Nalu always managed to escape capture—even in those huge Cadillac Eldorados from the 1970s.

A mother of three, Aunty Nalu defiantly rejected the state's treatment of Hawaiians. She often tore down NO TRESPASSING signs in the mountains and near the ocean if they were posted by the state, and she refused to register her car to an illegally occupying government entity. Moreover, she did not fit the gendered proscriptions emboldened by the state. She dressed in men's jeans, T-shirts, and tank tops and gave motherhood a masculine swagger by challenging the colonizing gendered expectations placed on her body. Except for a high-pitched cackle inherited from the Aken and Carlisle bloodlines, she was pretty "butch." She drank Budweiser, occasionally strummed the ukulele and, at family gatherings, argued with my cousin Kaipo about going rogue and taking back the 'āina (land, all that feeds). "I may be living on da beach but brah, I not homeless, I '*home-free.*' I take care of dis 'āina and dis 'āina takes care of me." She would then add, "Nobody going give us our land. We gotta give it our all and grab what we can before we lose everything that belongs to us."

At some point in my adolescence, Aunty Nalu began teaching away the problematic image of homeless Hawaiians from my mind, replacing it with an intimate, empathic solidarity for Hawaiians living out of a tent on the beach. When my mom was in prison, I'd go and stay with Aunty Nalu at Nānākuli Beach Park. It was there that I began to challenge the assumptions about Hawaiian bums mooching for money—stereotypes I had heard about from middle-class relatives living in single-family houses in the mountain valleys. Aunty Nalu refused being boxed in by the category of "homeless loser" that people like my cousins and other family members complained about. Instead, she was aware that the problem of displacing Hawaiians was the result of systemic and intergenerational trauma—the overthrow of our nation and the resultant state of Hawai'i being only the tip of the iceberg. She was concerned about the laziness of complacent Hawaiians and embodied an 'Ōiwi (Hawaiian in the bones) poetics—taking the runoff water from public beach showers to grow kalo or taro at a time when the US occupation became increasingly militarized and hostile to Hawaiian tent cities, particularly tent village residents at Mākua, who were evicted in 1996.

In 2014, after almost twenty years of beach bum living, Aunty Nalu moved to Alaska to care for a daughter with special needs. Nonetheless, it is through Aunty Nalu's teachings that I come to approach a "home-free" rather than an "anything less" kind of perspective. Framed within a distinctly queer theorization and a broader houseless or homeless discourse—a home-free perspective repositions, and indeed transforms, libelous poison into medicine and enables us to regard all people as whole and complete unto themselves. Processes of coloniality, active resistances to it, and simultaneous reclamations of the self in defiance of it—distinguish a "home-free" subjectivity from that of being merely houseless or homeless. I cherish the relatives who, like Aunty Nalu, remind me that they may be without a house but are, in fact, home-free. These relatives see land and family as a site of direct action to reclaim ʻāina—including one's own body, mind, and soul—and the broad sense of inclusive nourishment that results from this reclamation.

Layla

In 2011, Layla, a tall and thin sixty-two-year-old Kanaka Maoli māhūwahine (transgender woman), walked out of her Chevrolet van for the last time and headed for what she then referred to as "the bush"—a tent village wedged between a high school and a boat harbor on the leeward coast of Oʻahu, now referred to as Puʻuhonua o Waiʻanae. After being fired from a nine-year janitorial job, she lost her apartment and, eventually, her van. Though at first Layla despised Puʻuhonua o Waiʻanae, she came to acknowledge and accept that life there was better than having to serve the interests of a workplace built on the systematic discrimination of māhū people. At Puʻuhonua o Waiʻanae, she lived free of such violence and survived on less than thirty dollars a week—a manageable rate subsidized by dumpster diving, bartering, and reciprocal gift giving.

Moreover, the indifference Layla once enjoyed while living in her apartment, free from the raids and evictions taking place in public parks, was no longer an option. She was booted from parking lots, kicked off beaches, and disrespected in shelters by police officers and security guards. Puʻuhonua o Waiʻanae saved her life and shielded her from this harsh reality. At Puʻuhonua o Waiʻanae, the community polices itself and provides for its residents without the economic and political support of the cistem, a systemic privileging of cisgender and heteronormative nuclear family structures. Layla and other Puʻuhonua o Waiʻanae residents work tirelessly to keep the place clean. Many of them know the intimate tortures of having one's belongings thrown into dumpsters. They hope that by organizing themselves and taking initiative they might stave off such violence.

At first, Layla was nervous to enter the village. She didn't know when a raid would happen, or how she would defend her meager belongings from thieves. The blue and black tarps, the tents—the perceived harshness of the people—weren't exactly welcoming. Nonetheless, Layla persevered and was pleasantly surprised to find a well-organized village setting protected by a group of queer Hawaiian women. One of the residents even hosted her for a few days until Layla was able to get on her own two feet.

In this essay, I focus on gender nonconformity and home-free Kanaka resilience. Such stories situate a queer cosmology of aloha ʻāina; that is, a theory of gender-nonconforming origination, persistence, and evolution within a broader social movement to "soften" the hardness of violence. I am particularly interested in unsettling and transforming "cissettler" family formations that shun rather than embrace their queer and transgender kin.

Pu'uhonua is a Hawaiian concept of place. On one hand, it literally translates to "earth barrier," and on the other, it means "city of refuge." In this essay, I observe the queerness of pu'uhonua—the inclusive atmosphere it provides and the free-flowing social nature of its culture within and against the state. This piece focuses on anarcha-indigeneity to demonstrate how respect for one's self and others builds upon a social network that diverges, however unequally, from its original intended purpose: to serve as a temporary holding zone for the state.

As an indigenous and autonomous space for gender-nonconforming Kānaka, displaced Pacific families, and abandoned settlers from the continental United States, the village is rebranding itself not simply as a tent city but as a model refuge for the 'ohana, a fully functional and inclusive chosen family system. This essay stems from the trust established with people in this 'ohana and the emo-spiritual labor of organizing political dissent toward addressing the urgent, everyday needs of Pu'uhonua o Wai'anae residents. The stories shared here are generally overlooked in mainstream news reports. However, these narratives are profoundly influential in weaving together the broader experiences and critiques of colonial land displacement, homophobia, and transphobia experienced by and among Kānaka in contemporary Hawai'i. More importantly, the village allows us to plant the seeds of an increasingly important project to address the issue of land displacement through the active repossession of lands, waters, and tools to empower our own liberation from the bottom up.

For Layla, Pu'uhonua o Wai'anae offered not only the promise of escapement and safety, but also a queer sense of belonging and healing without the added pressures of paying for costly rent and bills. In particular, it enabled a re(knewed) sense of freedom within herself to reject the gendered social expectations placed on her body resulting from the cistem in which she had lived and worked throughout her life. Despite ongoing challenges such as access to public sanitation, Layla expresses that her well-being has improved since moving to the village. As she lovingly points out, "Everybody here is ugly, just like me" (meant as a term of endearment). For some people, Pu'uhonua o Wai'anae represents economic and political abandonment, a place where people are sent to die. And for others still, it is a last resort. For Layla, however, Pu'uhonua o Wai'anae has become a reliable home where a queer love ethic activates the transformation of violence.

In her poem "The Second Gift," Brandy Nālani McDougall describes the everyday violence of houseless raids and evictions in contemporary Hawai'i as something that no longer shocks us. In this essay, I want to push McDougall's depiction to the horizon by showing how the *people* of Pu'uhonua o Wai'anae, including the aforementioned māhūwahine, transform themselves and their larger social support networks for the better. I argue that in the queer-managed space of Pu'uhonua o Wai'anae, there is a queer soul that challenges and indeed transforms the "gift" of US settler occupation and the economic and political landscape under which it stands. Such a soul supports the bare necessities: autonomy, land, privacy, sleep, and water. It disarms and indeed tenderizes the people to care again, to wake up and act upon that intuition. Today, the people of Pu'uhonua o Wai'anae are unfurling their "fists . . . to the smallest of handouts," and they are also advocating for new directions in the larger Hawaiian movement. Perhaps this is the seedling of possibility—the promise of contrasted visions for how we might better work together to resolve the gendered conundrums of our time and make us "green and tender once again" (McDougall, 2014, p. 253). In this restorative condition, might we overcome the numbing, everyday violence of eviction, scarcity, and indifference?

Today, it is nearly impossible to talk about Hawaiʻi without first confronting the crises of drugs, housing, and land. Scholars, doctors, community leaders, and activists all acknowledge the overwhelming increase of these scourges in contemporary Hawaiʻi. And yet, rather than generating on-the-ground, low-cost, indigenous, localized, and organic alternatives, colonial frameworks continue to dominate the perceptions of healing as a biomedical and statistical game without pleasure and fun. Entering the village in 2014, however, I was struck by the bold leadership against the cistem as a matter of fun and of pleasure. Thus, it became clear that a crucial part of both my internal and external spiritual journey back to this city of refuge, this ancestral place of indigenous well-being, was its capacity to promote aloha with dignity and calm in the face of overwhelming systemic chaos and failure, including the neocolonial regulation of Hawaiian subjectivity.

In line with Mark Rifkin's work, villagers are redefining the terms of indigenous autonomy within the social context of colonial land displacement and cultural repossession by defending their autonomy and freedom as Hawaiians (Rifkin, 2009, p. 102). Such villagers are simultaneously mobilizing collective self-sufficiency and political transformation of the "bare life" of tents on the beach by bringing people to consciousness about Hawaiian land struggles and by activating creative solidarities. It is presumed, according to Agamben (1998), that the bare life is incapable of making autonomous decisions. However, the people of puʻuhonua challenge this characterization and do so with increasing regularity as the village itself continues to grow its political power, digital presence, and cultural importance for all people of Hawaiʻi who can relate to being priced out of paradise. The village embraces the bare life and demands a second look at the analytical capacity it offers for transforming oppressive settler relations. Within this transformation the future is optimistic, however cruel or bleak it may at first appear.

Puʻuhonua o Waiʻanae challenges the discursive limits of homelessness as a category for purposes of policy and protocol. Unlike state-based programs that focus on providing shelter to transition out of homelessness as a matter of discipline, the village reaffirms the cultural restoration of ʻāina-based relationship building through direct action as a matter of mending relations of harmony. The distinction between those who are home-free, homeless, and/or houseless is mostly absent in contemporary debates about what to do about the "homeless problem." In this article, I reposition the conversation to explore how Kānaka Maoli, in particular, understand "re-placing" themselves temporally and spatially back on the land (Fermantez, 2012) rather than opting for other available housing "solutions" that are often taken as a stand-in for universalized care in larger legislative contexts.

Oh Back! To Paragraph 175

By the summer of 2015, Layla was doing odd jobs, recycling cans, and trading goods and services with fellow villagers at Puʻuhonua o Waiʻanae to meet daily needs.

She refused an offer for a room in a nearby shelter facility to maintain these relationships. Moreover, past experiences with transphobia by staff and residents at the shelter facility prompted her to turn down the offer. "They forced me to use the men's bathroom against my will," she told me (field notes, March 2017).

The effects of transphobia in her life have left Layla reluctant to accept offers for work and shelter from unknown sources. This is intergenerational trauma. In 2015, she declined a job offer at a nearby resort, afraid that she'd be fired for being māhū. "I'm too old to deal with that shit," she told me on a hot Sunday. "I just want to work in my yard and take these recyclables in to buy food for my cats and dogs" (field notes, November 2016). The shit Layla is referring to is racism, cisheteropatriarchy, and capitalism—institutionalized technologies of governmental control that moved from making her life hard to unbearable. These institutions have undergirded the various settler logics and assimilation technologies aimed at erasing Layla's Hawaiian ways of knowing and being. For Hawaiian transgender women, or māhū, the risk of state violence has compounded encounters with these technologies. Many transgender and queer people of color have a healthy distrust for law enforcement officers due to past experiences.

In 1963, the state of Hawai'i passed a public ordinance dubiously termed by the courts as "deception under the law," or paragraph 175, which forced māhū to wear a button that read, "I am a boy." The buttons were distributed at local nightclubs such as the Glades, a hotspot in Honolulu for māhū and drag performers. Layla recalls having to wear these buttons every night in town, especially in the 1960s and '70s when Vietnam soldiers were making their way to Honolulu for redeployment and recreation. She recalls police beating up "the queens"

(māhū) who refused to wear the buttons and the sheer brutality forced upon the girls who did. The ordinance was borrowed from the Nazi military code, also known as paragraph 175, which sent thousands to death camps during the Holocaust for trivial things like cross-dressing and homosexuality (Mancini, 2010). Penalties for not wearing the button carried a minimum sentence of a year in jail and a one thousand dollar fine.

Sheila, another village māhū in her sixties, a friend of Layla, recalls having to run from law enforcement with or without the button on. She explains, "They didn't care about us girls. All they wanted was to beat us up, rape us, and dispose of our bodies" (field notes, April 2017). Both Sheila and Layla lost a number of māhū friends during the 1970s and '80s. One girl, according to Layla, disappeared under mysterious circumstances, her body found mutilated and disposed of in the Ala Wai canal. Sheila, a friend of the murdered queen, recalls how lax law enforcement was with the handling of the investigation. She believes the officers were responsible for her friend's disappearance. "It was premeditated murder, those assholes took my friend's life" (field notes, April 2017).

A Refuge Fit for Queens

At the village, Layla expresses feeling like the days of people "clocking her t," or giving her weird double takes because of her transgender positionality, are behind her. She feels safe in the village. Adding to her level of comfort is the fact that the village is run almost entirely by gender-nonconforming Hawaiian women, including gay and transgender women, as well as those who position themselves as politically queer and/or accepting of LGBTQ people. Pu'uhonua o Wai'anae is a Hawaiian cultural sanctuary that naturally includes protections for transgender and queer individuals from the dehumanization of capitalism and cisheteronormativity, two systems upheld by a belief that only two genders (male and female) and heterosexuality serve as the only productive norms for market economics. The village offers a queer alternative to such a belief. Hawaiian and other Pacific families, for example, have long carved out a place for māhū (trans) and aikāne (gay) individuals in society. Aunty Laka, the village's second-in-command, was raised by "da kine" (queer and transgender) relatives and pledges to maintain the village's queerness in this way.

However, it isn't all sunshine and roses. "Living in the village is a full-time job," Layla reminds me. "You have to haul your own water, build your own hale (house), and carry out at least ten hours of community service once a month to remove rubbish from the village." Such cleanups are made possible with the help of Hawaiians from the nearby community. One person, a hefty Hawaiian man from the nearby Hawaiian homestead, donates his semitruck to haul the trash once a month. On these days, volunteers from local church, school, and governmental organizations lend a hand. Still, despite all the help and support, the village has unmet needs.

The nearest bathrooms and water spigots are located hundreds of yards from the village, making it especially difficult for disabled and elderly villagers to access. Cruel optimism, as defined by Lauren Berlant (2011), is a relational double bind where one's attachment to an object sustains life, but the object itself is actually a threat to flourishing. The village represents this cruel optimism. As Layla points out, "It's better to be in a jungle that loves you than in a house that doesn't. If we had bathrooms and showers, things would be a lot better for

us." By stapling flower-print sarongs to wooden pallet walls, Layla has enough privacy to bathe fully naked. She uses water jugs to complete the task, an important ritual for her. "I don't want boils," she tells me one day, alluding to the prevalence of skin infections among villagers who bathe near the garbage-filled dumpsters and water spigots in the boat harbor parking lot. She continues, "I don't understand why the government doesn't provide us with basic stuff like toilets and showers. They know we're here" (field notes, September 2017).

The simple answer to Layla's question is that the state sees the village as an obstacle to long-term, stable, permanent housing. To build accessible sanitation facilities for the village would make it appear as though the state supports an obstacle rather than a solution. Meanwhile, public health concerns of the villagers remain an ongoing problem that has less to do with those who are without resources and more to do with those who have resources but choose not to help. An ongoing component of my research involves actively organizing partnerships, collaborating with political and community stakeholders, and working with village leaders to challenge this reductive depiction of the village.

The Fluidity of Home

Anela is a twenty-one-year-old Hawaiian-Samoan transgender resident at Puʻuhonua o Waiʻanae. She is a defiant, philosophical "spartan" with curly brown locks, ʻehu blonde streaks, and muscly calves. Her no-nonsense attitude meets with a tenacity of will that is humble, honest, and genuine. Working hard to keep the village organized and clean, Anela believes that "home" is what you make it. She spends much time caring for this idea in a multiroom tent house shared with several other young Hawaiian adults and children.

Residing with Aunty Tina, the village's "commander in chief," Anela and the crew of young folks live and conduct daily chores under sage tutelage and guidance. The campsite reminds me of my own childhood in the house on Puhano Street, where my grandma ruled. Aunty Tina is the matriarch, the glue of the 'ohana, who keeps everyone working together to make sure there is food on the table and that there is a strong sense of belonging for everyone. Anela is known as Aunty Tina's "son," an endearing term since being informally adopted by the stern leader a few years back. This informal adoption practice, or hānai kinship, is a key strength of 'ohana relationships mediated through more-than-bloodline relations rooted in intimate care and reciprocity.

Understanding the 'ohana relationship within a queer cosmology of aloha 'āina disrupts and expands ideas about Hawaiian belonging in contemporary life and the important embrace of our queer and Pacific kin. Aside from creating solidarity across racial, gender, 'āina, and housing divides, being home-free enriches the 'ohana relationship and animates the undertheorized political terrain for an expansive queer indigeneity that refuses to settle and disappear. Hawaiian epistemologist Manulani Aluli-Meyer asserts that basing a movement on money is a mistake. In this vein, I argue that a queer cosmology of aloha 'āina expresses a refusal of capitalist exploitation through chosen family arrangements of mutual reliance and collective autonomy, which are generative and effectively mobile in subverting social alienation in everyday life.

"I'm not fish like you yet," Anela tells me one day as we hike up pillbox, a mountain trail in Maile. "I don't have a preferred gender pronoun or whatever you call it. I'm okay with either 'he' or 'she,' but who knows what the future holds?" Like the tent she now lives in, home for

Anela's gender identity and expression is liminal, constructed, and flexible. It transcends the hegemonic sphere of biologically determined dichotomies that fail to capture her wholeness as "male" or "female," just as owning a rambler fails to define what it means to be "home-free." Instead, home appears to evolve, move, and adapt to the social and physical environments and orientations in which she finds herself. "Tida," she explains, as we sit on a bomb shelter to enjoy panoramic views of rolling mountains and pristine beaches, "one day I will be on hormones, go to college, and buy a house." I reply with an encouraging smile and a chuckle. This isn't a topic of discussion we'd normally have back at the village, around people who are not trans-identified. Anela is a healer, and her optimism about the future, a rare phenomenon in our village, is palpable. I am afraid that offering critical concerns might dissolve this hopeful disposition. I don't push sensitive questions and tensions. She and I are both well aware that things can, and indeed do change, with the high probability that they won't be in our favor. "I'm here to support you, Anela," I tell her while hopelessly struggling to descend down the mountainside. "Take my hand, Tida," she responds, preventing me from falling off a steep embankment. I gather my composure as we sit for a few minutes on a large gray rock surrounded by tall yellow grass near a tree with exposed roots. "We help each other," she reminds me. "Home is a journey, not a destination."

Home is a journey. For Hawaiians, working-class immigrants, and trans folk alike, this journey often involves structural violence defined and redefined by an Empire that moves from making life difficult to intolerable. In this work, we examine alterNative economies of solidarity between Hawaiians, settlers, and arrivants at Pu'uhonua o Wai'anae through the 'ohana principle, an inclusive Hawaiian concept of family that emphasizes mutual respect for all individuals making up the extended family and kinship network. We pay particular attention to its anarcha-indigenous home-making capacity within a third space of counter-Empire resistance to settle claims to land, language, and water in contemporary Hawaiʻi. Taking environmental justice, class struggle, and indigenous economies seriously, I situate the village at Puʻuhonua o Waiʻanae within a milieu of Hawaiian resistance and resurgence outside the dominant housing social structure of contemporary Hawaiʻi. In this article, I look at how villagers of Puʻuhonua o Waiʻanae perform and/or enact an anti-oppressive and non-statist form of self-determination in the largest outdoor "homeless" encampment in the United States.

According to post-Marxist philosophers Negri and Hardt, "The creative forces of the multitude that sustain Empire are also capable of autonomously constructing a counter-Empire, an alternative political organization of global flows and exchanges" (2000, p. xv). At Puʻuhonua o Waiʻanae, that counter-Empire is sustained by the ʻohana, that dwelling place of social interconnection and responsibility. Borrowing from Tongan anthropologist Epeli Hauʻofa (1993), the ʻohana serves as "our sea of islands" in the village. That is, ʻohana is a s/Pacific third space of relational belonging shared between people, place, and the more-than-human, beyond-colonial mappings of our island homes, bodies, and ideas as small, isolate, and violable.

"We use to live like dat, you know," my Aunty Mandy told me one day after hearing about my research project. "Me, your dad, everybody up-house in Waiʻanae Valley. Before the construction money, we slept outside. Those were the days. Grandma played music and we all sang, talked stories, and laughed ourselves to sleep." Aunty Mandy is my dad's sister. She is a small-framed, warm-spirited Hawaiian mahjong player from Waiʻanae who smokes American Spirit menthol lights. She lives in a four-bedroom, three-bathroom rambler in the Hawaiian Homestead of Kapolei along with her son, his wife, and their three kids. Her role in my upbringing at the house on Puhano Street cannot be overstated. She is the aunty who took me out for ice cream the year everyone forgot about my ninth birthday, the one who always said "I love you" when it counted, and the one who cried for me when I returned to Washington state for high school. "The aloha of our ʻohana is more powerful than money," she reminds me one night in Kapolei, as she lights up a cigarette. "It is aloha and ʻohana that keep us safe when we need to be cared for and loved." Interestingly, this notion of aloha, staying connected, and re-membering ʻohana, moves from up-house in Waiʻanae Valley, the new tract housing development in Kapolei, to the tent structures of Puʻuhonua o Waiʻanae, where the ʻohana continues to grow in large numbers. The ʻohana is a safety net for individuals and families facing displacement and dispossession. The strength of ʻohana lies in its ability to resist structural violence at the individual, community, and transnational level. The decentralized but closely knit organization of the ʻohana comforts the individual. It manifests itself by linking local officials and community organizations to individuals and families needing support to stop an eviction from their home. It finds expression in "talk story" among politically situated relatives to make land, water, and food resources accessible to people who need it most and can instill in the hearts and minds of the larger community that protecting people and places serves as a benefit to everyone caught in the inevitable fall of Empire.

Mapping the Counter-Empire

Some tents are canoes. Some are ramblers. Some are canoe ramblers. A few of them have multiple bedrooms. Living rooms. Kitchens. Dining areas. Upstairs, downstairs, houses made of pallets. Front yards. Backyards. Communal meeting spaces.

Beyond the design of architectural bricolage that uses available materials to make shelter, Puʻuhonua o Waiʻanae has its own map drawn and routinely updated by Aunty Laka, a middle-aged Hawaiian mother of three. Tediously documenting the 130+ campsites is no simple task, requiring periodic updates as people come and go. The map challenges the colonial techniques used to displace Native peoples from their territories through the cadastral survey, which mapped subdivisions for sale and profit.

Though not formally recognized by the state, the camp's map, the village, and what they stand for, are a radical departure from the state's portrayal of tent cities as dangerous and disorganized sites of disposability for Hawaiians who have failed to assimilate. Here, at Puʻuhonua o Waiʻanae, Hawaiians have not failed to assimilate. Rather, they have refused to accept the economic and state violence that makes life unbearable under capitalism. Here, I borrow from Mohawk anthropologist Audra Simpson the concept of refusal to better understand how the assemblage at Puʻuhonua o Waiʻanae is really about housing aloha (deep love and care) in a time of crisis beyond and within the call for economic and policy reform (Simpson, 2007).

The village is a well-known home to a restoration project for a distinctly Hawaiian place of refuge. This kind of home, however precarious, is proving surprisingly effective despite the imperfect balance of power in contemporary Hawaiʻi, which disproportionately alienates Hawaiians from the land. Hawaiian women lead the project's everyday affairs in Waiʻanae and are known for being the camp's most devoted residents.

Aunty Pearl, a Hawaiian woman in her sixties, for example, has lived here for more than twenty years; Aunty Tina, ten; and Aunty Laka, seven. On nineteen acres of undeveloped land, these Hawaiian women are leading the charge to reclaim the now radical idea that people can and indeed do create "free" and "safe" places to affirm life outside of capitalism and do so with little to no help from the state government. Taken in this vein, the village can be read as housing aloha ʻaina within a "Hawaiian Dream" that protects those suffering under the destructive spell of the American one.

Admittedly, the village is an unusual scene of chaos and confusion for the newbie and is not completely removed from the state apparatus and its policies to evict tent cities. However, there is something about tent village life here in Waiʻanae that transcends the politics of visibility and liberal recognition. Picture Gilligan's Island meets Mad Max. Mopeds, dune buggies, wooden pallets, roaming dogs, rugged men with tattoos, and tin roofs meet with well-manicured dirt pathways, home gardens, and neatly divided campsites headed by sixteen strong female defenders. At first, the village appears as a kind of postapocalyptic scenario that should be avoided at all costs. However, after taking time to become a part of it, building friendships with the people residing in it, and feeling the sunrise change the morning temperature on the skin as roosters crow to greet the day, the village becomes less scary and more like a place worth returning to.

Homeless Discourse as Settler Colonial Violence

Kānaka, or Hawaiians, are reported to make up the majority of the homeless population in Hawai'i. As alarming as this statistic appears to be, without a nuanced historical and contemporary context of land struggles, it can be misleading. In particular, statistics have the effect of entrapping Hawaiians within a settler colonial occupation that frames failure by quantifying what Hawaiians are said to be lacking. The lack of rambler housing, for example, almost always entails some kind of political intervention to justify the use of force to discipline precariously housed Hawaiian bodies. This is an old biopolitical technique with contemporary vestiges, requiring critical assessment by scholars on the consequences of Empire and how home is defined and redefined by affective relationships in the twenty-first century. Through the effect of Empire, or the ways in which imperialism shapes and structures the way people feel about homelessness, we can better understand affordable housing policies from a different perspective. Affordable housing sounds like a well-intended political intervention for homeless individuals. However, as Aunty Laka points out, "Such policies will not help the people living at Pu'uhonua o Wai'anae, because affordable housing is still out of reach for most of us and doesn't resolve our land crisis."

Along the Wai'anae coast, where the largest Hawaiian population anywhere in the world is said to reside, anarchical and indigenous forms of autonomy at Pu'uhonua o Wai'anae disrupt the naturalization of homelessness as a particularly Hawaiian social problem caused by a failure to assimilate. This autonomy challenges political interventions by delineating a critique of the current state's ongoing failure to respect Hawaiian sovereignty, our people, and our place-based values over time. It juxtaposes the limits of the state's bureaucracy with the collaborative and queer cosmology offered by an alterNative land system that prioritizes indigenous well-being, non-statist freedom, and more-than-human relations above profit and social control. This is a critical departure from state-based systems ruled by capitalist values, institutions, and settler state ideologies of indigenous elimination.

The people of Pu'uhonua o Wai'anae who are reclaiming their displaced, sometimes broken, and socially abandoned bodies as sites of spiritual import, cultural resilience, and autonomous refuge articulate an alterNative economy of solidarity and epistemic disobedience that refuses to settle for a land management system that is devoid of aloha. The aloha I seek to index here is not the "aloha" bought and sold in market economy fantasies for touristic consumption. Rather, it is aloha 'āina beyond monetary and political gain and the elite social structure of liberal recognition. It rests, instead, within the building up of intimate relationships between variously positioned people banding together to make places like Pu'uhonua o Wai'anae feel possible, like this a good place for all of us to stand as one.

REFERENCES

Berlant, L. (2011). *Cruel optimism*. Durham, NC: Duke University Press.

Fermantez, K. (2012). Re-placing Hawaiians in dis place we call home. *Hūlili: Multidisciplinary Research on Hawaiian Well-Being, 8*(1), 97–131.

Hardt, M., & Negri, A. (2000). *Empire*. Cambridge, MA: Harvard University Press.

Hauʻofa, E. Our sea of islands. (1993). In E. Waddell, V. Naidu, & E. Hauʻofa (Eds.), *A new Oceania: Rediscovering our sea of islands* (pp. 2–16). Suva, Fiji: University of the South Pacific School of Social and Economic Development, in association with Beake House.

Mancini, E. (2010). *Magnus Hirschfeld and the quest for sexual freedom: A history of the first international sexual freedom movement*. New York, NY: Palgrave Macmillan.

McDougall, B. N. (2014). The second gift. In A. Yamashiro & N. Goodyear-Kaʻōpua (Eds.), *The value of Hawaiʻi 2: Ancestral roots, oceanic visions* (pp. 250–253). Honolulu, HI: University of Hawaiʻi Press.

Nagourney, A. (2016, June 3). Aloha and welcome to paradise. Unless you're homeless. *New York Times*, p. A1. Retrieved from https://www.nytimes.com/2016/06/04/us/hawaii-homeless-criminal-law-sitting-ban.html.

Rifkin, M. (2009). Indigenizing Agamben: Rethinking sovereignty in light of the "peculiar" status of native peoples. *Cultural Critique, 73*, 88–124.

Simpson, A. (2007). On ethnographic refusal: Indigeneity, "voice" and colonial citizenship. *Junctures, 9*, 67–80.

ABOUT THE AUTHOR

Kalaniopua Young is a radical māhūwahine scholar-activist of color, a trans woman survivor of cis-sexist heteropatriarchy and racial gender violence, and a former community organizer with Puʻuhonua o Waiʻanae and United Territories of Pacific Islanders Alliance. She is a recent doctoral graduate of the Department of Anthropology at the University of Washington. Her dissertation, "Constellations of Rebellion: Home, Makeshift Economies and Queer Indigeneity," is a critical ethnography that centers emergent connections between the dissonance of home, Queer Indigeneity, and tent cities across and within settler states. Giving focus to ʻŌiwi ethnographic epistemology and ontology, the work conjures innovative practices, principles, and priorities that reconfigure questions about people, time, space, place, social belonging, community health, environmental justice, and spiritual well-being.

NOTES

1. Queer kid—gender nonconforming, māhū (transgender).

2. In this article, aliases instead of real names are used for confidentiality purposes.

Mapping Abundance on Mauna a Wākea as a Practice of Ea

CANDACE FUJIKANE

This article recounts the stand that Kānaka ʻŌiwi and their allies took to protect Mauna a Wākea from the construction crews who tried to make their way to the summit on June 24, 2015. As Kānaka stood in lines across the road leading up the mauna, they chanted about the abundance that grows from their genealogical connectedness to Mauna a Wākea. The occupying state has long mapped Mauna a Wākea as a wasteland, and the proponents of the proposed Thirty Meter Telescope have employed the figure of a "threshold of impact" to depict the mountain as so "degraded" by existing telescopes that the addition of more would not have a significant impact. By contrast, the movement to protect Mauna a Wākea maps ancestral knowledge about the waters of life on Mauna a Wākea as part of an education in "ea," a word meaning life, breath, sovereignty, and a rising. In this stand, the people are enacting a decolonial future on ancestral lands, and it is upon this abundance that the people of the lāhui are rising.

CORRESPONDENCE MAY BE SENT TO:
Candace Fujikane
English Department, University of Hawaiʻi
1733 Donaghho Road, Honolulu, Hawaiʻi 96822
Email: fujikane@hawaii.edu

Hūlili: Multidisciplinary Research on Hawaiian Well-Being, Vol. 11, No. 1

O hanau ka Mauna a Wakea	Born of Kea [Wakea] was the mountain,
O puu a'e ka mauna a Wakea	the mauna of Kea budded forth.
O Wakea, ke kane,	Wākea was the husband,
O Papa, o Walinuu ka wahine	Papa Walinu'u was the wife.
Hanau Hoohoku, he wahine	Born was Ho'ohoku, a daughter,
Hanau Haloa he 'lii	born was Hāloa, a chief,
Hanau ka Mauna,	born was the mountain,
he keiki mauna na Wakea	a mountain-son of Kea.

(Poepoe, 1906, p. 1; Trans. by Pukui & Korn [1973], p. 23)
—Verses from "He kanaenae no ka hanau ana o Kauikeaouli,"
chanted by kia'i mauna, protectors of Mauna a Wākea, on June 24, 2015

Nā Moʻokūʻauhau: Genealogies

Mauna a Wākea is "ka makahiapo kapu na Wakea," the sacred firstborn of the union of Papahānaumoku, She who is the foundation birthing islands, and Wākea, He who is the wide expanse of the heavens (Poepoe, 1906). As the highest point in the Pacific, Mauna a Wākea is "ka piko o ka moku," the piko of the island in the many senses of the word (Edith Kanakaʻole Foundation, p. i). The mauna is the piko or summit where the earth meets the sky. The mauna is also the elder sibling of both the kalo plant and the Kānaka, the people, all fathered by Wākea. Through this moʻokūʻauhau, this genealogy, Mauna a Wākea is the piko as the umbilicus, the cord that binds the people to their ancestors and all of their pulapula, the seedling descendants, all those who came before and all those who will come after. Mauna a Wākea thus embodies a profound sense of familial connectedness to the past, present, and future.

The genealogy of water on Mauna a Wākea also speaks of currents of connection and abundance. Water that collects on the piko of the kalo plant, which also refers to the junction of the stem and kalo leaf, is sacred because it has not yet touched the earth, and water on Mauna a Wākea is most sacred because it is the highest source of water that flows to the aquifer to feed the island (Nā Maka o ka ʻĀina, n.d.). This water from Kāneikawaiola, Kāne of the life-giving waters, comes from the hau, the snow, and the lilinoe, the mists that gently meander over the mauna. Out of Kāne's great love for the summits were born the water deities of the mountain: his daughter, Poliʻahu, the woman wrapped in the snow mantle of Mauna a Wākea, and her sisters, Līlīnoe of the fine mist; Waiau, of the swirling waters of the lake where Poliʻahu resides during the summer months; and Ka Houpo o Kāne, master kapa maker who beats the brilliant, snow-white bark cloth. Ka Houpo o Kāne throws the waters on her kapa, which become the heavy rains, beating her kapa thunderously, and when she flips the bright new kapa over, this is the lightning flashing in the skies. In the winter months of hoʻoilo, the sisters wear the kapa hau, the mantle of snow, and in the summer months of kauwela, they wear the kapa lā, beaten with the golden kukunaokalā, the rays of the sun (Haleole, 1863). Moʻoinanea is the reptilian water deity, the matriarch of moʻo akua throughout the islands, who watches over Poliʻahu in Waiau during the warm summer months. When the snow or the red dirt of the mauna glows with the rising or the setting of the sun, we see Poliʻahu's lover Kūkahauʻula embracing her, his cloak wrapped around her snow forms. These deities are manifested in the mauna itself and the water forms on the mauna—from the fine mists to the snowfall to all of the bodies of sacred water on the mauna.

I begin with these genealogies to foreground the connectedness and abundance of Mauna a Wākea in moʻolelo, reminding us of the intimate connections between Kanaka and akua, gods or elemental forms.[1] In the face of this abundance, the settler/occupying state has historically represented Mauna a Wākea as a wasteland, a barren desert. Through these representations, it has sought to profit from the construction of observatories on this sacred land. In 1968, the Land Board issued a lease for the construction of a single telescope, but since then, that one telescope has multiplied to thirteen observatories, or twenty-two, if we consider that some observatories house multiple telescopes (Pisciotta, 2015).

More recently, in 2010, the University of Hawaiʻi at Hilo filed a Conservation District Use Permit (CDUP) application on behalf of the Thirty Meter Telescope (TMT) Corporation for the proposed construction of what would be the most massive observatory yet. The proposed telescope would be eighteen stories tall—taller than any existing structure on Hawai'i Island—with a footprint of more than five acres, which would require excavating twenty feet into the northern plateau of the sacred mountain. In the permit application, the university argued that the TMT would meet the conditions of eight criteria for the Conservation District. Protectors of Mauna a Wākea immediately requested a contested case hearing. In a procedural error, the Board of Land and Natural Resources (BLNR) approved the CDUP for the TMT in February 2011 before the contested case hearing was held in August 2011, and in 2013, the BLNR confirmed its approval. A group of six petitioners, who came to be known as the Mauna Kea hui, or collective, took the case to the courts on the issue of both the procedural violation and the failure of the University of Hawai'i to prove that the TMT would meet the eight criteria for the Conservation District. The case then made its way up to the Hawai'i Supreme Court.

In this article, I begin with the stand that Kānaka and their allies took to protect Mauna a Wākea from the state officers and construction crews who tried to make their way to the summit on June 24, 2015. As Kānaka stood in lines across the road leading up the mauna, they chanted about abundance and their genealogical connectedness to Mauna a Wākea. I then examine the state forms of mapping that represent Mauna a Wākea as a wasteland and the ways proponents of the proposed TMT have employed a "threshold of impact" figure to depict the mauna as so "degraded" by existing telescopes that the addition of more would not have a significant impact. I turn to the impact these arguments have on Hawaiian well-being and the ways that the movement to protect Mauna a Wākea has been reconceived as a celebration of the abundance of Mauna a Wākea. I then turn to the

ways 'Ōiwi have mapped the abundance of Mauna a Wākea as it extends from ma uka to ma kai, from the mountains to the sea, to mobilize the lāhui, the nation, the people, around the protection of the mauna.

In these arguments, I look at the mapping of ancestral knowledges of the abundance that is Mauna a Wākea as part of an education in "ea," a word meaning life, breath, sovereignty, and a rising—the rising of the people to protect the 'āina, the land that feeds physically, intellectually, and spiritually. The word ea is likened to the birth of the living land itself. Hawaiian language scholar Leilani Basham describes a beautiful image of ea: "'O ke ea nō ho'i ka hua 'ōlelo no ka puka 'ana mai o kekahi mea mai loko mai o ka moana, e la'a me ka mokupuni" (Basham, 2010, p. 50). In her introduction to *A Nation Rising: Hawaiian Movements for Life, Land, and Sovereignty*, Noelani Goodyear-Ka'ōpua sets the foundation for the collection by engaging Basham's words. She explains,

> Indeed, ea is a word that describes emergence, such as volcanic islands from the depths of the ocean. In looking to mele Hawai'i—Hawaiian songs and poetry—Basham points out that the term "ea" is foregrounded within a prominent mele ko'ihonua, or creation and genealogical chant for Hawai'i: "*Ea* mai Hawaiinuiakea / *Ea* mai loko mai o ka po." The islands emerge from the depths, from the darkness that precedes their birth. Basham argues that, similarly, political autonomy is a beginning of life. (Goodyear-Ka'ōpua, 2015, pp. 4–5)

Rooted in genealogy, the principle of ea also reminds us that life, breath, land, and political independence cannot be separated from each other. Goodyear-Ka'ōpua further explains that when a British captain seized the islands in 1843, the success of Hawaiian emissaries to restore the sovereignty of the kingdom was celebrated in the Lā Hoʻihoʻi Ea national holiday, and Davida Kahalemaile's 1871 speech on ea on that holiday continues to teach us about the richness of that word and its importance for a sovereign future.

Noʻeau Peralto elaborates on the protection of Mauna a Wākea as a practice of ea. He describes Mauna Kea as the ʻōpuʻu, the whale tooth pendant that must be recovered in the struggle for ea. He writes,

> In 1959, the United States transferred control of these ʻāina [lands of Mauna a Wākea] to the state of Hawaiʻi, establishing the Public Land Trust. Since this seizure occurred and American occupation began in these islands, control of the allodial title to these ʻāina mauna has framed the ongoing struggle by Kanaka ʻŌiwi and many others to mālama this keiki mauna na Wākea, in the face of increasing pressure to impose further desecration upon its summit. Thus . . . our struggle to recover the ʻōpuʻu that is Mauna a Wākea, parallels our enduring struggle to reestablish our ea in these islands. (p. 236)

Peralto goes on to explain that the genealogy of Mauna a Wākea tells of not only the birthing of the land but also the birthing of a unified Hawaiian consciousness.

I myself do not have the genealogy of Kanaka ʻŌiwi, nor am I from Hawaiʻi Island. As a fourth-generation Japanese settler ally, I grew up in Pukalani, Maui, on the slopes of Haleakalā, learning aloha ʻāina by growing pili to the ʻāina mauna, close to the mountain lands of Haleakalā. As a settler ally, I work for the restoration and affirmation of Hawaiʻi's independence through both statist and non-statist forms of self-governance. That is, I work to support both actions to establish state-centered independence as well as community-based actions enacting land-centered independence without a governing state entity.

There has been much discussion and debate about the term "settler" and whether people of color who have suffered from racism and discrimination can be positioned as settlers. Haunani-Kay Trask explained that it is settler colonialism itself as a set of political conditions that institutes the genealogical distinction between Natives and settlers (2000, p. 21; 2008, p. 47). She was the first to identify people of color as "settlers of color," but she also opened up a space for settler allies by reminding us, "For non-Natives, the question that needs to be answered every day is simply the one posed in the old union song: 'Which side are you on?'" (2000, p. 20; 2008, p. 62). This question emphasizes that as settlers, people of color have agency and can choose whether to identify with the settler state or as settler allies in decolonial struggles for independence.

Goodyear-Kaʻōpua expands on Trask's question and discusses the importance of settler allies who exercise settler kuleana, the responsibilities, rights, and privileges given to them, but do not lose sight of their settler privileges. She writes, "Perhaps, such a positioning might be thought of as a *settler aloha ʻāina* practice or kuleana. A settler aloha ʻāina can take responsibility for and develop attachment to lands upon which they reside when actively supporting Kānaka Maoli who have been alienated from ancestral lands to reestablish those connections and also helping to rebuild Indigenous structures that allow for the transformation of settler-colonial relations" (2013, p. 154).

27

In writing this article, I have asked myself, what is my settler kuleana in writing about Mauna a Wākea? I feel the pain deep in my own core as I have stood with Kānaka and other settler aloha 'āina, bearing witness to the unjust processes of the settler state that amended the legislative language of HB1618 CD1 from requiring the BLNR to have a seat for a member with expertise in native Hawaiian traditional and customary practices in order "to better administer the public lands and resources with respect to native Hawaiian issues and concerns" to a seat for a "cultural expert" who does not represent Hawaiian concerns.[3] The governor subsequently appointed an Asian settler to this seat on the BLNR, a board member who voted to approve the permit for the TMT on three separate occasions.

Instead, settler kuleana is about sharing the 'eha—the 'eha in the na'au, the pain that Kānaka and settler allies feel to the very core of our being when we see Kānaka ancestral knowledges being discredited by settler decision-making boards, the 'eha of standing in boardrooms, quasi-judicial meeting rooms, and courtrooms and listening to the degradation of ancestral knowledges and the disregard for the health and well-being of Kānaka, the 'eha of seeing aloha 'āina being handcuffed and arrested like criminals in front of their children for protecting the sacred mauna.

This is why I call myself a Japanese settler ally, a settler aloha 'āina: because non-Hawaiians are still trying to seize places meant for Kanaka cultural experts, and as settler allies, we need to work against that theft. As Asian settler allies, we can help bear that 'eha by doing the difficult work that Kānaka do, such as taking our places on the front lines of decolonial struggles in toxic boardrooms and courtrooms and standing for the kulāiwi and the 'āina. This means exposing and working

toward lifting that 'eha by growing ea, cultivating life, breath, and political independence.

In this way, I see the term "settler ally" as one that opens up possibilities. The term has its own capaciousness, one that grapples with the social processes of US occupation, one that contains the seeds within itself of a decolonial future. The term "settler ally" engages settler colonialism so that we never lose sight of those conditions or the privileges we derive from them, even as we seek to rearticulate our own positionalities. In this way, "settler ally" encompasses the *imaginative possibilities* for our collaborative work on ea and growing a land-based lāhui.

As a member of Huaka'i i Nā 'Āina Mauna, I have walked with our alaka'i, our leader, Kūkauakahi, on the ancient kuamo'o, trails, of Mauna a Wākea since 2012. We walk across the uplands of Mauna a Wākea in the traditional Hawaiian practice of ka'apuni māka'ika'i, the practice of traveling on spiritual huaka'i, or journeys, taken as occasions to view, remember, and teach the mo'olelo of the wahi pana, or celebrated places. On these huaka'i, we walk in the footsteps of Kamiki, the warriors of 'Umi, the kupua Māui, and Queen Emma to different parts of the mauna, all of which are sacred, and all of which are related to other land formations through both view planes and genealogies. As Kūkauakahi explains, walking across Mauna a Wākea changes us:

> We go up there to learn about the mountain and how we can learn to live with its most intimate moods and attributes. We go up there to discover who we are and to learn about our special inner workings—and each other. The lines of sight and the land formations you see will become mapped in your na'au. Being able to experience the

intangibles, to experience the experiences of the ancients, brings the kind of special intimacy of real feelings and identification. It's all beautiful.[3]

The mauna is not just mapped in the mind but in the naʻau, the gut, the deep visceral core of our knowledge and emotions, for all of us as ʻŌiwi and as settler allies.

In the quiet of Mauna a Wākea, with only the sound of the Kīpuʻupuʻu wind whipping our jackets and the crunch of our footsteps on lava cinders, we have walked in Kamiki's footsteps, making our way down loose, flat rocks, stacked tiles forming gorgeous mosaics of gray, blue, red and gold, shifting ground beneath our feet. We have looked out over nā ʻāina mauna, the mountain lands, the steeply sloping terrain of rocks, and we have seen the land open up to a stunning vista as the late afternoon sun casts a golden light on the yellow, grassy slopes below, evoking a vision of Poliʻahu and her sisters, Līlīnoe, Waiau, and Ka Hopou o Kāne, wearing the golden kapa pounded by the rays of the sun. We have seen a view of red puʻu, cinder cones, below us, rising out of a rolling surf of clouds like Kānehūnāmoku, the twelve hidden islands of Kāne guarded by Moʻoinanea.

We remember the fourteenth-century moʻolelo of Kamiki, telling of the travels of two supernatural brothers, Kamiki and Makaʻiole, on a huakaʻi around Hawaiʻi Island along the ala loa and ala hele, the ancient trails and paths, competing with ʻōlohe, experts in running, fishing, debating, or solving riddles (Wise & Kihe, 1914–1917). They were empowered by their ancestress Kauluhenuihihikoloiuka, who instructs Kamiki to travel along "ke ala kapu," a sacred trail, to the home of Poliʻahu, one of their elder relatives, to collect the sacred water of Kāne for ʻawa. Kamiki creates the springs below when the water overflows from Hōkūʻula, the ʻawa bowl.

We have walked to these springs, Houpo o Kāne spring, Kawaihūakāne, and Līlīnoe below it.[4] At Houpo o Kāne, the water streams down from a massive moss-covered boulder that is the breast of Kāne. From there, we have looked out over the plains of Pōhakuloa to imagine the springs that stretch out across military-occupied lands all the way to Hualālai, the springs of Waikiʻi near Puʻu Keʻekeʻe, Anaohiku at Hanakaumalu, Honuaʻula, and Kīpaheʻewai on the slopes of Hualālai.

Kūkauakahi teaches us the cultural practice of kaʻapuni mākaʻikaʻi to enable us to bear witness to extraordinary beauty, and he also teaches us that this practice of ea comes with the kuleana of documenting and testifying to the devastation of these places. Kūkauakahi has been a petitioner in both the 2011 and 2016–17 contested case hearings against the proposed TMT. He is also a plaintiff in a case against the renewal of the BLNR permit to the US Army and its use of Pōhakuloa for live-fire training exercises at the Pōhakuloa Training Area at the base of Mauna a Wākea, 133,000 acres across which the springs from Waiau extend.

From these sacred places on Mauna a Wākea, we recall and visualize other wahi pana and wahi kapu, the many places celebrated in moʻolelo for the life-giving waters of Kāne. It is the mapping of this abundance in our naʻau that sustains us in our daily practices of ea as we seek to bring into being a rich and fertile decolonial future for the pulapula.

"Kū Kiaʻi Mauna!" Standing for Mauna a Wākea on June 24, 2015

Kanaka ʻŌiwi practitioners, environmentalists, and others have stood as protectors of Mauna a Wākea since the construction of the first telescope in 1968. Although the media has sought to cast them as "protesters against astronomy," "telescope detractors," or "opponents," each phrase is a narrow description that centers astronomy and positions certain people against it. The people who stand for Mauna a Wākea have made it clear that there is a distinction between protesters and protectors: "Protester" centers astronomy, while "protector" centers the mauna and protection of Mauna a Wākea. Shelley Muneoka, an outreach coordinator for KĀHEA: The Hawaiian-Environmental Alliance, who has presented testimony on Oʻahu at every BLNR meeting regarding the TMT, explains, "The moʻokūʻauhau, the genealogy of this movement doesn't start with people fighting UH, but with people loving Mauna Kea, which extends even further back than that."[5]

In the first 2011 BLNR contested case hearing, the Mauna Kea hui intentionally emphasized the word "protector" to describe themselves. The hui includes Kealoha Pisciotta of Mauna Kea Anaina Hou, E. Kalani Flores and B. Pualani Case of the Flores-Case ʻOhana, Clarence Kūkauakahi Ching, Paul Neves, Deborah J. Ward, and Marti Townsend, assisted by Bianca Isaki, Lauren and Shelley Muneoka, and Miwa Tamanaha, representing KĀHEA. Later, as the movement to protect the mauna grew across the islands and around the world, the rallying call, "Kū Kiaʻi Mauna!" (Protectors Stand for the Mountain!) helped to convey what it means to stand for the mauna and to affirm ea.

In June 2015, as attorneys were preparing for the August 27 Hawaiʻi Supreme Court hearing on the legality of CDUP issued to the TMT, the kiaʻi mauna, protectors of the mauna, learned that the TMT was planning to commence construction, despite the fact that the court case had not yet been resolved. Three months prior to this, there had been thirty-one arrests of kiaʻi on Mauna a Wākea on April 2, when kiaʻi were protecting the mauna from construction crews. The kiaʻi had linked their arms and chanted on the northern plateau, preventing the construction crews from doing any work. Although these efforts had halted work temporarily, workers were scheduled to begin construction once more. The protectors sent out the kāhea, the rallying call, and many of us flew to Hawaiʻi Island to stand for the mauna.

On June 24, 2015, at 4:00 in the morning, hundreds of us gathered at Hale Pōhaku on Mauna a Wākea under the dim glow of lights from the Visitor Center. One of the kiaʻi, Kahoʻokahi Kanuha, explained that the strategy would be to have sixteen lines of kiaʻi on the state road. Some of the kiaʻi would first gather at the Legendary Crosswalk, or the Aloha ʻĀina Checkpoint, located on the county road in front of the Visitor Center. This became the focal point where the kiaʻi practiced kapu aloha, the highest form of love and respect extended to one's opponents, even as they stood kūpaʻa, steadfast, against construction crews for months.[6] Sixteen lines would then be positioned above the county road on the graded state road, each with an alakaʻi, to line up about fifty feet apart to the summit. The county police and state officers would have to explain their rights to every line of protectors before any arrests could be made. As Kanuha spoke, I could see in my mind's eye what the Legendary Crosswalk would look like, multiplied sixteen times up the mauna on the state road. He later explained that the sixteen lines of protectors corresponded with the wā, or eras of the Kumulipo, the koʻihonua chant of the creation of the world: "I wanted sixteen lines, to represent the sixteen wā of the Kumulipo. The county and state officers would have to get through the seven wā of Pō [night] before they got to other wā of Ao [day]. We try as much as possible to ground our resistance in cultural understanding, hence the idea of sixteen lines and sixteen alakaʻi [leaders] representing each wā of the *Kumulipo*."[7]

The kiaʻi called for volunteers to be legal observers to ensure that the Division of Conservation and Resources Enforcement (DOCARE) officers were following procedures. As an older Japanese woman who would remind the DOCARE officers of their aunties and school-teachers, and as a university professor, I knew settler privileges would enable me to intervene if kiaʻi were being mistreated. As a legal observer, I planted myself with the first line of kiaʻi on the state road.

By 7:00 a.m., Hawaiʻi County police arrived at the Aloha ʻĀina Checkpoint in front of the Visitor Center. Kiaʻi there had improvised and had added additional lines on the county road in advance of the sixteen rows on the state road. Rows of kiaʻi chanted in lines twenty feet apart up the quarter mile of county road. The officers were greeted by children who extended kapu aloha to them with lei lāʻī, ti leaf lei, to ensure that all would be safe. For three hours, police talked with multiple lines of hundreds of protectors who stretched across the expanse of the county road leading to the state road, explaining their rights to them, as protectors chanted oli in ceremony. Lines of protectors on the county road were able to delay the police for three hours, resulting in only one arrest.

At 10:00 a.m., we saw protectors making their way up to the state road where I stood. We all watched as DOCARE Hawaiʻi Island Branch Chief Lino Kamakau approached Lākea Trask, the alakaʻi of the first line, and talked with him about their needing to stand down. They talked for forty-five minutes before the line dispersed only to move up to support the line of protectors behind it. At the second line, Kahoʻokahi Kanuha stated clearly, "I give you my word. I will not block traffic. I *will* block desecration." When the DOCARE officers realized that there were more lines ahead, they pushed forward more aggressively and began arresting the kiaʻi.

Line after line, the protectors stood in red kīhei tied over one shoulder and red shirts, holding their ground as long as they could. In the mana wahine line (fig. 1), Nohea Kawaʻa-Davis, Kaleinohea Cleghorn, Alohilani Keohuloa, Mehana Kihoi, Kuʻuipo Freitas, Naaiakalani Navas, Hōkūlani Reyes, and many others stood with arms linked, holding a long lei lāʻī, chanting "Mālana mai Kaʻū" in powerful unison, calling together the peoples of the different districts of Hawaiʻi Island in the building of a canoe sealed together by Mauna a Wākea. Everyone felt the enduring strength of mana wahine that day, and this photo continues to be circulated to rally kiaʻi at times when Mauna a Wākea is most in need of protection.

In the ʻōpio line, Movement for Aloha No ka ʻĀina (MANA) organizer Kerry Kamakaokaʻilima Long led young people who were growing into their own leadership kuleana. The DOCARE officers moved forward aggressively, arresting eleven people along the way, including Kahoʻokahi Kanuha, Kaleikoa Kaʻeo, Hualālai Keohuloa, and Andre Perez, leaders in the Hawaiian independence movement. These leaders sat on the ground when arrested and, as the DOCARE officers carried them away, the people wailed "Auē!" out of grief and concern.

With the mists of Līlīnoe enveloping us and the icy, black, biting Kīpuʻupuʻu and Kuauli rains[8] warding the crews away from the summit, the officers were stopped at the eleventh line, where ʻOhulei Waiaʻu led the kiaʻi,

31

Figure 1. The mana wahine line. Photo courtesy of Te Rawhitiroa Bosch.

who chanted and danced to "He kanaenae no ka hanau ana o Kauikeaouli" (cited in the opening of this article) to assert the genealogies of Mauna a Wākea and Kanaka. The kiaʻi who stood in that line, Pumpkin Waiaʻu, ʻOhulei Waiaʻu, Leialoha Kaleohano, Winter Hoʻohuli, Kini Kaleilani Burke, and Michelle Tomas, chanted in rhythmic unison, their voices ringing strong and clear in the mist and the rain (fig. 2).

This powerful moment illustrates the fullest expression of ea, an upsurging of a sovereign people profoundly connected with the world and the surrounding elements. The mana, or life force of the rain, the stones, and the people converged as genealogy was chanted: the ua, the rains, and the mists watering the Kānaka,

the pulapula seedlings of Papahānaumoku and Wākea; the pōhaku, who embodied Papahānaumoku, standing as kūpuna, as ancestors, with their descendants that day; the Kānaka who chanted their genealogical relationship to the mauna, steadfast in their protection; and the mauna itself. In this powerful moment, the kiaʻi faced a modern threat but stood for Mauna a Wākea, firmly rooted in their ancestral knowledges, offering their leo, their voices, up to the akua of the mauna. All of these things stopped the convoy from continuing up the mountain.

The state officers gave different reasons for calling off construction that day. They initially said the rain and the lack of time would make it difficult for construction crews to work. Then they said the pōhaku, stones, that had been planted in the road were the deterrent. They refused to acknowledge the power of the unified leo of the people and the ancestral elemental forms that stood with them that day.

The Occupying State and Its Mapping of Wastelands

Maps generated by the occupying state and developers seek to erase and empty out wahi pana and wahi kapu, to produce wastelands for the development of settler homes, infrastructures, and industries. The state does so through static maps paralyzed in time, two-dimensional documents that abstract and encode the intimacies of land into lines, dots, grids, letters, and numbers, as well as tax map keys, degrees, minutes, seconds, decimals, and other geographic coordinates. As the substance of land is abstracted in this way, the state then condemns abundant lands as "wastelands" to pave the way for urbanization and industrialization.

My own critical settler cartography foregrounds the settler state's use of what I refer to as the logic of subdivision: the occupying state's erosion of the integrity of land and its continuities to produce wastelands as a part of the ongoing process of land seizure in Hawai'i. Under the conditions of a capitalist economy, the state and developers engage in the structural operations of subdivision, producing terra nullius, "land belonging to no one," eviscerating land of history and meaning. In a settler colonial system premised on the logic of subdivision, the state and developers draw red boundary lines around isolated "parcels" of land, fragmenting wahi pana and wahi kapu into smaller and smaller isolated, abstracted spaces that have no continuities and thus,

Figure 2. The eleventh line. Photo courtesy of Te Rawhitiroa Bosch.

they claim, "no cultural significance." The occupying state must compulsively seize land through this piecemeal process to secure its own future; however, precisely because the state never completely captures the occupied territory, there is always the possibility that this territory will escape the state's grasp. It is this precariousness of US occupation that is leading to its own demise while enabling an Indigenous futurity.

By mapping abundance, we identify what settler colonial capital fears. David Lloyd has argued that it is precisely the fear of abundance that is inscribed in colonial capital. Abundance raises the possibility of just distribution, conditions of satiation and fullness, which threaten a capitalist economy. Capitalism depends upon stories of hunger, the competition for limited resources, the production of markets and profits; thus, capitalist production depends on desiccating abundance to manufacture conditions of scarcity. Lloyd writes,

Perhaps, then, we need to recognize that precisely what neoliberal capital fears is abundance and

33

what it implies. Abundance is the end of capital: it is at once what it must aim to produce in order to dominate and control the commodity market and what designates the limits that it produces out of its own process. Where abundance does not culminate in a crisis of overproduction, it raises the spectre of the redistribution of resources in the place of enclosure and accumulation by dispossession. The alibi of capital is scarcity; its myth is that of a primordial scarcity overcome only by labor regulated by the private ownership of the means of production. (Lloyd, 2016, p. 209)

I would add that capitalist economies offer us instead ideological regimes of excess that proffer an imaginary plenitude. Such plenitude takes monetary form as well as the form of international "recognition" in the annals of science. Yet the interests of capital behind this imaginary plenitude are not the same as an ancestral abundance that feeds or sustains us for generations. If capital's fear of abundance produces a narrative about the conditions of people competing for scarce resources, then an economy of abundance is what creates a space for a radically different kind of economy, one of māʻona, fullness, that comes from sharing, trading, conserving, and adapting. The processes of restoring abundance, of course, will still contend with globalized and militarized capitalism. Practitioners of this economy of abundance strive to balance critical analyses of the circuits of globalization with the moʻolelo about the currents of the ocean, winds, and rains that teach us to better care for the planet. In this commitment to restoring abundance, Kanaka ʻŌiwi stand with other Indigenous peoples who are on the front lines against global climate change.

The settler/occupying state has actively worked to produce wastelands through mapping practices leading up to

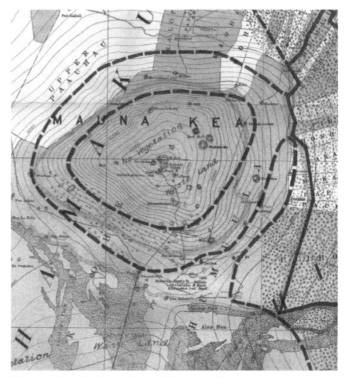

Figure 3. Detail of 1901 Hawaiʻi Territory Survey map

and continuing after the 1893 overthrow of the Hawaiian government and the illegal annexation of Hawaiʻi in 1898. An early 1891 map by American surveyor C. J. Lyons inscribed Mauna a Wākea with the words, "Barren Rock and Sand" (Lyons, 1891), illustrating American perceptions of this sacred place as land that did not conform to capitalist notions of agricultural productivity. A decade later, a Hawaiʻi Territory Survey map (Donn, 1901) labeled Mauna Kea as a "Waste Land" (fig. 3).

This designation is reminiscent of Ngugi wa Thiong'o's assertion about the cultural bomb that extends imperialism into colonialism by making Native people see their past as a wasteland:

But the biggest weapon wielded and actually daily unleashed by imperialism against that collective defiance is the cultural bomb. The effect of the cultural bomb is to annihilate a people's belief in their names, in their languages, in their environment, in their heritage of struggle, in their unity, in their capacities and ultimately in themselves. It makes them see their past as one wasteland of non-achievement and it makes them want to distance themselves from that wasteland. (Ngugi, 1986, p. 3)

The seizure of land through the designation of wastelands reveals that it was precisely land that was at stake in the erasure of Hawaiian forms of knowledge. In the larger historical context, settler colonial depictions of the land as "lying in waste" were aimed at seizing political control over both people and land and to erase a vast ʻŌiwi knowledge base.

The condemnation of lands on Mauna a Wākea signaled that the location was already being seen as scientifically valuable. Cartography went hand in hand with astronomy, as can be seen as early as 1889, when E. D. Preston, an astronomer with the US Coast and Geodetic Survey, began correspondence with W. D. Alexander, and in 1892, both traveled to the summit with a small telescope and a pendulum for the purpose of perfecting the survey of the summit lands and setting up a gravity and magnetic station for determining the mean density of the earth (Maly & Maly, 2005, p. 176). By 1901, then, this Territory Survey map had already marked a place for the "Waiau Astron Sta." The pretense for condemning land as wasteland, in agricultural terms, paved the way for the settler state to make such "public lands" available for increasingly industrial astronomical uses.

Representations of the summit of Mauna a Wākea as a wasteland persist into the present. For example, in the second contested case hearing in 2017, the University of Hawaiʻi at Hilo and TMT International Observatory stated, in their filing of "Joint (Proposed) Findings of Fact," that nineteenth-century ʻŌiwi historian Davida Malo had called Mauna Kea a wasteland: "He made no mention of traditional or historic practices atop the summit of Mauna Kea and reported that it was considered wasteland or the realm of the gods" (University of Hawaiʻi at Hilo & TMT International Observatory, 2017, p. 102, #646).[9] I tracked their quotation from *Hawaiian Antiquities: Moʻolelo Hawaiʻi* and found that it provides only Nathaniel Emerson's English translation. The phrase "waste places" appears not in the translation itself but in Emerson's *footnote*. Emerson's translation reads,

> 12. The belt below the *wao-eiwa* was the one in which the monarchs of the forest grew, and was called the *wao-maukele*, and the belt below that, in which again trees of smaller size grew was called *wao-akua,* [sic], and below the *wao-akua* comes the belt called *wao-kanaka* or *mau*. Here grows the *amau* fern and here men cultivate the land.[10]

As W. D. Alexander's "Introduction" to the book explains, the footnotes were written by Emerson.[11] This is Emerson's footnote 6:

> [6]Sect. 12. In the phrase wao-akua, which means wilderness of the gods, we have embodied the popular idea that the gods and ghosts chiefly inhabit the waste places of the earth.

Emerson could articulate only a settler colonial imaginary in which the realm of the gods is conceived of as the "waste places of the earth."

Malo himself never said that Mauna a Wākea is a waste-land. Malo's text is not about Mauna a Wākea; it provides an account of "Ke Kapa Ana i Ko Loko Mau Inoa o ka Moku" (The Naming of What is Found on the Islands), a description of the different realms on the islands. Malo describes the wao akua as the places on the land where vegetation grows through the cultivation of the gods, the elemental forms. Here are Malo's own words and a translation by Malcolm Naea Chun:

> 12. O kahi o na laau loloa e ulu ana makai mai o ka wao eiwa, ua kapa ia aku ia, he wao maukele ma ia poai, ao kahi makai mai, o ka wao maukele e liilii hou iho ai na laau, ua kapa ia aku ia he wao akua, ma ia poai kahi makai mai o ka wao akua e ulu ana ke amaumau, he wao kanaka kahi inoa, he mau kahi inoa oia poai, kahi a na kanaka e mahiai ai.

> 12. The place where the tall trees grow seaward from the wao eiwa is called wao maukele where it encircles the kua mauna. Seaward from the wao maukele, where the vegetation is small with new growth is called wao akua.[3] [sic] Seaward of the wao akua grow the 'Ama'uma'u fern and it is called wao kanaka. There are several terms for the area where people farm. (Malo, 2006, p. 12)

Malo's own words define the wao akua, the realm of the gods, as the places where vegetation grows through the elemental powers of the akua, in contrast to the wao kanaka, where vegetation must be cultivated by peo-ple. The fact that the university and the TMT attorneys failed to consult Malo's Hawaiian language text and con-sulted only the English translation illustrates both their own inability to read 'ōlelo Hawai'i and their disregard for 'Ōiwi knowledges.

From these contrived depictions of Mauna a Wākea as a wasteland emerges one of the most egregious logics of the occupying state: the construction of a "threshold of impact." In preparing the final environmental impact statement, project manager James T. Hayes, of the firm Parsons Brinckerhoff Americas, was mandated by a pre-vious ruling to assess the cumulative impact of the TMT on Mauna a Wākea. NASA's final environmental impact statement for the Keck Outrigger Telescopes project in 2005 states unequivocally that "From a cumulative perspective, the impact of past, present, and reasonably foreseeable future activities on cultural and biological resources is *substantial, adverse, and significant*" (NASA, 2005, p. xxi, emphasis mine). The TMT final environ-mental impact statement, prepared for the University of Hawai'i, attempted to counter NASA's finding of adverse impact by establishing what it calls "Thresholds Used to Determine Level of Impact" (University of Hawai'i at Hilo, 2010, p. 3-3). The section concludes that all of the activities on Mauna a Wākea have a significant and adverse impact on the summit and that the threshold of adverse impact has been crossed; therefore, the sum-mit lands are so "degraded" by industrialization that the addition of the eighteen-story, industrial TMT to the Conservation District will have an effect that is "less than significant." The final environmental impact state-ment states:

> In general, the Project will add a limited incre-ment to the current level of cumulative impact. Therefore, those resources that have been sub-stantially, significantly, and adversely impacted by past and present actions would continue to have a substantial, significant, and adverse impact with the addition of the Project. For those resources that have been impacted to a less than significant degree by past and present actions, the Project

would not tip the balance from a less than significant level to a significant level and the less than significant level of cumulative impact would continue. (University of Hawaiʻi at Hilo, 2010, p. S-9)

In a rhetorical move of smoke and mirrors, Parsons Brinckerhoff, the multinational corporation that prepared the environmental impact statement for the University of Hawaiʻi, attempted to dissipate the adverse impact of the TMT through the figure of a "threshold," what it constructs as the "tipping point" of impact. In this way, the final environmental impact statement attempts to bury the TMT's impact under the existing impact of the thirteen other telescopes, while manufacturing a false narrative of the mauna being irreversibly wasted by degradation.

I would dispute Parsons Brinckerhoff's analysis by pointing to the logarithmic, exponential nature of environmental impact. As we are seeing with global climate change, a mere two-degree Celsius increase in global temperatures above preindustrial levels will have catastrophic effects, including loss of sea ice, sea level rise, acidification of the ocean, species extinction, droughts, hurricanes, and heat waves. Although Parsons Brinckerhoff is attempting to minimize the appearance of impact by calling it an "incremental impact," the point here is that environmental impacts are systemic and involve entire ecological systems. These impacts are what scientists call cascades, meaning that a small change multiplies in effect, from trophic cascades downward as well as upward cascades. In the case of the TMT, cultural practitioners and environmentalists testified to tremendous, extensive impacts that are cultural and natural, beyond any institutional attempts to contain impact to a "limited increment."

This formula of "threshold of impact" has larger implications as an assertion of the inevitability of settler colonialism as a foregone conclusion. Like the trope of the "vanishing Indian," this argument isolates colonization to a past point in time as the threshold that has already been crossed, and in this way the settler state and its agents seek to foreclose the possibility of decolonization. This occupying state formulation for settler colonial inevitability must shore itself up, however, precisely because of the movement of Native resurgence, which is demanding decolonization.

It is within this Indigenous resurgence that we see ʻŌiwi challenging the settler colonial argument about tipping points of impact, pushing back against such rhetorical fallacies, and standing for the restoration of Mauna a Wākea and Hawaiʻi's independence. In response to the argument that Mauna a Wākea has been laid to waste by the current observatories, petitioner Kūkauakahi Ching points to an irreducible fact: The addition of an eighteen-story industrial complex to a conservation district can only add significant impact. In his closing argument in the first contested case hearing, he stated, "While mental hocus-pocus, along with alchemy and witchcraft, might have attained credibility in the Dark Ages, my modern mind tells me that one cannot subtract or mitigate by adding" (Ching, 2013, p. 98). Petitioner Kealoha Pisciotta further explains that this "increment," emphasized by the TMT, would not only cause irreparable harm to the mauna and to the people but would also become an enormous falsehood that will expose and crush the fragile juridical underpinnings of the state: "If the BLNR allows the legal limits to be exceeded, they will be in breach of trust in excess of their authority. And in any case, the TMT is not only the straw that breaks the camel's back, it's the elephant that will cause the entire system to break down" (Pisciotta, 2013, p. 124).

We can further see the state's logic of subdivision in the way that the final environmental impact statement's proposed location for the TMT, known as the "13N site" within "Area E" within the 525-acre "Astronomy Precinct," already provides a visual illustration of abstracted land in nested subdivisions, one within the other. A total of 263 historic properties are identified on the northern plateau, but the TMT final environmental impact statement recognizes only three places of significance, stating, "The TMT Observatory will be placed at the 13N site where it will not be visible from culturally sensitive locations, such as the summit of Kūkahauʻula, Lake Waiau, and Puʻu Lilinoe" (University of Hawaiʻi at Hilo, 2010, p. P-3, S-13). The impact, therefore, appears to be limited to the red boundary lines drawn around these three sites and their singular view planes to the TMT.

However, as cultural practitioners have argued, all of the mountain lands of Mauna a Wākea, including the northern plateau itself, are sacred. In their testimony against the TMT project, Kanaka cultural practitioners emphasized repeatedly that the Mauna a Wākea summit cannot be subdivided because of the integrity of these sacred lands. The ʻāina mauna, or mountain lands were historically not divided precisely because they were not for human use and, as the realm of the akua, represented the highest expression of the integrity of land. For example, Victoria Kamāmalu relinquished these lands as *undivided* lands to Kauikeaouli at the time of the privatization of land with the Māhele in 1848—lands that became the government lands, later seized at the time of the overthrow and "ceded" by the settler oligarchy of the Republic of Hawaiʻi to the United States at the time of annexation (Kauikeaouli, Na Lii, & Kalama, 1848, p. x).

Kealoha Pisciotta, a cultural practitioner who has stood for Mauna a Wākea in contested case hearings and courts for the past twenty years, points to the problems that occur when the state maps these puʻu and limits their extent to the boundary lines drawn around them or the view planes from these three bounded sites alone. She reminds us that such mapping obscures the fact that the entire summit is the body of Poliʻahu. As Pisciotta explains,

> And then one day I walked out and the snow had been perfect and there was a cloud bank, a typical cloud bank that always is on the mountain, and right there you could see her whole body, her face, her hair, her shoulder, and her arm, her nene [nipples of a woman's breast] and then of course the telescopes are right there by her ʻōpū [belly, stomach] and her nene and then you go down and then two puʻu on the mountain that if you look from Hilo side, like looking from Mokuʻula is a good way to see, and then you can see her two feet. Then what happens is that she floats like a cloud of the tree line. (quoted in Simonson & Hammatt, 2010, p. 143)

Pisciotta's description recalls Herb Kāne's paintings of Poliʻahu, which depict ancestral knowledges of Poliʻahu as embodying all of the snow on the mountain, her body draped over Mauna a Wākea, far exceeding the red boundary lines that attempt to contain single cinder cones in isolation. In the moʻolelo of Mauna a Wākea, we see the mauna come alive as the akua embody the entire summit.

To emphasize an expansive ʻŌiwi perspective, Pisciotta submitted a new map (fig. 4) as Exhibit C-5 in the contested case hearing in 2011. Drawn by Community by Design, a planning group from the University of California–Berkeley, this map depicts traditional Hawaiian view planes (Pisciotta, 2011). It is a partial map that also provides a visual representation of some of the solstice and equinox ceremonies.

Pisciotta refutes the university's claims that the view planes would not be affected by the TMT. She explains,

> Most of our practices rely on some kind of view plane, because they are about the relationship between Papa and Wākea (our relationship with and to the earth and the celestial bodies and heavens). For example, we have repeatedly included concerns for the impacts on various ceremonies exercised on Mauna Kea, such as the solstice and equinox ceremonies that we along with many other Hawaiian groups collectively participate in throughout the year on Mauna Kea and other sacred sites around the islands. . . . The ceremonies I just described are specifically dependent upon our ability to observe and track the motion of the sun and other celestial bodies in order to find our way and to determine when and how to perform certain things for the care of the land and sea. Our traditional resource management models are dependent on these ceremonies. Our ancient knowledge relating to our relationship to other Pacific peoples is also a part of this knowledge. And lastly our sacred prophecies are based in this knowledge. (Pisciotta, 2011)

Based on this deeper cultural understanding, the TMT would be in the direct line of sight of Maui from the northwestern plane used for ke ala ao solstice and equinox ceremonies. The map extends out from Mauna a Wākea as the center, connecting to Poliʻahu heiau on Kauaʻi, Ahu a ʻUmi Heiau, Puʻu Koholā Heiau in Kawaihae, and even beyond to Moku Manamana (Necker Island) in Papahānaumokuākea, or the Northwestern Hawaiian

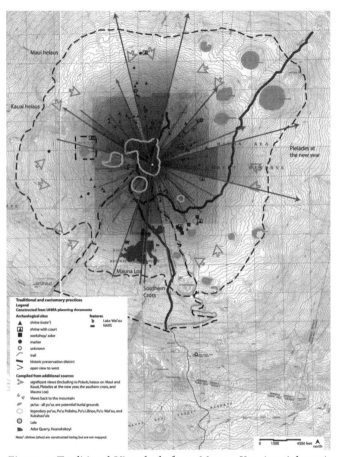

Figure 4. Traditional Viewsheds from Mauna Kea (partial map). Map by Community by Design.

Islands. The view planes look out from Mauna a Wākea, and to Mauna a Wākea, from these different places across the island and extending across the archipelago. The view planes not only direct our vision and ceremony, they also chart channels of energy that run between these sacred places. E. Kalani Flores, a petitioner in both contested case hearings representing the Flores-Case ʻOhana, has shifted the frame of reference of these hearings from an American context to one that honors

39

the knowledge base of Mauna a Wākea. His family has consulted with the akua, kupua, and kūpuna of Mauna a Wākea, and he explains, "Sacred mountains such as Mauna a Wākea, due to their geological composition and extreme height, are a piko (portal) that allows for the transference of energy from one source to another" (Flores, 2016, p. 20).

Not surprisingly, the university attorneys' interpretation of the expansive view planes demonstrated by Pisciotta's map attempted to contain these continuities once more by arguing that it presented view planes from a single isolated spot on the summit, thus further deploying the logic of subdivision. The hearing officer presiding over the contested case hearing reiterated these arguments, concluding that "all of those view planes emanate from a single point: the actual summit of Mauna a Wākea, located on Puʻu Wekiu. It is undisputed that the TMT Observatory will not be visible from Puʻu Wekiu" (Aoki, 2012, p. 66, #379). In the state's mapping of Mauna a Wākea, not only were the sites themselves cordoned off and contained, the cultural practitioners were also depicted as being so limited in their practice that they engage in it only at a single place on the summit—despite repeated testimony that practitioners engage in practice all over the summit.

In their response, the Mauna Kea hui pointed to the untenable premise of the university attorneys' claims. Pisciotta explains,

> Now, when we practice on Mauna Kea, we don't only go to the summit as the university would have everyone believe. Practices are dependent on the reason for the ceremony being conducted, and the hundreds of cultural and historical shrines placed around the summit region

> demonstrate practice is widespread. View planes, viewscapes, are public trust resources. The TMT being placed in the middle of the ring of shrines that contains hundreds of these sites will totally impact our practice. (Pisciotta, 2013, p. 123)

Hawaiian customary and traditional practices show us that places on the mauna cannot be isolated from each other. Hawaiian practices take place over the entire mauna, not just the summit.

Against Colonial Despair: Mapping Joy in Standing for Mauna a Wākea

For those familiar with the genealogy of Mauna a Wākea and all the deities who reside on the mauna, he ʻāina kamahaʻo, a sacred land of wonder, it is painful to witness Mauna a Wākea described as a wasteland. The very proposal to build a massive, industrial structure on Mauna a Wākea fills people with ʻeha and kaumaha, a heavy sadness. As many who were interviewed for the Cultural Impact Assessment of the TMT explain, this ʻeha is intergenerational. It is the ʻeha of hearing again and again the dismissal of not only the genealogy of this mauna but also an expansive ʻŌiwi knowledge base. In the pro-TMT arguments that the observatory represents progress and the future, we hear the voices that claim ʻŌiwi scientific knowledges to be "backward" and that relegate these knowledges to the past.

The proposed TMT also violates Hawaiʻi Revised Statute 711-1107 on "Desecration," which defines desecration as "defacing, damaging, polluting, or otherwise physically mistreating in a way that the defendant knows will outrage the sensibilities of persons likely to observe or discover the defendant's action."[12]

The statute states that "A person commits the offense of desecration if the person intentionally desecrates" "(b) A place of worship or burial." J. Kēhaulani Kauanui stated in her testimony for the 2011 contested case hearing,

> The telescopes are a constant reminder of the State's willing degradation of Hawaiian culture, religion, and therefore, the well-being of the Hawaiian people. They are a legacy of a continuing process of colonization that fractures communities who live in Hawai'i. As the 1993 Apology Resolution correctly recognizes, "the health and well-being of the Native Hawaiian people is intrinsically tied to their deep feelings and attachment to the land[.]" (Joint Resolution, US Public Law 203-150). The existence of an eighteen-story structure that takes up the area of nine football fields in Wao Akua, the home of our gods, our 'Aumakua (ancestral beings), and the place of the conception of the Hawaiian people by Papa and Wākea is the most atrocious violation of our attachment to the entire archipelago. (Kauanui, 2011, p. 2)

Hawaiian well-being, then, has been documented in Public Law 103-150, the Apology Resolution, as being tied to the land: when the land suffers, so do the people.

For the thirty-one kia'i arrested on April 2, 2015, twelve arrested on June 24, eight arrested on July 31, and eight arrested on September 9, their arrests testify to the great love they have for Mauna a Wākea and the lengths they will go to protect the mauna. Mehana Kihoi, who had been handcuffed on April 2 and was a petitioner in the second contested case hearing against the TMT, asked the TMT project manager in that hearing,

> Would there be any outreach provided to our Native Hawaiian children who have been emotionally, physically, mentally, and spiritually traumatized by this project? More specifically, my child who was present for the arrest on the mountain, who saw me being handcuffed while I was in pule [prayer ceremony] on the summit of Mauna Kea by the very DLNR officers that fill this room. What does your project have in place to address her concerns, her pain, and her suffering? I am speaking on behalf of my daughter who is here with me today who does not have a voice. I am her voice. (Kihoi, 2016, pp. 216–217)

The trauma that Mehana described points to the intergenerational trauma that the augmented desecration of Mauna a Wākea would have—the far-reaching genealogical consequences as trauma is passed down through generations.

A beautiful Facebook post by Pua Case to the family of Mauna a Wākea protectors reminds us there is joy, too, in these practices of growing ea. Pua explained that we have to be healthy, that we cannot be driven to anger or rage or depression, because our children will look to us to see what they should do, and we have to stand for the mauna with joy. This movement will have longevity and will be intergenerational:

> Although we are seriously strengthening ourselves and standing steadfast . . . we honor the healing, the joy, and above all the laughter . . . for we must remain healthy and our children must see that we are in harmony and balance and as we stand as leaders and in service, and as we work hard we remain in peace within ourselves and we breathe the same breath as Mother Earth . . . and we will not let anyone drive us to anger or rage, to

41

depression. For our children, let us remain light-hearted, in peace as we move onward and forward . . . Idle No More . . . Eō![13]

As Pua suggests, desecration has intergenerational effects for all Indigenous peoples. In the full post she connects the struggles of the kiaʻi at Mauna a Wākea to the Indigenous water protectors around the world, to the First Nations peoples and their allies in the Idle No More movement in Canada, and to the many American Indian tribes and their allies who came together at Standing Rock to protect the Missouri River from the Dakota Access Pipeline. As she further explains, however, the practices of aloha ʻāina also have intergenerational effects that are necessary to the longevity of these movements for ea.

In the face of colonial despair, the protectors of the mauna have turned to mapping the collective protection offered in joyous celebration of the mauna. One of the oli that has come to represent this collective effort is "Mālana mai Kaʻū" (see fig. 1 above), which has been chanted to celebrate the genealogy of the voyaging canoe Hōkūleʻa. "Mālana mai Kaʻū" is a map that describes the people of the different districts of Hawaiʻi Island—from Kaʻū, Puna, and Hilo, to Kona, Kohala, Hāmākua, and Waipiʻo, to Waimea, Kawaihae, to Mauna a Wākea—who gather together, each a different part of the canoe being built, with Mauna a Wākea being the sealant that binds us all together ("Mālana mai Kaʻū," 2001). This chant is particularly important because it counters colonial despair with the articulation of a collective, decolonial joy. When Pua Case teaches this chant to those who stand for Mauna a Wākea, she focuses on the final line, "Ohohia i ka hana ʻana aku e / Rejoicing at the activity, the building of the canoe." She explains, "The most beautiful word is in that last line. The first word ʻohohia' ['to rejoice']

is going to remind us what feeling, what spirit we are in. We are in the joy of being in the mauna, in the joy of being aware, conscious enough to know that we remember our mauna is sacred and the joy in that" (Case, 2014). Ohohia is an integral part of kūʻē, resistance: it is what sustains people in struggle, what brings us together again and again as a collective, rather than the colonial despair and attrition that can happen when there isn't a recognition of joy in protecting land, people, and lāhui.

Mapping the Abundance of Mauna a Wākea through EAducation

Central to the restoration of Hawaiʻi's independence is the restoration of the health of the land and the health of the people, which are mutually dependent. Under the pressures of US occupation that has sought to seize land by burying Hawaiian knowledge systems, we are seeing now a great flowering throughout the islands and across the globe that has been brought about by Mauna a Wākea and the abundance of the pulapula, the new generations of leadership that are being planted on Mauna a Wākea and the rising of the lāhui through a revival of these knowledge systems, as well as the ways that knowledge systems are interrelated.

As more and more people traveled to Mauna a Wākea to support the kiaʻi mauna, we have seen the emergence of what Hawaiian-medium preschool teacher Kahoʻokahi Kanuha has termed "EAducation," a philosophy of education that directs educational projects on the Hawaiian historical and cultural foundations for political autonomy. Kanuha organized the Hawaiʻi Aloha ʻĀina series of EAducation workshops on the mauna, which have grown into a widespread movement to educate people about ea, political sovereignty, Hawaiian history, and politics.

"EAducate" is a word that I used at the beginning of the Mauna Kea movement. On September 20, 2014, I started Hawai'i Aloha 'Āina, a monthly series of free presentations for the community in Kona. I made Aloha 'Āina messaging on T-shirts to support this series financially. Our first shirt was "a hiki i ke Aloha 'Āina hope loa (until the very last Aloha 'Āina)." These were the words spoken by James Keauiluna Kaulia in a speech against the annexation of Hawai'i by the United States where he famously stated that Kanaka would stand for Hawai'i's independence until the very last aloha 'āina, the very last patriot of the lāhui, the nation. The idea was to EAducate, a philosophy of education that would give the lāhui the ability to rise, to ea. EAducation is about learning your culture, your history, your language, your stories. That is what will empower the lāhui. EAducation is what will return breath and life to our lāhui, it will give us the ability to have sovereignty, rule and independence over all the decisions we make and over the future of our lāhui.[14]

It has developed into a free Hawaiian educational series that aims to overcome the indoctrination, denationalization and Americanization of our people that has been occurring ever since the illegal overthrow of our queen Lili'uokalani on January 17, 1893. It is comprised of various presentations and lectures on anything related to Hawaiian history and culture. There are many meanings to the word "ea." These include sovereignty, life, air, breath, to rise and to swell up. All of these meanings are goals for Hawai'i Aloha 'Āina, to raise awareness and knowledge that the history we thought we knew was in fact all lies. We are in a time of great change, and so I believe the meaning of this slogan "EAducate" is to educate in the Hawaiian way; to see things the same way our kūpuna saw things. It's an amazing time to be witnessing this. (Quoted in Hermes, 2016)

As Freitas has explained, there has been a shift and, now is a time of ea, a time of 'Ōiwi resurgence that has transformed our understanding of the terms of this struggle.

Kanuha's work has conditioned the soil for a strong foundation for the EAducational movement as ea workshops and events have been planted in other communities across the islands. These workshops give us visual image of the ea that is flourishing and bursting through the cracks in the concrete institutional structures of settler colonial education.

Ku'uipo Freitas, another kia'i mauna of this new generation of leaders, who was arrested twice on the mauna and is a teacher at Pūnana Leo o Kona, explains how EAducation has grown:

Kanuha taught schoolchildren about ea at the very site of struggle: at the basecamp on Mauna a Wākea. He speaks to the haumāna about the reason why the kia'i are standing for Mauna a Wākea in the larger picture of US occupation in Hawai'i. He explains,

The reason for our being here, for all these pilikia, development, not just on Mauna Kea . . . is due to the fact that we are not able to govern ourselves and determine for ourselves what is pono and unpono for our people and our 'āina. So I'm going to get into a political realm, but it's not so much politics as 'oia'i'o, as it is the truth of the matter. And so we determined that instead of trying to

43

pick the fruits of the tree, instead of trying to trim the leaves and the branches, let's huki this whole kumu out of the ground, and let's get the roots out of it. The source of this pilikia is an illegal occupation by the United States of our people dating back to the overthrow in 1893. Again, I teach preschool, so I try to keep it basic as possible. I teach it to those keiki as well. (Kanuha, 2015)

As Kanuha suggested, ea grows out of an education in ʻoiaʻiʻo, truth, and that kind of education must question the very foundations of education in occupied Hawaiʻi. An EAducation is one that is rooted in the abundance of ancestral knowledges, bearing the fruit of children who will be able to choose a future that is pono, right, balanced, and sovereign.

ʻŌiwi maps are kīpuka, a term referring to oases of old forest growth during a lava flow that are seedbanks for the future, and we can look to the ways that visual artists create maps that are kīpuka of ancestral lessons about ea that are rooted in particular places. I want to turn to the work of an artist who maps a visual illustration of ea through the genealogy of Mauna a Wākea. Haley Kailiehu, an artist from the ʻili ʻāina of Kukuipuka in the ahupuaʻa of Kahakuloa on Maui, has done much to help us remember the abundance of Mauna a Wākea. She works to "allow the current and future generations of Kanaka ʻŌiwi to (re)learn and assert their kuleana, (re)establish connections to our moʻolelo and kūpuna (ancestors) and (re)affirm our rightful place in our homeland."[15] On October 12, 2013, with ʻIlima Long, Andre Perez, and other members of HauMANA, a student arm of the Hawaiian independence group MANA, she organized a community-painted mural at the University of Hawaiʻi at Hilo to call public attention to the university's role in supporting the construction of the TMT and to mobilize the community against the DLNR's renewal of the university's leases for the Mauna Kea Science Reserve. More than a hundred students, faculty, and people from different communities gathered over the course of one weekend to contribute to this mural (fig. 5). In this mural of Mauna a Wākea, Kailiehu focuses on the beauty of the moʻolelo that inspires a shared vision

Figure 5. Photo courtesy of Haley Kailiehu.

of a decolonial future. The mural is a kīpuka that maps the genealogical path of the waters of Mauna a Wākea.

The painting depicts the sacred water streaming down the mountain from Waiau, shaped as a kalo leaf, feeding the Kānaka as plant people, siblings of the kalo, their leafy arms outstretched to Wākea, Sky Father, their malo the corm of the kalo. At the center of the mural is a visual illustration of the genealogical chant that stopped the construction crews, beginning with Papahānaumoku and Wākea. To the right of them is their daughter, Hoʻohōkūkalani, holding a baby in her arms. Her first child by her father Wākea was born as an unformed fetus and when buried, grew into the kalo plant, Hāloanakalaukapalili of the long stem whose leaves tremble in the wind. The second child she carries in her arms is Hāloa the aliʻi, the younger sibling to the kalo, and also to Mauna a Wākea. These ancestors fill the land in the mural, reminding us of the genealogical descent of Mauna a Wākea, kalo, and kanaka from Papa and Wākea, all fed by the life-giving waters of Kāne at Waiau, the mural a reminder of their familial relationships and their kuleana to care for each other.

The text accompanying the mural criticized the university for representing the Thirty Meter Telescope:

UH CANNOT BE A
HAWAIIAN PLACE OF LEARNING
WHILE LEADING THE DESECRATION
OF MAUNA A WAKEA.
HEY UH . . . BE ACCOUNTABLE
BE A HAWAIIAN PLACE OF LEARNING . . .
STAND WITH THE PEOPLE . . .
STOP THE DESECRATION . . .
STOP THE THIRTY METER TELESCOPE!

After the completion of the mural on Sunday, a *Ka Leo* staffer painted over the message, then printed "Ka Leo Arts Fest" over the above message. HauMANA quickly organized a protest attended by over two hundred students, faculty, and staff who were outraged by the censorship. Kailiehu reflects on the power of the mural:

> I feel an overwhelming sense of hope. I can recollect the experience as if it happened just yesterday. I can remember the people, the keiki with parents, friends with more friends, and the kūpuna, who we were all there painting together. Our Mauna a Wākea mural was an attempt to convey our message to the rest of society, to bring awareness to a concern that we felt all people should understand and know fully. Our Mauna a Wākea mural was a venue where people from within the scope of consciousness and others, not so much aware, could come and learn and actively engage in taking a stance.[16]

In this way, the mural's moon, in her Hoaka crescent phase, also sets the intention of the mural as the unification of the people. As Katrina-Ann R. Kapāʻanaokalāokeola Nākoa Oliveira notes, Ka Pae ʻĀina Hawaiʻi, the Hawaiian archipelago resembles the Hoaka moon phase, and Kailiehu's image of the moon in this mural appears in Oliveira's *Ancestral Places: Understanding Kanaka Geographies* as an illustration (Oliveira, 2014, p. 46). In the mural, the evocation of the Hoaka moon is a way to inspire all the people of Ka Pae ʻĀina Hawaiʻi to be united through Mauna a Wākea in a greater vision of a sovereign future.

Another one of Kailiehu's pieces, "Huliau," depicts a turning point where the pulapula, the new generations of leadership, are being planted on Mauna a

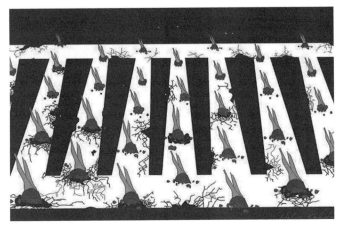

Figure 6. "Huliau," by Haley Kailiehu. Image courtesy of the artist.

Figure 7. The Legendary Crosswalk. Photo courtesy of Naaiakalani Navas.

Wākea (fig. 6). As children join their parents and families in the struggle, they lift up the Hae Hawai'i (fig. 7), the Hawaiian flag that was lowered at the time of the overthrow and cut to pieces when Hawai'i became a republic. The children are the huli, the kalo tops who are planted in what became the Legendary Crosswalk for the protection of Mauna a Wākea. "Huliau" also refers to a turning point, and Kailiehu illustrates this turning point through the image of the children being EAducated, huli taking root, their young, green abundance busting through the asphalt of the crosswalk that represents capitalist economies that industrialize sacred lands. The huli represents knowledge, ideas, all the people of the lāhui. Such abundance cannot be contained, covered over, or stifled. Kailiehu writes in her artist's statement for the piece, "The huli has already been planted, and it will continue to grow. This one is for the poe aloha aina maintaining a continuous presence at the aloha aina crosswalk checkpoint. Mahalo for planting the huli for the huliau in us all."

Personal stories can also become powerful 'Ōiwi maps that illustrate different kīpuka. One such example comes from the eleventh line, where TMT construction workers were stopped. 'Ohulei Waia'u, the alaka'i who led the kia'i in chanting "He kanaenae no ka hanau ana o Kauikeaouli," describes a beautiful mapping of the lines of protectors on the mauna that day. She explains,

> We were in line 11 and from our perspective, we could see all of the lines and we heard about what was happening below us. Once they got past one row, the next row would come up. We heard that our strong leaders Kaleikoa, Kaho'okahi, and Hualālai were taken and that everybody was afraid because we knew they had been hand-picked for arrest as our leaders, but I said to them,

"Don't worry, we're like the teeth of the manō. When one shark's tooth falls out, there's always another to replace it." Not like, watch out, we're going to bite you. No, what we realized is that there are always many, many rows behind that front, many, many leaders who are coming into their own and are willing to step up to lead us. (Waiaʻu, 2015)[17]

The lines of protectors, then, were rows of shark's teeth, resilient, regenerative, and abundant. Sharks tear their prey so violently that they break or lose their teeth daily. New teeth are continuously growing in rows that move forward, up to seven rows of replacement teeth and as many as thirty thousand teeth. The teeth are as the lehulehu, the multitudes that stand for Mauna a Wākea—the four hundred, the four thousand, the forty thousand, the four hundred thousand protectors being regenerated in the ʻōpio on the mauna.

This image illustrates what Kūkauakahi describes as the *decentralization* of organizing on Mauna a Wākea, the suppleness of this organizing structure, and when the leaders have been arrested, others have stepped in to take their places, including the ʻōpio who have come into their own as leaders, and still others who have taken the lead in organizing ʻAha Aloha ʻĀina gatherings in their own communities across Ka Pae ʻĀina o Hawaiʻi, to grow relationships, economies, systems, and structures for independence. This nonhierarchical, horizontal leadership is also mapped along the land, illustrating a land-based conception of the lāhui. Waiaʻu's words present us with an example of indigenous cartography that illustrates the visual mapping of the independence movement on Mauna a Wākea premised on ʻŌiwi economies of abundance, connectedness, and regeneration.

Figure 8. *"ReKALOnize Your Naʻau," by Haley Kailiehu. Image courtesy of the artist.*

Kailiehu also represented this image of the lines of kiaʻi on Mauna a Wākea in a way that maps a genealogical return to the piko as the source of ea. In July 2015, Kailiehu depicted the lines of kiaʻi in a piece entitled "ReKALOnize Your Naʻau" (fig. 8). In this image, Kailiehu inverts the process of colonization by depicting the lines of protectors on the mauna on a spiraling path back to the source, to the kalo leaf, an image reclaiming the naʻau, the mind and the inner core of one's being, from colonization. The kiaʻi hold the lei lāʻī before them, in lines reaching up to Waiau, which is depicted as the leaf of the kalo. This image brings together the piko as the point where the stem attaches to the kalo leaf from which veins radiate out, the piko as the summit and as the umbilicus that connects past generations of kiaʻi to future generations. Kailiehu writes,

This image depicts our kiaʻi mauna standing in lines up on the mauna walking together to the piko of our ea, ka piko o Wākea, at Waiau. The shape of Waiau, I often see as similar to that of the kalo leaf. And like the piko of the kalo leaf, the piko of the mauna connects us to our ʻāina and akua, the sources of our ea. It is thus in our returning to the piko to strengthen these ancestral connections that the consciousness of our lāhui is re-kalo-nized, re-centered, and re-born.[18]

Thus, reKALOnizing the naʻau is an act of ea and indigenous resurgence that turns inward. Waiau is the poʻowai, the place from which the headwaters and ʻike, knowledge, flow to the people and to which the people return to regain ea, life, breath, and political sovereignty.

"ReKALOnize Your Naʻau" gains further resonance when we look at the June 24, 2015 images of the pōhaku, or rocks that were planted in the road near the summit to protect the mauna. One of the kiaʻi, Kaukaohu Wahilani from Puea, Waiʻanae, was above the eleventh line and describes what he saw:

> Līlīnoe covered both our lāhui and DLNR, however, where we were higher up, it was clear and sunny. We could only hear the chanting and cries of our lāhui. We were all waiting for our lāhui to join us, and that is when this older kāne spoke and said, "Hui lāhui! Looks like nā kūpuna are ready to come down the mauna and join us!" As soon as those words left his mouth the lāhui started to halihali the pōhaku and place them on the road! It was amazing. From pōkiʻi to kūpuna, everybody was doing the hana lima![19]

The pōhaku were planted in the road, some here and there, and others in low rock walls that formed a labyrinth through which people, but not vehicles, could pass. Kailiehu's image, then is also a mapping of moʻokūʻauhau, from the keiki in the first line on the county road, through to the ʻōpio line, and other lines up the mauna and to the pōhaku above, the pōhaku as kūpuna, as the last lines of ancestors standing for Mauna a Wākea. On that day, the kiaʻi stood with the kūpuna in the lines leading to the piko of Mauna a Wākea. Jada Anela Torres was planted there on Mauna a Wākea (fig. 9) with her older brother Jonah and her parents, Meleana Smith and Kaleo Torres, as an ʻohana, a family, standing with their kūpuna pōhaku that day.

The hearing officer in the second 2016–17 contested case hearing has recommended to the BLNR that it reaffirm its approval of the Conservation District Use Permit for the TMT. Richard Naiwi Wurdeman, attorney for the Mauna Kea hui, stood kūpaʻa for the mauna in both Supreme Court cases. On September 30, 2018, the Hawaiʻi Supreme Court majority opinion affirmed the BLNR's approval of the Conservation District Use Permit issued to the TMT. In his lone dissenting opinion, Justice Michael Wilson (2018) points to the ways this conclusion is "fraught with illogic" (p. 14), and that the

Figure 9. Jada Anela Torres with the kūpuna pōhaku, June 24, 2015. Photo courtesy of Etihu Keeling, with permission of Jada Anela Torres and Meleana Smith.

majority decision authorizes a dangerous new "degradation principle" that "dilutes or reverses the foundational dual objectives of environmental law—namely, to conserve what exists (or is left) and to repair environmental damage" (p. 4).

One thing is certain: We will continue to fight for Mauna a Wākea a hiki i ke aloha 'āina hope loa (until the very last aloha 'āina). We stand fast, 'onipa'a, knowing that the kūpuna pōhaku, and the myriad other forms the kūpuna take, are protecting the mountain, and that we will be standing there with them when the construction crews try to make their way back up the mountain. The movement to protect Mauna a Wākea has rippled out to become part of a unified global movement against the capitalist economies driving climate change. As late settler capitalist economies in crisis are beginning to wither away in their manufactured wastelands of scarcity, we are collectively transforming the conditions of US occupation and settler colonialism, looking to the kīpuka provided by Kanaka 'Ōiwi maps, rebuilding social relationships and cultivating the land base that is both the 'āina momona, the abundant lands, and the 'āina kamaha'o, the wondrous land. We are bringing into being a decolonial future on the abundant ancestral lands—the national land base—and it is upon this abundance that the people of the lāhui are rising.

REFERENCES

Ahuena (Emma Ahuena Davison Taylor). (1931, July). The betrothal of the Pink God and the Snow Goddess. The pink snow is always seen upon Mauna Kea. *Paradise of the Pacific*, 13-15t.

Aoki, P. (2012). *Board of Land and Natural Resources, State of Hawai'i, Hearing officer's proposed findings of fact, conclusions of law, and decision and order for the contested case hearing for the Thirty Meter Telescope.* DLNR Docket No. HA-11-05.

Basham, L. (2010). Ka Lāhui Hawai'i: He mo'olelo, he 'āina, he loina, a he ea kākou. *Hūlili: Multidisciplinary Research on Hawaiian Well-Being, 6*(1), 37–72.

Case, P. (2014, October 5). Mālana mai Ka'ū, TMT orientation [Video file]. Retrieved from https://www.youtube.com/watch?v=kBNaGlbojeo

Ching, C. K. (2013, February 12). *Oral argument before the Board of Land and Natural Resources.* Transcript by J. McManus. Hilo, Hawai'i.

Donn, J. M. (1901). Territory survey map, Hawai'i. Territory of Hawai'i.

Edith Kanakaʻole Foundation. (2009). "Cultural anchor." In *Mauna Kea comprehensive management plan*. Prepared for the University of Hawaiʻi by Hoʻakea, LLC dba Kuʻiwalu.

Flores, E. K. (2016). *Exhibit B.02a: Written direct testimony of E. Kalani Flores in the State of Hawaiʻi, Board of Land and Natural Resources contested case hearing for the Thirty Meter Telescope*. Retrieved from https://dlnr.hawaii.gov/mk/files/2016/10/B.02a-wdt-EK-Flores.pdf

Goodyear-Kaʻōpua, N. (2013). *The seeds we planted: Portraits of a Native Hawaiian charter school*. Minneapolis, MN: University of Minnesota Press.

Goodyear-Kaʻōpua, N. (2014). Introduction. In N. Goodyear-Kaʻōpua, I. Hussey, & E. K. Wright (Eds.), *A nation rising: Hawaiian movements for life, land, and sovereignty* (pp. 1–33). Durham, NC: Duke University Press.

Goodyear-Kaʻōpua, N. (2017). Protectors of the future, not protestors of the past: Indigenous Pacific activism and Mauna a Wākea. *South Atlantic Quarterly, 116*(1), 184–194.

Haleole, S. N. (1863, January 24). "Ka moolelo o Laieikawai." *Ka Nupepa Kuokoa,* Vol. 2, No. 4, p. 1.

Hermes, K. L. (2016, March 10). Interview with Kuʻuipo Freitas. *The Hawaiʻi Independent*. Retrieved from http://hawaiiindependent.net/story/a-new-eaducation

Kanahele, P. K. (2011). *Ka honua ola: ʻEliʻeli kau mai / The living earth: Descend, deepen the revelation*. Honolulu, HI: Kamehameha Publishing.

Kanuha, K. (2015). Wākea—basecamp: Kahoʻokahi Kanuha [Video file]. Retrieved from https://www.youtube.com/watch?v=BJueh2moX5c&t=101s

Kauanui, J. K. (2011). *Exhibit B-20. Written direct testimony of J. Kēhaulani Kauanui in the State of Hawaiʻi, Department of Land and Natural Resources contested case hearing for the Thirty Meter Telescope*. Retrieved from http://kahea.org/files/b-20-kehau-kauanui-wdt/view?searchterm=Kauanui

Kauikeaouli, Na Lii, & Kalama, S. P. (1848). Buke kakau paa no ka mahele aina: I hooholoia iwaena o Kamehameha III a me na lii a me na konohiki ana [Buke Mahele]. Honolulu, HI: Hale Alii.

Kihoi, M. (2017, January 3). *Cross-examination of TMT project manager Gary Sanders*. Transcript by J. McManus. Hilo, Hawaiʻi.

Lloyd, D. (2016). "The goal of the revolution is the elimination of anxiety": On the right to abundance in a time of artificial scarcity. In Critical Ethnic Studies Editorial Collective (Eds.), *Critical Ethnic Studies: A Reader* (pp. 203–214). Durham, NC: Duke University Press.

Lyons, C. J. (1891). "Government survey map: Kaohe and Humuula, Hawaii." Registered map 1641. Kingdom of Hawai'i.

"Mālana mai Ka'ū." In M. P. Nogelmeier (Ed. & Comp.). (2001). *He lei no 'Emalani: Chants for Queen Emma Kaleleonālani* (pp. 268–269). Honolulu, HI: Queen Emma Foundation.

Malo, D. (1903). *Hawaiian antiquities: Mo'olelo Hawai'i.* (N. B. Emerson, Trans.). Honolulu, HI: Hawaiian Gazette Co. (Original work published 1898)

Malo, D. (2006). *Ka moolelo Hawaii: Hawaiian traditions.* (M. N. Chun, Ed. & Trans.). Honolulu, HI: First People's Productions. (Original work published 1838)

Maly, K., & Maly, O. (2005). *Mauna Kea—Ka piko kaulana o ka 'āina (Mauna Kea—The famous summit of the land): A collection of Native traditions, historical accounts, and oral history interviews for: Mauna Kea, the lands of Ka'ohe, Humu'ula and the "'āina mauna on the island of Hawai'i."* Prepared for the Office of Mauna Kea Management (University of Hawai'i at Hilo). Hilo, HI: Office of Mauna Kea Management.

Nā Maka o ka 'Āina (Puhipau & Joan Lander) (n.d.). "Mauna Kea—from mountain to sea." Retrieved from http://www.mauna-a-wakea.info/maunakea/A2_lakewaiau.html

NASA. (2005). *Final environmental impact statement for the Outrigger Telescopes project: Mauna Kea science reserve, island of Hawai'i, Vol. 1.* Washington, DC: Author. Retrieved from https://dlnr.hawaii.gov/mk/files/2016/10/FEIS-Outrigger-Telescopes-VOL-1.pdf

Ngugi wa Thiong'o (1986). *Decolonising the mind: The politics of language in African literature.* Portsmouth, NH: Heinemann.

Oliveira, K.-A. R. K. N. (2014). *Ancestral places: Understanding Kanaka geographies.* Corvallis, OR: Oregon State University Press.

Peralto, L. N. (2014). Portrait. Mauna a Wākea: Hānau ka mauna, the piko of our ea. In N. Goodyear-Ka'ōpua, I. Hussey, & E. K. Wright (Eds.), *A nation rising: Hawaiian movements for life, land, and sovereignty* (pp. 232–244). Durham, NC: Duke University Press.

Pisciotta, K. (2011, August 14). Meet the Mauna Kea Hui—Kealoha Pisciotta. [web log comment]. Retrieved from http://kahea.org/blog/mk-vignette-kealoha-pisciotta

Pisciotta, Kealoha. (2013, February 12). *Oral argument before the Board of Land and Natural Resources.* Transcript by J. McManus. Hilo, Hawai'i.

Pisciotta, K. (Panelist). (2015, May 1). Should the Thirty Meter Telescope be built? *Insights on PBS Hawaiʻi.* Retrieved from https://www.youtube.com/watch?v=HMKgNSbicE0&t=1106s.

Poepoe, J. M. (1906, February 10 and 12). The chant is known as "He kanaenae no ka hanau ana o Kauikeaouli" and can be found in "Ka Moolelo Hawaii Kahiko." *Ka Naʻi Aupuni,* Vol. 1, No. 65, p. 1.

Pukui, M. K., & Korn, A. L. (Trans. & Eds.). (1973). *The echo of our song: Chants and poems of the Hawaiians.* Honolulu, HI: University of Hawaiʻi Press.

Quinn, Daniel S. (2014, March 28). "Request approval to enter into a memorandum of agreement (MOA) and right of entry (ROE) with the County of Hawaiʻi on the transfer of management for a portion of the Mauna Kea State Recreation Area (MKSRA)."

Simonson, M., & Hammatt, H. H. (2010). Cultural impact assessment for the Thirty Meter Telescope (TMT) Observatory project and TMT mid-level facility project, Maunakea, Kaʻohe Ahupuaʻa, Hāmākua District, Hawaiʻi Island. In University of Hawaiʻi at Hilo, *Final environmental impact statement: Thirty Meter Telescope (TMT) project, island of Hawaiʻi, Vol. 3 – Appendices.* Kailua, HI: Cultural Surveys Hawaiʻi.

Trask, H. (2008). Settlers of color and "immigrant" hegemony: "Locals" in Hawaiʻi. In C. Fujikane & J. Y. Okamura (Eds.), *Asian settler colonialism: From local governance to the habits of everyday life in Hawaiʻi* (pp. 45–65). Honolulu, HI: University of Hawaiʻi Press. (Original work published 2000)

University of Hawaiʻi at Hilo. (2010). *Final environmental impact statement: Thirty Meter Telescope (TMT) project, island of Hawaiʻi, Vol. 1.* Hilo, HI: Author. Retrieved from https://dlnr.hawaii.gov/occl/files/2013/08/2010-05-08-HA-FEIS-Thirty-Meter-Telescope-Vol1.pdf

University of Hawaiʻi at Hilo, & TMT International Observatory. (2017). *Joint [proposed] findings of fact, conclusions of law, and decision and order.* May 30, 2017. Retrieved from https://dlnr.hawaii.gov/mk/files/2017/05/671-UHH-TIO-joint-proposal.pdf

Wilson, M. (2018, November 9). *Dissenting opinion in the matter of the contested case hearing regarding the conservation district use application for the Thirty Meter Telescope.* Retrieved from http://www.courts.state.hi.us/wpcontent/uploads/2018/11/SCOT-17-0000777disamada.pdf

Wise, J., & J. W. H. I. Kihe. (1914–1917). Kaao hooniua puuwai no Ka-Miki. *Ka Hoku o Hawaii.*

ABOUT THE AUTHOR

Candace Fujikane is an associate professor of English at the University of Hawai'i. She coedited with Jonathan Okamura *Asian Settler Colonialism: From Local Governance to the Habits of Everyday Life in Hawai'i* (University of Hawai'i Press, 2008). She is currently completing her book, *Mapping Abundance against the Wastelands of Capital: Indigenous and Critical Settler Cartographies in Hawai'i*.

NOTES

I would like to thank the following people for their generous comments and suggestions: Cristina Bacchilega, Clarence Kūkauakahi Ching, Cindy Freitas, Ku'uipo Freitas, Bianca Isaki, Noelani Goodyear-Ka'ōpua, Haley Kailiehu, Kaho'okahi Kanuha, J. Kēhaulani Kauanui, Mehana Kihoi, Shelley Muneoka, Kealoha Pisciotta, Meleana Torres-Smith, Glen Tomita, 'Ohulei Waia'u, Pumpkin Waia'u, Deborah Ward, and Erin Kahunawaika'ala Wright. Two anonymous reviewers provided excellent comments and suggestions. The amazing women in my writing group have also given me invaluable feedback: Elizabeth Colwill, Monisha DasGupta, Cynthia Franklin, Linda Lierheimer, Laura Lyons, Naoko Shibusawa, and Mari Yoshihara. All errors are my own.

1. For a discussion of akua as elemental forms, see Kanahele, 5.

2. For HB1618 CD1, see: https://www.capitol.hawaii.gov/session2014/bills/HB1618_CD1_.HTM. For the current language of the Hawai'i Revised Statute, see https://codes.findlaw.com/hi/division-1-government/hi-rev-st-sect-171-4.html

3. K. Ching, personal communication, July 18, 2012.

4. Kepā and Onaona Maly note that the name for the spring is spelled "Houpokāne" (Maly & Maly, 2005, p. 450), but after consulting with Hawaiian language speakers, I will spell it "Houpo o Kāne" for clarity. The name of the deity sister of Poli'ahu is spelled as "Kahoupokāne," so I am recording her name as "Ka Houpo o Kāne."

5. Speech at Mauna Kea rally, 'Iolani Palace, Honolulu, Hawai'i, April 13, 2015.

6. For a discussion of how the checkpoint became a place where kiaʻi engaged others in dialogue, see Goodyear-Kaʻōpua (2017).

7. K. Kanuha, personal communication, October 28, 2017.

8. These rains are identified in Ahuena (1931).

9. UHH Exhibit A-130 quotes Emerson's footnote from *Hawaiian Antiquities: Moʻolelo Hawaiʻi* at p. 38. https://dlnr.hawaii.gov/mk/files/2017/01/UHH-Exhibit-A-130.pdf

10. Emerson's English translation of Malo, *Hawaiian Antiquities*, 17.

11. See Alexander's "Introduction" in Malo, *Hawaiian Antiquities*, xvii.

12. https://www.capitol.hawaii.gov/hrscurrent/Vol14_Ch0701-0853/HRS0711/HRS_0711-1107.htm

13. Facebook post, December 30, 2012.

14. K. Kanuha, personal communication, October 30, 2017.

15. See Haley Kailiehu, "Artist Bio," http://www.haleykailiehu.com/community-art.html

16. See Kailiehu, "Community Art," http://www.haleykailiehu.com/community-art.html

17. ʻO. Waiaʻu, personal communication, June 25, 2015.

18. This quotation is from the artist's statement for "ReKALOnize Your Naʻau," which was previously available on Kailiehu's website.

19. K. Wahilani, personal communication, May 21, 2016.

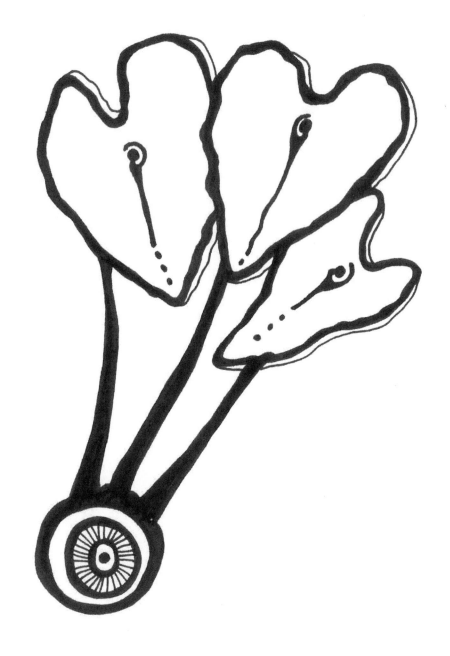

Resurgent Refusals: Protecting Mauna a Wākea and Kanaka Maoli Decolonization

DAVID UAHIKEAIKALEI'OHU MAILE

With construction of the Thirty Meter Telescope threatening to desecrate and destroy Mauna a Wākea, protection of the sacred mountain on Hawai'i Island has been steadfast in stopping the development. In this article, I investigate the complex and diverse discourses circulating in and around the movement to protect Mauna a Wākea. Using a makawalu method within a queer-Indigenous-anarchist methodological framework, I argue the corporeal refusals and collective resurgence against the Thirty Meter Telescope can forcibly be made complicit with, and undermined by, settler colonial state power. I demonstrate how this occurs in settler state law, science-neutral opposition, decolonization debates, and gendered public narratives. Nevertheless, I suggest that Kanaka Maoli activisms against astronomy-industry development illustrate non-statist forms of decolonization, which I theorize as "resurgent refusals" that offer interventions into both Hawaiian studies and critical Indigenous studies.

CORRESPONDENCE MAY BE SENT TO:
David Uahikeaikalei'ohu Maile
Department of Political Science,
University of Toronto
Sidney Smith Hall, Room 3018
100 St. George Street
Toronto, ON M5S 3G3
Email: maile.dave@gmail.com

57

Hūlili: Multidisciplinary Research on Hawaiian Well-Being, Vol. 11, No. 1
Copyright © 2019 by Kamehameha Schools

Discussing the undergirding philosophy of the movement to protect Mauna a Wākea from the Thirty Meter Telescope (TMT), Lanakila Mangauil said, "Our stance is not against the science. It's not against the science. It's not against the TMT itself" (Callis, 2015). Mangauil, alongside other Kānaka Maoli (Native Hawaiians), is a kiaʻi (guardian, protector) of our sacred mountain, Mauna a Wākea.

In 2014, the TMT International Observatory organized to construct an eighteen-story industrial telescope complex on Mauna a Wākea, a sacred mountain on Hawaiʻi Island. As Brown (2016) suggests, there are many examples that Mauna a Wākea is sacred to Kānaka Maoli. For instance, Mauna a Wākea is the genealogical kin of Papahānaumoku and Wākea, detailed in the birth chant crafted for Kauikeaouli, King Kamehameha III (Pukui & Korn, 1979), called "Hanau-a-Hua-Kalani" (Silva, 2017) as well as "He Kanaenae No Ka Hanau Ana O Kauikeaouli" (Peralto, 2014). According to Chang (2016), "The birth chant of Kauikeaouli evokes an identification between the newborn chief and the land," which "sacralized the aliʻi and also the land" (p. 203).

From the TMT International Observatory's earliest incarnation in 2003 as the Thirty Meter Telescope Observatory Corporation, kiaʻi have physically stopped construction of the TMT, since it aims to desecrate and destroy the mountain. In 2015, protection of Mauna a Wākea continued in the form of corporeal refusals and collective resurgence. However, the TMT threat remains, as proponents of desecration entwine capitalist development and settler colonial domination in the name of scientific knowledge production. This nefarious menace has resulted in kiaʻi being repeatedly arrested, incarcerated, and criminalized. Between April and September of 2015, the State of Hawaiʻi made fifty-nine arrests and has

suggested, ironically, that protectors are an "imminent peril to the public health or natural resources" (Lincoln, 2015). In opposing construction of the TMT, kiaʻi have emphasized that the issue is not about science. And yet, the TMT, as a state-supported project, would exact violence upon the land—the ʻāina (that which feeds)—and on Kānaka Maoli *in the name of science.*

This article therefore interrogates the multiple, complex, and competing discourses circulating in and around the movement to protect Mauna a Wākea from the TMT. I do this by addressing the following questions: Why has the defense of Mauna a Wākea made repeated claims that kiaʻi, in general, and Kānaka Maoli, in particular, are not anti-science? How is the protection of Mauna a Wākea regulated and disciplined by settler colonial state power? How do the corporeal refusals of and collective resurgence against the TMT jibe with non-statist forms of Kanaka Maoli decolonization?

To examine Kanaka Maoli resistance to the TMT, I analyze, in the words of Cacho (2012, p. 27), an "eclectic and unruly" archive by reading together seemingly disparate sources. These sources include legal documents and cases, news articles and reports, political cartoons, and a TMT public relations artifact. "Assembling these varied and often disjunctive primary sources," Puar (2007) writes, "is crucial to countering the platitudinous and journalistic rhetoric that plagues those public discourses most readily available for consumption" (p. xv). This chaotic archive of mine is activated by a makawalu method. Translating literally to "eight eyes" (Pukui & Elbert, 1986, p. 258), makawalu holds kaona (hidden meaning) that conveys a diversity of perspectives. In theorizing makawalu, hoʻomanawanui (2014) observes that Kānaka Maoli "accept and even appreciate multiple and sometimes conflicting accounts," which she states is "reflected in the ʻōlelo noʻeau (proverb), ʻaʻohe pau ka ʻike i ka hālau hoʻokahi (not all knowledge is contained in one school)" (p. xxxi). Makawalu offers a Kanaka Maoli method for analyzing the legion of discourses produced in the movement to protect Mauna a Wākea from the TMT. Engaging makawalu methodology, I argue that corporeal refusals and collective resurgence against the TMT can forcibly be made complicit with, and undermined by, settler colonial state power. In this article, I demonstrate how this occurs, as discursive grids of intelligibility, in settler state law, science-neutral opposition, decolonization debates, and gendered public narratives. I conclude that Kanaka Maoli activisms against astronomy-industry development illustrate non-statist forms of decolonization, which I theorize as *resurgent refusals* that provide interventions into both Hawaiian studies and critical Indigenous studies.

Queer-Indigenous-Anarchism

The methodological approach I use to orient my analysis of the protection of Mauna a Wākea integrates tools from anarchism and queer theory within a central framework of critical Indigenous studies. This *queer-Indigenous-anarchism* offers a methodology in the spirit of what Goodyear-Kaʻōpua (2016) calls selective promiscuity, which "draw[s] heavily on our ʻŌiwi [Indigenous] lineage" while "selectively bring[ing] in other lineages or thinkers who provide us with traction to move the lāhui [people, nation] forward" (p. 9). In this section, I briefly map out scholarship from anarchism, queer theory, and critical Indigenous studies, discussing some of the key debates and contributions, in order to establish my unruly methodology.

Claiming anti-state critiques of oppression, anarchism has neglected settler colonialism. Lewis (2015) states,

"The desire to resist all forms of oppression and domination is perhaps one of the hallmarks of anarchism" (p. 146). For anarchist studies, the state and its techniques of power are targeted for critique. Yet, Lewis posits that "fighting the state and capitalism is not enough" (p. 146). He suggests US and Canadian state power exists through white supremacy, which is animated via settler colonial dispossession of land, accumulation of capital, and Indigenous genocide. As such, Lewis implores white settler anarchists to engage with Indigenous movements for decolonization. He intimates, however, this could repurpose decolonization for incorporation. On this point, Walia (2015) asserts that incorporation can "subordinate and compartmentalize indigenous struggle within the machinery of existing leftist narratives" (p. 42). She exclaims, "We have to be cautious to avoid replicating the state's assimilationist model" (p. 42).

Despite anarchism's affinities with Indigenous theories and movements, my methodology moves away from a flattened equivalency that would position anarchism as an Indigenous philosophy or even Kanaka Maoli protectors of Mauna a Wākea as anarchists. Taking a cue from Ramnath's (2015) caution, I'm not looking for anarchism. The more productive imperative is for an Indigenous-centered anarchism that pursues anti-racist, anti-colonial, and anti-capitalist critiques of the settler state. This is the line of critique I follow in this article.

The impulse of my methodology is an Indigenous anarchism that makes critiques of the settler state accountable to what Brandzel (2016) calls the "violence of the normative." *Queer Indigenous Studies*, the edited volume and its attendant analytic, has simultaneously intervened into queer theory and Indigenous studies by "pay[ing] attention to the ways that heteronormativity—the normalizing and privileging of patriarchal heterosexuality and its gender and sexual expressions—undermines struggles for decolonization and sovereignty" (Driskill, Finley, Gilley, & Morgensen, 2011, p. 19). This approach also works to queer anarchism by, in the words of Daring, Rogue, Volcano, and Shannon (2012), "making anarchism strange" (p. 14), or making it estranged from white supremacist, settler colonial, and heteronormative structures of power. With this queer-Indigenous-anarchist orientation as a backdrop, the next section analyzes the protection of Mauna a Wākea and critiques the violence manufactured by the TMT's settler colonial capitalism.

Protecting Mauna a Wākea

The State of Hawai'i's Board of Land and Natural Resources (BLNR) issued a general lease in 1968 to the University of Hawai'i for the purpose of building a single telescope complex at Mauna a Wākea. Upon doing so, multiple telescope complexes began developing, and public protest emerged, claiming that the new development violated the state's initial general lease. After the University of Hawai'i applied in 2011 for a Conservation District use permit for permission to build the TMT, a petition was filed with the BLNR for a contested case hearing. However, the BLNR steamrollered the process and approved the use permit before holding the contested case hearing. This occurred even as the language in the university's application, on page 158 under environmental assessment, explicitly declared, "The impact on cultural resources has been, and would continue to be, substantial, adverse, and significant." However, the Hawai'i Supreme Court ruled, on December 2, 2015, this was "putting the cart before the horse" and was a violation of due process. The court therefore invalidated the building permit and remanded the case back down to the BLNR to hold a new contested case hearing. This new contested case hearing concluded with the hearing officer recommending that the BLNR approve the building permit for the TMT. On September 28, 2017, the BLNR voted in favor of granting a Conservation District use permit for the TMT. This brief synopsis poignantly shows how the state, despite the Supreme Court decision against the TMT, has played a significant role in authorizing the project.

With the pattern of decision-making about land use in mind, I suggest Hawai'i's settler state is co-constitutive of astronomy-industry development. Arguing that state-sanctioned astronomy-industry development is tied to empire, Byrd (2011) contends:

> Transit refers to a rare astronomical event, the paired transits of Venus across the sun, that served in 1761 and again in 1769 as global moments that moved European conquest toward notions of imperialist planetarity that provided the basis for Enlightenment liberalism. The imperial planetarity that sparked scientific rationalism and inspired humanist articulations of freedom, sovereignty, and equality touched four continents and a sea of islands in order to cohere itself. (pp. xx–xxi)

In other words, astronomy-industry development emerged through the dispossession and elimination of Indigenous peoples by imperial nation-states trying to universalize absolute truth of Enlightenment science. When the State of Hawai'i sanctions the TMT, it not only marks how the state entity constitutes itself on stolen lands via settler colonial dispossession, but it also demonstrates that the state's support of astronomy-industry development proliferates settler colonial power so as to reinforce its institutionalization in the formation of Hawai'i as a settler state. Such proliferation of power, at the expense of Hawai'i's Indigenous lands and people, is the centerpiece of the settler state.

Settler colonial state power, therefore, regulates the protection of Mauna a Wākea. Even as the settler state sanctions the TMT it has simultaneously interpellated, or hailed and coerced, protection of Mauna a Wākea to conform to settler state law. In discussing legal discursive formations, Barker (2011) asserts:

> The law is a discourse that operates in historically contingent and meaningful ways, articulated to other discourses ideologically, strategically, and irrationally. It informs the constitution and character of power relations and knowledge between Native peoples and the United States, and within Native communities. (pp. 7–8)

Because the settler state mediates social relations through law, Indigenous people face a double bind where "the state is assumed to be the center of political life, and people seek sanction within an already assimilative, disempowering and unequal framework" (Goodyear-Ka'ōpua, 2011, p. 131). My trepidation with relying on settler state legal frameworks as *the* avenue for liberation or *the* horizon of freedom to protect Mauna a Wākea aligns with Goodyear-Ka'ōpua's reflection: "What concerns me is the way sovereignty discourse has contributed to shifting emphasis and energy," she laments, "away from direct action land struggles—confrontations on the 'āina (land, literally 'that which feeds') over its usage—toward court battles, state and federal legislation, and research about historically appropriate legal strategies" (p. 134). Regulation's partner in crime is indeed discipline.

Protection of Mauna a Wākea against TMT has been disciplined into science-neutral opposition. Kealoha Pisciotta, a kia'i, cultural practitioner, and legal advocate, said in an interview with *Discover Magazine*, "It's not a question that we're against astronomy. We're just for Mauna Kea" (Hall, 2015). In a report by *Big Island Video News* (Corrigan, 2015a), kia'i Kaho'okahi Kanuha made similar remarks, suggesting that opposition to TMT is impartial and neutral to science. If the settler state of Hawai'i buttresses violence through a scientific project like the TMT then Kānaka Maoli *are not responsible to defend science*. This is particularly poignant as proponents of the TMT, like Richard Ellis from Caltech, an institutional member of the US-based consortium that funds the project, have unabashedly boasted, "We're searching for truth and knowledge. . . . We don't need to apologize" (McFarling, 2001, p. 2). And yet, Kānaka Maoli are callously expected and even demanded to apologize. I am not arguing against the corporeal refusals of the TMT enacted by kia'i confronting construction crews on the 'āina. Rather, I take issue with resurging against the TMT without opposing science, because this leaves settler colonial state power unscathed. The TMT is an astronomy-industry development proposed in the name of science, mediated and sanctioned through the settler state, which will in fact desecrate and destroy Mauna a Wākea, if constructed. This is neither neutral nor apologetic. Our critiques of the TMT must name scientific knowledge production and the settler state of Hawai'i as the perpetrators they are.

In a political cartoon by Dave Swann (fig. 1), published in the *Honolulu Star-Advertiser*, science-neutral opposition is structured by discourses of scientific progress. In the left panel, kia'i defending the Mauna are relegated to "THE PAST" whereas, on the right, "THE FUTURE" ushers in a fully constructed TMT, gazing at the stars

61

above. The image manufactures a primitivism in which the TMT's construction is inevitable and protection of Mauna a Wākea is futile, simultaneously signifying astronomy-industry development as modern and Kānaka Maoli as anachronistic.

Figure 1. A future of capitalist-colonialist violence disguised as scientific progress. Credit: Dave Swann and the Honolulu Star-Advertiser.

This signification of scientific progress camouflages capitalism's racist, and also colonial, developmentalism: develop through time by developing space. In his retooling of Karl Marx's theory of so-called primitive accumulation, Coulthard (2014) argues that settler colonial dispossession of Indigenous peoples' territories opens up proletarianization, or the insertion of subjects into labor markets, capitalist modes of production, and the accumulation of profit. For Coulthard, this is how spectacular violence transitions into concealed forms of violence cultivated vis-à-vis settler colonial state power, or what he refers to as "colonial governmentality" (p. 15). Swann's political cartoon is a visual portrayal of scientific progress disguising the TMT's capitalist-colonialist violence. As science-neutral opposition to TMT neglects,

and perhaps excuses, this structural dynamic of astronomy-industry development, it reifies settler colonialism and capitalism.

In an "Elevator Talk Brochure" (fig. 2) for the TMT, crafted by the TMT International Observatory and circulating as a public relations artifact, science and astronomy open up "new frontiers." By asserting the TMT's scientific mission will unlock new frontiers, reminiscent of Fredrick Jackson Turner's (1893) thesis, the message produced by this brochure indicates the universe is a new frontier requiring penetration, presupposing Hawai'i as a frontier already tamed. The logic suggests that Hawai'i has been conquered, which is simultaneously the condition of possibility as well as the motivational impetus to open up new frontiers and conquer additional sites. This hierarchicalization of frontiers elucidates, as Wolfe (2006) suggested, settler colonialism's irreducible element of territoriality, whereby astronomy-industry development has an insatiable hunger for land. It is an unyielding desire for our 'āina. The TMT's language of new frontiers invokes US empire's murderous conquest of Native Americans and is deployed, like manifest destiny's western frontier, to produce and camouflage violence against Kānaka Maoli.

Published in *Indian Country Today*, Marty Two Bulls's political cartoon (fig. 3) reveals the TMT as a scientific project tethered to settler colonialism and capitalism, which furthers the destruction and desecration of Mauna a Wākea.

This signification, I believe, is an important foil and lesson for science-neutral opposition. The image exposes the facile rationalizations of "scientific benefit" and "public good" that funnel critiques of the TMT into impartiality for science. For Two Bulls, protection of

Figure 2. TMT brochure suggesting the need to penetrate new frontiers and conquer new sites.

Figure 3. Opposing construction of the TMT while challenging scientific ideology. © 2019 by Marty Two Bulls Sr.

the sacred mountain crucially connects how "HAWAII AWAKENS" by refusing the construction of the TMT, even as it impotently attempts to defend itself: "But I'm science!" The ideological force of science simply does not justify the building of the TMT at Mauna a Wākea. In sum, I argue that collective resurgence requires us to forge criticisms of the TMT as a project of astronomy-industry development that produces and is a product of settler colonial capitalism.

Resurgent Refusals

To conclude this article, I examine Kanaka Maoli decolonization in the context of Mauna a Wākea. Theorizing Indigenous decolonization, Simpson's (2014) politics of refusal offers an ethic and practice to interrupt racialized, gendered economies of capitalist-colonialist violence against Indigenous peoples by refusing the "gifts" settler states offer—the TMT being one such "gift" offered to us in Hawai'i. She asserts, "To accept these conditions is an impossible project for some Indigenous people, not because it is impossible to achieve, but because it is politically untenable and thus normatively should be refused" (p. 22). In a similar vein, Coulthard (2014) advocates Indigenous resurgence in the face of settler colonial state recognition and its concealed violence. He recommends "redirect[ing] our struggles *away* from a politics that seeks to attain a conciliatory form of settler-state recognition for Indigenous nations toward a *resurgent politics of recognition* premised on self-actualization, direct action, and the resurgence of cultural practices" (original emphasis, p. 24). Refusal and resurgence, together, offer an Indigenous anti-state politics that antagonizes settler colonialism, capitalism, and heteropatriarchy, which I theorize as *resurgent refusals*. It is a theoretical concept, political philosophy, and embodied practice that exercises decolonization beyond the orbit of settler colonial state power.

Resurgent refusals emanate from on-the-ground struggles at Mauna a Wākea against the TMT. On June 24, 2015, more than seven hundred kiaʻi organized on Mauna a Wākea, chanting "hewa" and "aloha ʻāina," calling the TMT wrong, and standing in love of the land. As settler state law enforcement—officers who specifically were deployed from Hawaiʻi County Police and the Division of Conservation and Resource Enforcement—escorted TMT crews to the northern plateau, protectors mobilized multiple blockade lines and spread out across the access road. Kahoʻokahi Kanuha mentioned, "The plan wasn't to get arrested. But, the plan was to kūpaʻa, to stand, and stand until physically taken away" (Corrigan, 2015b). When the standoff culminated, twelve kiaʻi were arrested, and all construction was blocked. The strategy was to stall TMT crews. He stated, "Ten minutes, sixty-four lines, eight hours, and they're done." Kanuha also crystallized their solidarity, asserting, "Every inhabited island, we got em here. This is not a Hawaiʻi Island issue" (Corrigan, 2015c). In an interview after being released from his arrest at the June 24 blockade of the TMT, kiaʻi Kaleikoa Kāʻeo noted, "It really showcased the power of our people. The power of aloha ʻāina ʻoiaʻiʻo, which is the love—the genuine love. Love, the land, and truth" (Corrigan, 2015c). These are direct action blockades, embodied performances of decolonial love, and inter-island coalitions that operate exterior to structures of the settler state for protecting and repatriating Mauna a Wākea. They are resurgent refusals by Kānaka Maoli against astronomy-industry development as a project of settler colonial capitalism. "We have a word in our culture," Pua Case powerfully said on *Viceland*, in criticism of the TMT's settler colonial capitalism, "it's called mahaʻoi. It's when you overstay. And not only do you overstay your welcome, but you move in. And not only do you move in, but you push the original owners out" (Latimer, 2017). These resurgent refusals expose what is mahaʻoi and what is hewa by fighting to aloha ʻāina.

For decolonization to succeed, Kanaka Maoli movements, and other movements championed by Indigenous peoples, must be reflexive. I conclude by discussing two examples to make this point. First, the protection of Mauna a Wākea has deployed legal rhetoric from international law to claim that TMT construction is illegal insofar as its jurisdiction is legislated by a US state that illegally occupies Hawaiʻi. While Sai's (2008, 2004) arguments mobilize international laws of occupation to claim rights of national sovereignty to refuse TMT construction against the occupying US nation-state, this logic tends to flow in a direction whereby de-occupation is incommensurable with decolonization, which Kauanui (2008) has crucially described. Such an argument for de-occupation re-centers international law in a way that normalizes the Westphalian nation-state system, miscasting Indigeneity as inapplicable via claims that "Hawaiian" is purely a marker of nationality. Writing about how Native peoples invoke international legal systems, Barker (2011) reflects:

> Given histories of genocide, dispossession, assimilation, and discrimination are enacted and rationalized through the law, it is perhaps ironic or simply confusing that the law would continue to be regarded by indigenous peoples or other disenfranchised people as a tactic of resistance or reform. (p. 10)

"The question that lingers is not *why* Native peoples would use the law as a means of reformation," she further observes, "but *how*, in those uses, they seek to rearticulate their relations to one another, the United States, and the international community" (original emphasis, p. 11). Similar to using settler state law as a tactic, the question that must be asked is *how* international law gets mobilized in assertations of Kanaka Maoli sovereignty. Protecting Mauna a Wākea by separating Indigeneity and decolonization from de-occupation and nationalism, thus, is not a resurgent refusal.

Second, kiaʻi Brannon Kamahana Kealoha has openly criticized the TMT and Mailani Neal, a young Kanaka Maoli wahine (female), for creating a pro-TMT petition. Publicized on social media and further narrativized through news media, Kealoha's remarks asserted Neal should be "dealt with blows" (Walden, 2015)—a serious threat of physical violence. It is curious, as an informative anecdote, that my invocation of this story for analysis has been dismissed and silenced by some scholars, including a reviewer of this particular article. Let me be clear here. I am not suggesting that kiaʻi in the movement to protect Mauna a Wākea, or Kānaka Maoli

at large, be generalized, essentialized, or universalized as patriarchal, misogynistic, or sexist. To make such an interpretation would be a gross misreading. Kealoha's remarks, unfortunately, demonstrate how patriarchal domination and gendered violence have been rhetorically justified as a way to protect Mauna a Wākea. This, quite simply, should not be tolerated. We should not shy away from or compromise this point, nor should it be dismissed and silenced. Calling attention to these forms of hewa does not weaken our claims and movement but rather strengthens them in profoundly intersectional ways. It is as both Coulthard (2014) and Simpson (2014) assert: Indigenous peoples' decolonization *requires* gendered justice. Any heteropatriarchal violence in the movement to protect Mauna a Wākea must be abolished.

Resurgent refusals provide a grounded project to guide non-statist practices of decolonization. As such, my theoretical contribution intervenes into both Hawaiian studies and critical Indigenous studies. By utilizing makawalu as a Kanaka Maoli method of discourse analysis, and by utilizing a selectively promiscuous methodology of queer-Indigenous-anarchism, the arguments in this article provide preliminary answers to Goodyear-Kaʻōpua's (2011) question, "how do we *unsettle* settler state authorities, without replicating the violences and exclusions we aim to stop?" (p. 132). And in theorizing resurgent refusals as a non-statist form of decolonization by examining Kanaka Maoli activisms against astronomy-industry development, this article has engaged and intervenes within Coulthard's (2014) and Simpson's (2014) arguments for Indigenous resurgence and refusal. However, I do not intend to highlight these interventions over contributions by kiaʻi resurging and refusing the TMT on the ʻāina. And the fight is not over. This is especially true since construction still threatens to begin. My main hope is that this article can offer a guide, or blueprint, for resurgent refusals in the name of kiaʻi and for Mauna a Wākea.

From the deployment of de-occupation rhetoric to decolonize Mauna a Wākea, to the corporeal refusals of blockades on the ʻāina interrupting flows of settler colonial capital, protection of Mauna a Wākea elucidates how the politics of refusal and resurgence coalesce. Yet, as I have attempted to demonstrate, refusals of the TMT that re-center settler state law, remain neutral to astronomy-industry development, separate Indigenous decolonization from nationalist de-occupation, and bolster colonial heteropatriarchy, undermine resurgence against the settler state. Although queer-Indigenous-anarchism enables us to read these recuperations of settler colonial state power, we must continue to interrogate how decolonial movements for sovereign futures can be co-opted. Only when anti-state critiques within Indigenous movements are genuinely anti-colonial, anti-capitalist, anti-racist, and anti-sexist can decolonization manifest. While Mauna a Wākea signifies such a possibility, we must remain self-critical, coalitional, and altogether steadfast.

REFERENCES

Barker, J. (2011). *Native acts: Law, recognition, and cultural authenticity.* Durham, NC: Duke University Press.

Brandzel, A. L. (2016). *Against citizenship: The violence of the normative.* Chicago, IL: Illinois University Press.

Brown, M. A. (2016). Mauna Kea: Hoʻomana Hawaiʻi and protecting the sacred. *Journal for the Study of Religion, Nature and Culture, 10*(2), 150–169.

Byrd, J. A. (2011). *The transit of empire: Indigenous critiques of colonialism.* Minneapolis, MN: University of Minnesota Press.

Cacho, L. M. (2012). *Social death: Racialized rightlessness and the criminalization of the unprotected.* New York, NY: New York University Press.

Callis, T. (2015, March 31). TMT crews blocked. *Hawaiʻi Tribune-Herald.* Retrieved from http://www.hawaiitribune-herald.com/

Chang, D. A. (2016). *The world and all the things upon it: Native Hawaiian geographies of exploration.* Minneapolis, MN: University of Minnesota Press.

Corrigan, D. (2015a, April 1). Why block TMT on Mauna Kea? [Video file]. *Big Island Video News.* Retrieved from http://www.bigislandvideonews.com/

Corrigan, D. (2015b, June 25). Mauna Kea TMT showdown, part 1 of 3 [Video file]. *Big Island Video News.* Retrieved from http://www.bigislandvideonews.com/

Corrigan, D. (2015c, June 25). Mauna Kea TMT showdown, part 3 of 3 [Video file]. *Big Island Video News.* Retrieved from http://www.bigislandvideonews.com/

Coulthard, G. S. (2014). *Red skin, white masks: Rejecting the colonial politics of recognition.* Minneapolis, MN: University of Minnesota Press.

Daring, C. B., Rogue, J., Volcano, A., & Shannon, D. (2012). Introduction: Queer meet anarchism, anarchism meet queer. In C. B. Daring, J. Rogue, D. Shannon, & A. Volcano (Eds.), *Queering anarchism: Addressing and undressing power and desire* (pp. 5–17). Oakland, CA: AK Press.

Driskill, Q.-L., Finley, C., Gilley, B. J., & Morgensen, S. L. (2011). Introduction. In Q.-L. Driskill, C. Finley, B. J. Gilley, & S. L. Morgensen (Eds.), *Queer Indigenous studies: Critical interventions in theory, politics, and literature* (pp. 1–28). Tucson, AZ: University of Arizona Press.

Goodyear-Kaʻōpua, N. (2011). Kuleana lāhui: Collective responsibility for Hawaiian nationhood in activists' praxis. *Affinities: A Journal of Radical Theory, Culture, and Action, 5,* 130–163.

Goodyear-Kaʻōpua, N. (2016). Reproducing the ropes of resistance: Hawaiian studies methodologies. In K.-A. R. K. N. Oliveira & E. K. Wright (Eds.), *Kanaka ʻŌiwi methodologies: Moʻolelo and metaphor* (pp. 1–29). Honolulu, HI: Hawaiʻinuiākea School of Hawaiian Knowledge, University of Hawaiʻi Press.

Hall, S. (2015, May 9). Science and religion clash over telescope construction on sacred summit. *Discover Magazine.* Retrieved from http://blogs.discovermagazine.com/

hoʻomanawanui, k. (2014). *Voices of fire: Reweaving the literary lei of Pele and Hiʻiaka.* Minneapolis, MN: University of Minnesota Press.

Kauanui, J. K. (2008). *Hawaiian blood: Colonialism and the politics of sovereignty and indigeneity.* Durham, NC: Duke University Press.

Latimer, M. (Writer & Director). (2017). Hawaiian sovereignty [Television series episode 6]. In *Rise*. New York, NY: Vice Media.

Lewis, A. D. (2015). Anti-state resistance on stolen land: Settler colonialism, settler identity and the imperative of anarchist decolonization. In P. J. Lilley & J. Shantz (Eds.), *New developments in anarchist studies* (pp. 145–186). Brooklyn, NY: Thought Crimes, an imprint of Punctum Books.

Lincoln, M. (2015, July 14). Ige signs emergency rule restricting Mauna Kea access. *Hawaiʻi News Now*. Retrieved from http://www.hawaiinewsnow.com/

McFarling, U. L. (2001, March 18). Science, culture clash over sacred mountain. *Los Angeles Times*, p. 2. Retrieved from http://www.latimes.com/

Peralto, L. N. (2014). Portrait. Mauna a Wākea: Hānau ka mauna, the piko of our ea. In N. Goodyear-Kaʻōpua, I., Hussey, & E. K̄., Wright (Eds.), *A nation rising: Hawaiian movements for life, land, and sovereignty* (pp. 233–243). Durham, NC: Duke University Press.

Puar, J. K. (2007). *Terrorist assemblages: Homonationalism in queer times*. Durham, NC: Duke University Press.

Pukui, M. K., & Elbert, S. H. (1986). *Hawaiian dictionary: Hawaiian-English, English-Hawaiian*. Honolulu, HI: University of Hawaiʻi Press.

Pukui, M. K., & Korn, A. L. (Trans. & Eds.). (1979). *The echo of our song: Chants and poems of the Hawaiians*. Honolulu, HI: University of Hawaiʻi Press.

Ramnath, M. (2015). No gods, no masters, no brahmins: An anarchist inquiry on caste, race, and Indigeneity in India. In B. Maxwell & R. Craib (Eds.), *No gods, no masters, no peripheries: Global anarchisms* (pp. 44–79). Oakland, CA: PM Press.

Sai, D. K. (2004). American occupation of the Hawaiian state: A century unchecked. *Hawaiian Journal of Law & Politics, 1*, 46–81.

Sai, D. K. (2008). A slippery path towards Hawaiian Indigeneity: An analysis and comparison between Hawaiian state sovereignty and Hawaiian Indigeneity and its use and practice in Hawaiʻi today. *Journal of Law and Social Challenges, 10*, 68–133.

Silva, N. K. (2017). *The power of the steel-tipped pen: Reconstructing Native Hawaiian intellectual history*. Durham, NC: Duke University Press.

Simpson, A. (2014). *Mohawk interruptus: Political life across the borders of settler states*. Durham, NC: Duke University Press.

Turner, F. J. (1893). The significance of the frontier in American history. *Report of the American Historical Association, 1*, 199–227.

Walden, A. (2015, April 25). Anti-telescope leader calls for killing telescope supporters—HS girl targeted. Retrieved from http://www.hawaiifreepress.com/

Walia, H. (2015). Decolonize together: Moving beyond a politics of solidarity toward a practice of decolonization. In C. Milstein (Ed.), *Taking sides: Revolutionary solidarity and the poverty of liberalism* (pp. 41–47). Oakland, CA: AK Press.

Wolfe, P. (2006). Settler colonialism and the elimination of the native. *Journal of Genocide Research, 8*(4), 387–409.

ABOUT THE AUTHOR

David Uahikeaikalei'ohu Maile is a Kanaka ʻŌiwi scholar, activist, and practitioner from Maunawili, Oʻahu. He is an assistant professor of Indigenous politics in the Department of Political Science at the University of Toronto.

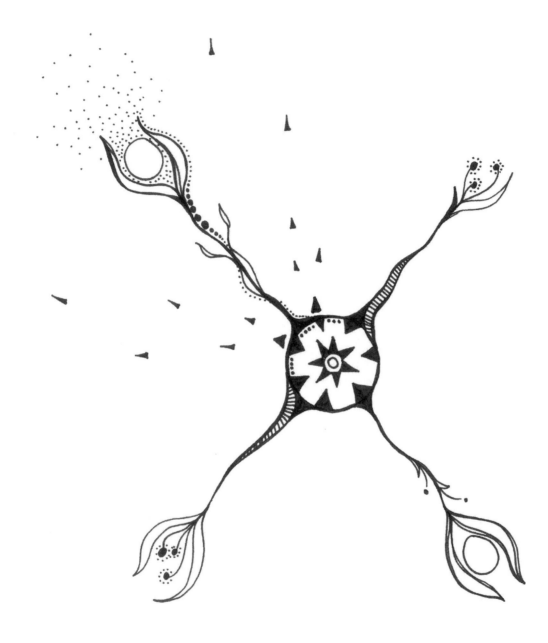

Aunty Alama: Lessons in the Value of Kūpuna

KAWEHI KINA

I heard many stories about the mean and strict science teacher at Waiheʻe Elementary School. Miss Ayers would whack her students with a yardstick if they did not listen, shame them in front of the whole class, and pick on them if she knew they were not paying attention. But no matter how hard she was on her students, she was remembered as a great teacher. Her former students have come up to me over the years, surprised to find out that Miss Ayers was my great-aunt. The stories they told me seemed unbelievable, because I never encountered such discipline with her. But her passion for education was something that all of us remembered.

CORRESPONDENCE MAY BE SENT TO:
Kawehi Kina
2108 Kahekili Highway, Wailuku, Hawaiʻi 96793
Email: kinak@hawaii.edu

Hūlili: Multidisciplinary Research on Hawaiian Well-Being, Vol. 11, No. 1

To me, Miss Ayers was Aunty Alama. Aunty Alama was an old, tall, Hawaiian-Chinese lady with a hunched back, who always wore a muʻumuʻu. She was also my neighbor. She was born and raised in the small town of Waiheʻe on the island of Maui. My aunt was a well-educated wahine who graduated from Kamehameha Schools for Girls in 1942. She obtained her bachelor's degree from Brigham Young University in Utah and earned her master's degree from Columbia University in New York. She also spent some time at Oxford University in England. She loved her home and wanted to give back by becoming a teacher.

Growing up, Aunty Alama would come over to my house about three or four times a week to visit my papa. She would either come early in the morning or late in the afternoon. When she was at my house, I had to be on my best behavior because she would always tell me what I did wrong. From a very young age, I could always remember hearing Aunty Alama walking to my house. She dragged her slippers on the asphalt as she walked on the side of the road. I assumed that her hunched back made her drag her feet. No matter where you were in the house—in the front parlor or in the back bedroom—you could always hear her slippers dragging. And if you couldn't hear her slippers, you could definitely hear her yell, "Manaku! I'm coming!"

Manaku was my papa and her older brother. As a child, hearing my aunt's feet and her yelling as she made her slow descent to my house made me laugh. I thought it

was so funny to hear this old lady, who was going deaf, yell at another old man, who was also going deaf. You could just tell these two were related. As she walked through the front door, she would yell for my papa, and these two buggahs would be screaming at each other. Not with anger, but because they could hardly hear each other.

"HI MANAKU!" my aunt would yell.

"WHAT?" my papa would yell back, as he tried to understand what she said.

"HUH?" she would reply.

Eventually they would carry on with their conversation, both acting like they could hear each other. Their conversation would meander all over the place, since they couldn't actually hear what the other was saying. But you could see that they enjoyed each other's company. Before my aunty would leave my house, she would be nīele and look in all the rooms. I would usually be on the computer, and she would always yell, "Eh, no sit close to da TV! You goin go blind. You like see or wat?" I would just laugh because she didn't know what a computer was. As she made her way out the door, she would yell, "Bye Manaku! Love you!" You knew she was home when you couldn't hear her slippers dragging anymore. I hold these memories close to me because as I got older, our lives changed drastically.

When I became a freshman in high school, I decided to board at Lāhaināluna High School. My papa and my two uncles had attended Lāhaināluna and boarded when it was an all-boys school, and I thought it was time for me to be independent and board as well. During my first three years at Lāhaināluna, there were many changes happening at home. We lost our family property. Six generations had been on that land, and it was devastating to no longer be part of that place. Aunty Alama would point to her chest and tell me, "My mother built that house, and me and Manaku grew up in it." Since I was boarding in Lāhainā during this transition, I wasn't able to see the pain that my mom and her brothers were going through. Our family was very small, and to have something so precious taken was heartbreaking. My aunt was silent during this time, but she was not angry. Although her family home was taken from her, it still stood there, holding all of her memories.

Aunty Alama at this time was getting old and needed more care since she lived on her own and did not drive. And because we didn't have a home anymore, my mom asked Aunty Alama if we could move in with her. She agreed, and my mom and sister moved in. Toward the end of my senior year, I got a life-changing call from my mother. She told me that Aunty Alama had fallen and broken her leg. My aunt's leg was in a cast and she could no longer walk. This was a difficult time for my mother. She lost her job as a result of caring for Aunty Alama, and she now relied on unemployment to help with the bills and food. When I graduated from high school, I moved back home. I saw the stress my mom was going through, trying to care for me and my sister, losing her job, and caregiving for Aunty Alama. It was then that I decided to take on this kuleana and became my aunt's full-time caregiver.

Caregiving was difficult, both physically and mentally. I couldn't imagine how Aunty Alama must have felt not being able-bodied anymore. During this time, my aunty and I spent a lot of time together, learning from each other. Even though she had dementia, we were able to have many conversations. However, the conversations were mostly short phrases, all jumbled up. She would always start off by proudly shouting, "I from Waiheʻe. Ayers is my name." And she would continue on about who her family was. She would go on and on, eventually telling me stories about growing up in Waiheʻe and attending Kamehameha. She would also tell me bits and pieces about her life as a teacher. I enjoyed listening, and as she opened up to me, we slowly created a bond.

While my aunt would rest, I would clean her room. I found many treasures in her drawers and closet. I found maps of the old Waiheʻe plantation town, old pictures of buildings like the old Waiheʻe Dairy, historical documents about Hawaiʻi, and even information about the Hawaiian Kingdom. Some documents were written by my aunt as well. There were also old newspaper articles about how involved my aunt had been within the Waiheʻe community and with other communities. It was amazing!

MY AUNT, WHO HAD GIVEN SO MUCH OF HER TIME AND KNOWLEDGE TO THE PEOPLE OF WAIHEʻE, WAS TRULY AN INSPIRATION.

One day, I told my mom what I had found in her room, and she told me that Aunty Alama had been a historian at the Bailey House Museum, so it wasn't a surprise for my mom to hear about these types of documents lying around the house. I was filled with awe, learning all this about the person I was caring for. My aunt, who had given so much of her time and knowledge to the people of Waiheʻe, was truly an inspiration.

On days when I was absent from her care, Aunty Alama would ask my mom where I was and when I was coming back. She could never pronounce my name, so she would ask, "Where the girl?" Other times, she would refuse to eat or drink unless I was there. I remember one day, I was doing a project for school, and I asked my mom to care for Aunty. As my mom was trying to feed her, all I heard was grumbling from the two of them. Then I heard a yell, "Kawehi! Come here." I went to my aunt's room and found her putting her hand over her mouth. She refused to eat what my mom was giving her. I gave Aunty Alama "the stare," and she looked down and slowly opened her mouth. My mom just laughed and couldn't believe the type of bond that had grown between Aunty Alama and me.

I cared for Aunty Alama for almost five years. Caring for her was the most difficult time in my life. I learned so much about caregiving and how it affects families. There were days when I felt alone, stressed, and depressed. But my aunt had taught me to always love and to always have patience.

If it was not for my Aunty Alama, I would not be where I am today. I graduated from the University of Hawai'i at Mānoa and am now working toward a master's degree. The experience of being my aunt's caregiver opened my eyes. I now do things not for myself, but for the next generation, while also remembering what our kūpuna have taught us. Looking back on the life of my aunty, the stories I was told about her were true. She was mean and strict. But she was a great teacher. I would not have become the person I am today without her.

ABOUT THE AUTHOR

Kawehi Kina is a Kanaka ʻŌiwi Hawaiʻi from Waiheʻe on the island of Maui. She is a master's student in the Department of Educational Administration at the University of Hawaiʻi at Mānoa. Her time as a caregiver for her great aunt, Alama Ayers, inspired her to pursue higher education.

Kānāwai LAW

Lawaiʻa Pono: Community-Based Fishing

TED KAWAHINEHELELANI BLAKE & CHARLES YOUNG

We are the families and descendants of Hawaiʻi's native fisherfolk. Drawing on our customary and traditional knowledge, we see a pressing need for more closures of fisheries to ensure long-term sustainability. Closures not only allow fish to reproduce and replenish, but also provide a sustainable fishery and greater regulation. We are taking a stand today by providing the general public with proven traditional community-based fishing rules that are sensible, responsible, and consistent with the fishing traditions of our ancestors.

Lawaiʻa pono—to fish in a Hawaiian way—isn't about the take. Rather, it's about taking care. Lawaiʻa pono is about our responsibility to practice restraint and make sacrifices today for the long-term benefit of generations to follow.

CORRESPONDENCE MAY BE SENT TO:
Ted Kawahinehelelani Blake
PO Box 96
Kōloa, Kauaʻi, Hawaiʻi 96756
Email: tblake@mac.com

Hūlili: Multidisciplinary Research on Hawaiian Well-Being, Vol. 11, No. 1

Reconciling these rights and responsibilities is a simple task. However, a breakdown in native culture and a disconnection from that which truly feeds us has caused confusion. Even talking about kuleana in some circles can cause conflict and gives rise to questions and accusations like, "Who are you to tell me what I can and cannot do?"

In previous generations, one's position and status were automatic—something you were born into. This idea of knowing your place is still present in local culture today. Our elders recall their "bag boy/bag girl" days of their youth, carrying the catch bag as youngsters, as foundational to their skill and practice as lawai'a.

As lifestyles, economies, and attitudes about our rightful roles as Kānaka change, so does our behavior. Vehicular shoreline access, larger coolers, and readily available freezers have changed the fishing landscape. For example, vehicular accessibility to fishing spots, hauling coolers in vehicles, and advanced fishing gear allow modern-day fishers to take more than they can consume in two to three days. This puts a strain on the fishery and inhibits our responsibility to take care of and provide for generations that follow.

As the posterity of kūpuna who knew their places well, we understand that to perpetuate lawai'a pono, we need to adapt to changing times, attitudes, and issues. We do so by remaining steadfast to our values and by living our island values of reciprocity, respect, and trust in each other. As descendants of keen observers of place, we also understand that managing people is the most effective way to manage fish populations sustainably.

Though the State of Hawai'i is mandated to manage our resources, we recognize that the people of this place know their resources best. Therefore, we assert that regulations need to be placed-based and come from the ground up. Blanket rules and regulations do not work. For example, spawning seasons in neighboring ahupua'a can vary along the same shoreline. Our methods for managing resources should remain traditional, yet we should be adapting to our observations. We need to pay attention to every detail of the watershed, shoreline, and sea, because one change is an indicator for another, and these change variations are all interconnected.

Community-based subsistence fishing areas (CBSFA) are legally designated areas per HRS §188-22.9 (1994), where our Hawai'i fishing communities establish fishing rules, in partnership with government, based on customary and traditional practices of that area.

Hā'ena, Halele'a, Kaua'i

In 2006, the legislature passed a law designating Hā'ena as a CBSFA (HRS §188-22.9). After a decade of interviews, studies, stakeholder and public meetings, and more than twenty drafts and ten rounds of agenda review, the Hā'ena rules package was signed in 2015 by Governor Ige (HAR §13-60.8). The Hā'ena community rules make sense for that place.

For example, the rules stipulate not using more than two poles per person, and that 'ula needs to be gathered by hand only, with a bag limit of two. Also, kūpuna identified a juvenile pu'uhonua (fish nursery), and scientists supported their evidence. The rules for the pu'uhonua state that no one go within that papa so as to not disturb the breeding and growth process. They do not say to stay out, but just to swim around. Lawai'a are so attuned to the ocean, they know that even their shadows affect the i'a, so they walk carefully along the shore.

Kaʻūpūlehu, Kona, Hawaiʻi

Though not a CBSFA, Kaʻūpūlehu's ten-year rest period gives kamaʻāina families the time needed for manini and other important food fish to reproduce and replenish the area, from Kīkaua to Kalaemanō, while families continue to monitor their grounds and create a comprehensive management plan. Seeing their fishery depleted, they said, "Try wait" to give the reef a rest before it's too late. Kaʻūpūlehu is within the West Hawaiʻi Regional Fishery Management Area (FMA) created by Act 306, which was passed by the Hawaiʻi State Legislature in 1998 in response to concerns about commercial aquarium harvesting. The ten-year rest period was attained through a rule amendment and approved by Governor Ige in mid-2016.

Moʻomomi, Koʻolau, Molokaʻi

From 1994 to 1996, Hui Mālamaʻo Moʻomomi piloted a CBSFA and is working today with the Hoʻolehua Hawaiian Homestead to establish an expanded CBSFA from ʻĪlio Point to Kaholaiki Bay.

Communities throughout the pae ʻāina are creating lawaiʻa pono initiatives They are taking steps by finding solutions appropriate for their unique places, ma uka to ma kai. They are restoring loʻi, replanting native plants, compiling moon calendars, passing down traditions of hānai koʻa, hosting family fish camps, running monitoring programs like Makai Watch, implementing ʻopihi rest areas, surveying fishers and ocean users, convening and connecting people, creating outreach and educational programs, and volunteering hundreds of selfless hours to tend our resources and bring back abundance for all.

Reciprocity in our relationships with others and with our resources can restore abundance. For lawaiʻa pono, join us as we ʻauamo kuleana in putting forward community-based fishing rules and solutions and seek to partner with the state and others in ways that mālama sustainable fishing customs and traditions of our community.

ABOUT THE AUTHORS

Ted Kawahinehelelani Blake serves as executive director of Mālama Kōloa and is a member of E Alu Pū. His formal education includes Kamehameha Schools, Orange Coast Community College, College of Idaho, and the University of Hawaiʻi. He was born on Kauaʻi. Residences include Kōloa, Kona, Kauaʻi and Tiahura, Moʻorea, Niamataʻi.

Charles Young is a lawaiʻa, educator, and kamaʻāina of Hoʻokena, South Kona, Hawaiʻi. He also serves as the secretary of Kamaʻāina United to Protect the ʻĀina / Friends of Hoʻokena Beach Park, a nonprofit organization focused on the preservation of cultural and natural resources and culturally sensitive economic development in Hoʻokena.

The 2016 Naʻi Aupuni Congregation: A Brief Study in a Practice of Indigenous Self-Determination

PŌKĀ LAENUI

This article reviews a broad environment of Hawaiian activities—from a historical and decolonization pattern to a specific recent process in indigenous affairs. It analyzes the process taken, the procedures put into effect, and the high and low points of the Naʻi Aupuni gathering held at Maunawili, Kailua, Oʻahu in 2016. This article also evaluates the product of the gathering, comparing it with that of an earlier and different process, the Native Hawaiian Convention. It then compares the product of the 2016 gathering against the final rule of the US Department of Interior and against general principles of international law. The article concludes with lessons learned and suggestions for improvement going forward.

CORRESPONDENCE MAY BE SENT TO:
Pōkā Laenui
86-641 Puʻuhulu Road, Waiʻanae, Hawaiʻi 96792
Email: plaenui@hawaiianperspectives.org

Hūlili: Multidisciplinary Research on Hawaiian Well-Being, Vol. 11, No. 1

Historical Backdrop

Hawaiian sovereignty has been a topic of public and private discussions in Hawai'i for many years. It is a fundamental part of what some have called the "Hawaiian revolt." A potential starting point for the revolt is the "Kalama Valley" period of the late 1960s, when Kōkua Hawai'i stood up to powerful land developers to protest the eviction of Hawaiian residents from the valley. This was followed by the uproar in the wake of the appointment of yet another non-Native Hawaiian as trustee of Kamehameha Schools Bishop Estate. On the heels of these events was the "Kaho'olawe movement," which questioned the supremacy of the US Navy in Hawai'i's political life and sought to elevate the place of Native Hawaiian cultural and spiritual values in Hawai'i.

New musical approaches also came to the fore, challenging prevalent views on Hawaiian history, loyalty, royalty, and patriotism, with names such as Don Ho and Kui Lee leading the pack, bringing a new sense of pride, confusion, and critical debate about "proper" Hawaiian entertainment with the singing of songs such as "Nā Ali'i" and "Hawai'i Pono'ī," followed by "God Bless America." Hula hālau multiplied during this period with the graduation of a profusion of kumu hula (hula masters), many tracing their roots to the Margaret Aiu Hula Studio, which changed to the Hula Hālau 'O Maiki and is presently the Hālau Hula 'O Maiki—its name changes from pre-1950s to 1974 reflecting growth in awareness of Native Hawaiian culture.[1] The Polynesian Voyaging Society also entered the arena with Hōkūle'a and its journey to the South Pacific. New expressions of Hawaiian culture flourished during these decades.

From the underground, a sweep of Hawaiian pride emerged, somewhat uncertain, yet firm in challenging the superiority and supremacy of non-Hawaiians, questioning why gambling and other vices in Hawai'i should be controlled by Koreans, Chinese, Japanese, or other immigrants, while Hawaiians and other Polynesians were simply used as "muscle" to keep everybody in line. Hawaiians, under the leadership of "Nappy" Pulawa, formed a coalition with Samoans organized under Alema Leota and removed the "non-natives" who had been controlling Hawai'i's gambling. This "native power," having organized, was now able to put up barriers against the Yakusa invasion from Japan as well as the Mafia from Italian-America, in their attempt to move in on the local market. One popular story is that when the Italian Mafia sent men to Hawai'i to infiltrate the local underworld, the men were packed up in pineapple boxes and sent back to America with the message, "'Ono, send some mo!"[2] An infusion of local pride was forming and emerging from this sector of the community, finding its way into increased popularity in canoeing, local volleyball, and junior golfing in a wide exhibit of local talents.

The Federal Strike Force was brought into Hawai'i, and a concentrated attack against this native power was underway. Nappy Pulawa was convicted of federal tax violations and sent off to federal prison for a longer period than the notorious Al Capone, thus removing this charismatic leader for a time.

Pulawa was returned for a retrial on state charges of double murder and kidnap (*State v. Pulawa*, 1975). Having made a major media showing of his criminal organizing activities during his previous years in Hawai'i, the local newspapers, television, and radio stations again raised the matter of his criminal activities and of his return for a retrial, anticipating an outcome of life imprisonment for Pulawa.

From the circuit courtroom of Ali'iōlani Hale—that same building from which so many other memorable events occurred, including the proclamation of the end of Queen Lili'uokalani's reign and the formation of the Provisional Government of Hawai'i,[3] and the guilty jury findings of the Massie defendants for the murder of Joseph Kahahawai[4]—rang out the Pulawa reply to charges of kidnaps and murders, "I refuse to dignify this court by entering a plea. Instead, I ask, who are you foreigners to come into Hawai'i and charge us by your foreign laws? We are not Americans, we are Hawaiians!"

This modern Hawaiian revolution was thus cast into yet another expression: the "Hawaiian sovereignty movement."

Hawaiian sovereignty movement

The Pulawa trial resulted in a finding of not guilty and was soon followed by other challenges to the jurisdiction of the US courts: Hayden Burgess (Pōkā Laenui), attorney for Mr. Pulawa in the state charges, declared in Federal District Court before Sr. Judge Samuel King that he was not a US citizen, yet insisted on his right to practice law in all of the courts of Hawai'i; US v. Raymond Kamaka challenged the government's taking of Kamaka's family land at Waikāne Valley, also claiming his Hawaiian citizenship and the taking of Hawaiian land; US v. Lorenzo challenged US taxing authority over Lorenzo as a Hawaiian citizen; and US v. John Marsh, retired Honolulu police officer, questioned US taxing jurisdiction in Hawai'i and proclaimed Marsh's Hawaiian citizenship. In the Hawai'i State Courts, jurisdiction of the US laws often combined with land issues, such as the eviction of Sand Island "squatters," most of whom were Native Hawaiians who had established a fishing village and were arrested and evicted by the State Department of Land and Natural Resources (State v. Paulo et al., 1980). Another example is Mākua "beach people," blown off the beaches first by Hurricane Iwa and followed in a one-two punch by the state police arresting them as they tried to return to their homes on the beach (State v. Pihana, Nae'ole, Alana et al., 1982). Many others living along the beaches at Kahe Point, Nānākuli, Mā'ili, Kea'au, and Waimānalo were subsequently arrested, and they too raised the same defense of "Hawaiian sovereignty," challenging US jurisdiction over Hawaiian citizens and Hawaiian lands.

The movement expanded into schools, universities, political debates at the Office of Hawaiian Affairs (newly formed in the 1978 Constitutional Convention), and finally into the Hawai'i State Legislature, now impacting questions of the legitimacy of title in the "ceded" lands as well as US jurisdiction over Hawai'i. These questions were also raised at international venues such as the World Council of Indigenous Peoples and the International Indian Treaty Council, reaching the halls of the United Nations in Geneva primarily through the UN Working Group on Indigenous Populations, and receiving attention in New York before the UN General Assembly.

Hawaiian groups, sometimes noted for their individuality, began to take a new approach to the Hawaiian sovereignty question, forming Hui Na'auao, a study group of principally Native Hawaiians, to discuss and promote information regarding Hawaiian history, culture, politics, and other matters relating to Hawaiian sovereignty, agreeing, for a time, that this would be their sole purpose, not taking positions on any other matter.[5] One of the major events Hui Na'auao spearheaded in 1993 was the reenactment of the overthrow of Hawai'i one hundred years previously. Hawai'i Public Radio transmitted the program live across Hawai'i.

Involvement of state legislature

The Sovereignty Advisory Council (SAC) was formed by the state legislature in 1991 (Act 301), appointing a handful of organizational representatives and individuals to "develop a plan to discuss and study the sovereignty issue." In 1992 this council submitted a report to the state legislature that detailed the events of the overthrow and the remaining issues still unresolved, and made suggestions on the state's taking further action on the sovereignty issue. A Hawaiian Sovereignty Economic Symposium was held at the William S. Richardson School of Law on June 5, 1993, the first in-depth study of the economic consequences of models of Hawaiian nationhood, which was broadcast live by Hawai'i Public Radio.

Although the legislature refused to continue the work of SAC, it subsequently created the Hawaiian Sovereignty Advisory Council (HSAC) by Act 359 in the 1993 legislative session, to seek counsel from Native Hawaiians on:

1. Holding a referendum to determine the will of the Native Hawaiians to convene a democratically elected convention to achieve a consensus document proposing how Native Hawaiians could operate their own government

2. Providing a way to democratically convene a convention so Native Hawaiians could freely deliberate and decide the form of that government

3. Describing the conduct of fair, impartial, and valid elections including a referendum election

This council of twenty-one members, appointed by Governor Waihe'e, visited communities in Hawai'i and in America, to obtain opinions on how to proceed with self-governance. HSAC concluded it could not counsel the legislature on that matter because HSAC was not the representative voice of the Native Hawaiian people. Instead, the council suggested that a plebiscite be called, asking the Native Hawaiian population whether an election of delegates should be held to propose a form of Native Hawaiian governance. The legislature adopted the recommendations and appointed the HSAC commission members to the Native Hawaiian Elections Commission to conduct this Native Hawaiian vote.

Native Hawaiians of any citizenship or residence were eligible to register in the "Native Hawaiian Vote." Current or prior criminal convictions, or incarceration, were no basis for denial from voting. The only limitation was an age requirement of eighteen years by September 2, 1996, the scheduled date for the results to be announced.

In July 1996, 81,598 ballots[6] were sent throughout the world, asking, "Shall the Hawaiian people elect delegates to propose a Native Hawaiian government?" Discounting for returned mail, deceased addressees, and ballots returned by non-Hawaiians, the list was reduced to 81,507. Of that, 30,783 valid, signed ballot envelopes with ballots were returned, constituting 38 percent of the list. Of the resulting list, 2 percent were disqualified because of the failure to affirm their qualification to vote, and 360 ballots were disqualified due to torn stubs or empty secret ballot envelopes. The League of Women Voters did the final tally and reported that 30,423 (37 percent) of the ballots were counted, of which 22,294 (73.28 percent) voted YES, and 8,129 (26.72 percent) voted NO.

Genesis of the Native Hawaiian Convention

Following the approval of the majority of the ballots counted, an election of delegates was held. Candidates ran for delegate positions from places in which they lived in Hawai'i, divided into areas called moku. The

Figure 1. Elected delegates to the Native Hawaiian Convention on the steps of ʻIolani Palace, July 31, 1999.

continental USA also set aside delegates from that area. The Native Hawaiian Convention (hereafter NHC), also known as the ʻAha Hawaiʻi ʻŌiwi, was convened on July 1, 1999.

These delegates met over the course of one year, studying various models to recommend a form of governance (fig. 1).

On July 29, 2000, after weeks of meetings, strongly argued positions, intense studies, and hearing various voices, both foreign and domestic, on self-governance, the convention delegates selected two conceptual models to place before the people for their advice and recommendations, one for integration within the United States of America and the second for independence from the USA. While delegates themselves had strong positions toward one or the other model, they generally agreed that it was better to let the people decide between these models. They also agreed that the delegates would work on developing these two models for presentation to the people.

Work was done by the delegates to develop these two separate models. Over time, it was obvious that the

integration model was being influenced by versions of the Akaka Bill(s) being introduced into the US Congress, and further development of that model waned in the face of the Akaka Bill's development.

The independence model, however, took a different lead. There was a strong pull for independence—perhaps stemming from Hawaiʻi's history of its period of independence and its record of advocacy for independence, which has gained momentum over the past thirty years.

Fundamental questions needed to be addressed that revolved around an independence status. Following are some of these questions and the general direction of their responses.

(1) Who were the citizens of such an independent nation (to be defined racially, ancestrally, culturally, historically, or based on loyalty)? The Hawaiian citizens were to be identified similar to how they were identified under the Hawaiian Kingdom—by place of birth, by years of residence in Hawaiʻi and, if not native born, by an oath of loyalty to qualify for nationalization. It would also be required that Hawaiian citizenship not be imposed but would instead be a choice made by any person who qualified.

(2) Given the current makeup of Hawaiʻi society, and the fact that Native Hawaiians would be in a minority if all those qualifying under the definition of a Hawaiian citizen were to elect to be such a citizen, what protections would there be for the Hawaiian indigenous people? A separate political body (Kumu Hawaiʻi) would be created, autonomous to the general political body of the national government, consisting of only Native Hawaiians, and this body would have exclusive control over certain decisions affecting Hawaiʻi, including

population control, land demarcated from the former government, and Crown lands and assets set aside for Kumu Hawai'i; control over Native Hawaiian education, health, and justice systems; and the right to identify royalty for purposes of interacting with other monarchies should the general body decide that Hawai'i should also have a monarchy.

The drafting of the independence model has been a work in progress, without any final decision made about the document itself (fig. 2). The document referenced later in this article is currently the most advanced draft but is not considered as final by the full convention.

The state legislature and the Office of Hawaiian Affairs refused to fund this convention to completion. The convention now stands in recess, remaining unfunded, and thus unable to complete its work to be submitted to the Native Hawaiian population. The NHC today is in recess and has not adjourned sine die (without a day to reconvene, essentially closing the assembly). With the NHC in recess, the legislature and the Office of Hawaiian Affairs now started looking in another direction—toward the US Congress and federal recognition—to resolve the matter of Hawaiian self-determination.

Figure 2. Convention debate on self-determination, July 29, 2000

In pursuit of federal recognition

On July 20, 2000, in the 106th US Congress, the first Akaka Bill was introduced in both the US House of Representatives and in the Senate. The brainchild from the offices of Senators Daniel Akaka and Daniel Inouye of Hawai'i, the bill was an attempt to congressionally declare the Native Hawaiian people as a nation within the sovereignty of the United States of America. Once given this federal recognition, it was said that the Native Hawaiian people would have the right for special treatment as an indigenous nation, similar to the treatment given to American Indian or native tribes or nations. From the year 2000, every Congress until the 110th Congress of 2007 received the reintroduction of the Akaka Bill with various amendments. This attempt to formally recognize the Native Hawaiian people as a native, indigenous, or Indian people within the borders of the United States, subject to the superior jurisdiction of the United States, failed to pass the Congress every year.

In its 2011 session, the state legislature adopted Act 195, calling for the formation of a Native Hawaiian Roll Commission to create a list of voters to elect delegates to a new convention and to adopt a document to meet the requirements of federal recognition of a Native Hawaiian nation. The state's Office of Hawaiian Affairs was charged with financing this commission, electing delegates,[1] and funding a convention. Only those of Native Hawaiian blood were to be enrolled on the "roll of qualified Native Hawaiians" permitted to register to vote in the selection of delegates to the convention.[7] In passing Act 195, the state legislature stated: "The State has supported the reorganization of a Native Hawaiian governing entity. It has supported the Sovereignty Advisory Council, the Hawaiian Sovereignty Advisory Commission, the Hawaiian Sovereignty Elections Council, and Native

Hawaiian Vote, and the convening of the ʻAha Hawaiʻi ʻŌiwi (the Native Hawaiian Convention)."

Act 195 proceeded to (1) recognize Native Hawaiian people as the "only indigenous, aboriginal, maoli people of Hawaiʻi," (2) provide for and implement the recognition of Native Hawaiians to self-governance, and (3) create a Native Hawaiian Roll Commission to maintain a roll of qualified Native Hawaiians and to certify their qualifications as Native Hawaiians (e.g., tracing ancestry in Hawaiʻi to pre-1778 or being eligible for the Hawaiian Homes program). The roll also required members to be eighteen years of age or older and to have maintained a significant cultural, social, or civic connection to the Native Hawaiian community.

The Office of Hawaiian Affairs launched "Kanaʻiolowalu" to create the roll. The publication of the roll was to "facilitate the process under which qualified Native Hawaiians may independently commence the organization of a convention."[8] Five members appointed by the governor were to serve on the roll commission. Upon completion of the roll, the governor was to dissolve the commission.

Following a failure to register a sufficient number of Native Hawaiians on the Kanaʻiolowalu roll, an effort was made to cobble together names from other listings—not only those who registered directly with the Kanaʻiolowalu roll created by the commission, but also those registered with Kau Inoa, Operation ʻOhana, and the Hawaiian Registry through the Office of Hawaiian Affairs. It included persons of all ages, including those under the age of eighteen. Deceased persons also remained on the roll. The Roll Commission had more than 125,000 qualified Native Hawaiians on the list (*Judicial Watch, Inc. v. Namuʻo et al.,* 2015). There were no

citizenship or residency requirements, nor did the roll exclude convicted felons or those declared mentally incompetent (Native Hawaiian Roll Commission, 2014).

Following the work of the Roll Commission, in December 2014 there emerged a group called Naʻi Aupuni—five individuals who formed a nonprofit organization to "help establish a path for Hawaiian self-determination" (Naʻi Aupuni, 2015a). Its scope of service for the Office of Hawaiian Affairs called for "an election of delegates, election and referendum monitoring, a governance ʻAha, and a referendum to ratify any recommendation of the delegates arising out of the ʻAha."

There were 201 individuals nominated to fill forty delegate positions to a convention. Nominees were required to be nominated by ten individuals who were enrolled on the Kanaʻiolowalu roll. From these nominees, forty delegates were to be elected in an election conducted by mail-in ballots. The election was held, and ballots were mailed in, but the counting of the ballots was held up by an intervening lawsuit, Akina v. State of Hawaiʻi, 2015. That lawsuit challenged the legitimacy of the election, primarily due to its use of state funds and its limitation of voting to only those of the Native Hawaiian race. After losing at the Federal District Court and at the Appeals Court level, the case was taken to the US Supreme Court. A temporary restraining order was issued by the US Supreme Court, preventing the counting of the ballots until the court could consider the matter. Kūhiō Asam, chairman of Naʻi Aupuni, Inc., determined that the court could take years in reviewing the issue and announced the commencement of a convention without the counting of the ballots for electing delegates.[9]

Naʻi Aupuni, foregoing the counting of the ballots, declared that a gathering in Maunawili, Kailua, Oʻahu would be convened, in which all nominees who confirmed their participation would be seated. On February 1, 2016, 154 delegates were convened at a private venue, the Royal Hawaiian Golf Club, behind secured entrance gates.

Only the confirmed participants were allowed into the meetings. Exceptions included three trained mediators, a support staff, 'Ōlelo Community Media's TV crew, guest speakers for the first week of meetings, a security team, a registration team (Commpac) contracted by Na'i Aupuni, and food staff.

There were no copy machines, printers, or computers for use by the delegates. This required attendees to bring their own devices, making it difficult or nearly impossible to make and distribute handouts for all participants. Delegates were expected to bring their iPads, iPhones, or other similar devices to communicate via a custom-made electronic polling system (training included). This process took a lot of time and left many out of the loop because of the lack of equipment and the inability of the system to handle the load of input. Many participants, usually of the older generation, were not able to use or felt uncomfortable with the electronic media and were thus at a disadvantage for effective engagement in the affairs of the convention.

Because the number of delegates had increased dramatically from what was originally planned, Na'i Aupuni reduced the length of the congregation[10] from forty to twenty days and reduced the previously announced per diem to fifty dollars for O'ahu members, two hundred dollars for Neighbor Island members, and two hundred and fifty dollars for members outside of Hawai'i. Members' acceptance of the per diem was optional. Breakfast and lunch for the twenty convention days were provided by Na'i Aupuni. No other financial assistance (e.g., transportation and lodging) was made available.

There were no state or federal government officials, no trustees of the Office of Hawaiian Affairs in their official capacities, no legislative representatives in their official capacity, and no special guests other than three invited speakers who addressed substantive questions of constitution writing, US and international developments of indigenous rights, and Hawaiian constitutions. There was some suspicion, given the behavior of at least one individual member, that an agent of a government agency was also on assignment to be among the delegates.

By the conclusion of the congregation, two documents were produced: the Constitution of the Native Hawaiian Nation (attachment 1), and the Declaration of the Sovereignty of the Native Hawaiian Nation: An Offering of the 'Aha (attachment 2). The following month, on March 16, 2016, Na'i Aupuni announced it would not be following up on the ratification vote of the Constitution of the Native Hawaiian Nation, leaving the congregation participants to do it themselves. Na'i Aupuni returned to the Office of Hawaiian Affairs a balance of $82,509.86, the amount that was slated to be used for that vote.

Evaluation of the Na'i Aupuni Congregation

Although a valiant effort was made by the state legislature, the Office of Hawaiian Affairs, members of the Roll Commission, and the five private citizens who formed Na'i Aupuni and stepped up to undertake the ongoing work of that commission, this attempt to practice self-determination, against the backdrop of many years of colonization, posed many challenges for all, resulting in some movement forward but multiple failures.

This process was intended to create a "qualified Native Hawaiian roll" and from that roll, to elect delegates, conduct an ʻAha, and ratify the results of the ʻAha, presumably a constitution or a formative document that would meet the administrative rules of the US Department of Interior (DOI). The process created a roll of questioned legitimacy, which included dead people, and added names of those who never intended to have their names included. It failed to elect delegates to an ʻAha or convention, and the attendees of the gathering had no legitimate basis to claim a representative voice of a constituency other than, perhaps, the ten names that were used to nominate them. The gathering produced a haphazard document made up of bits and pieces of a governing entity, without a consistent theme or even a name for this Hawaiian nation. The congregation adjourned sine die, after which Naʻi Aupuni abandoned the ratification referendum of the congregation. The announced deadline by which a ratification vote was to have taken place (May 2016) has long passed, and the Constitution of the Native Hawaiian Nation now appears irrelevant.

Reflecting on the longer-term view, starting with the organization of Hui Naʻauao several decades ago, followed by the Sovereignty Advisory Council, the Hawaiian Sovereignty Advisory Commission, the Hawaiian Sovereignty Elections Council, the Native Hawaiian Vote, and the Native Hawaiian Convention, the Naʻi Aupuni process was a failure in moving the exercise of self-determination forward. The earlier processes, seen as a progression, had already accomplished a valid roll of Native Hawaiians, held a referendum to determine if the people wanted to adopt this process of calling their Native Hawaiian representatives to a deliberative body, elected that body, held their deliberations, and produced two draft alternatives. If the state legislature and

the Office of Hawaiian Affairs had not failed to fund the NHC to completion, two alternative proposals would have been presented to the Hawaiian constituency, one setting forth a design for integration within the United States of America, and a second for independence from the United States of America.

The NHC has not adjourned sine die and remains in recess until it is able to complete its mandate. Some have argued that the NHC, which was elected in July 1999, is outdated. That is an uninformed judgment. Like any other legitimate organization, the NHC had adopted a process that allows it to maintain its viability. The NHC is nearly twenty years old as of this writing, but that age only underlines the need to allow the NHC to complete its work and put before the Hawaiian constituency the proposals for determination. A great amount of earlier work, beginning with the Sovereignty Advisory Council in 1991 (Act 301) up through the NHC in 2000, was marginalized by Act 195.

Yet another agenda was at work, although not explicitly declared: The imminent departure of the Obama administration was assumed to close a window of opportunity to achieve a presidential executive order recognizing an organized Native Hawaiian "nation" under requirements of the US DOI. The struggle for recognition dates back to the early days of the rejuvenated Hawaiian sovereignty movement following the Alaska Native Claims Settlement Act (ANCSA) adopted by Congress in 1971. What followed was the Aloha Bill, which attempted to mimic the footsteps of the Alaska experience. Having failed in those early efforts, and seeing the US Congress adopt the 1993 Apology Resolution (Public Law 103-150) confessing the illegal role of the United States in the Hawaiian overthrow,[II] a new attempt by US Senators Inouye and Akaka was made to achieve recognition of the Native Hawaiian nation (the US House of Representatives having adopted such a bill on numerous occasions). Senate bills were introduced in different forms from 2000 until 2007 but were never successfully adopted, largely due to the manipulation and objections of a small Republican minority in that body.

A presidential executive order could have circumvented the political roadblock in Congress. At the time, the DOI was already in the process of developing its rules, had held contentious hearings in Hawai'i, and had issued proposed rules during the Roll Commission process. All that was needed was for the DOI to establish final rules—and for the Native Hawaiian people to accept a document through a plebiscite that would meet those minimum requirement of the final rules—and the Native Hawaiian "nation" would have become federally recognized. This would have been pleasing to those who support integration of the Hawaiian nation within the United States but hated by those in support of total independence. The process started by Act 195 failed to meet that objective of achieving federal recognition of the Native Hawaiian nation.

How did the Office of Hawaiian Affairs get into this situation? Trustee Peter Apo explained the following during an Asset and Resource Management meeting of the Office of Hawaiian Affairs:

> So here we are negotiating the ceded lands settlement, two hundred million Kaka'ako, and in the eleventh hour, that bill gets inserted in Act 195. Okay? You either have to agree with Act 195 or we may not give you the two hundred million dollar settlement. That's how we got into Act 195. We had no control over that unless you wanted to turn down the settlement and so when we move

forward and I don't know how many millions of dollars we're into that now. (Apo, January 27, 2015)

There is an answer to Apo's question about spending that resulted from Act 195: $4,521,515.37 was spent on the Roll Commission, another $2,598,000 was granted to Na'i Aupuni (through a fiscal agent, the Akamai Foundation), and $82,509.86 was returned to the Office of Hawaiian Affairs when Na'i Aupuni did not fulfill its grant requirement to ratify any recommendation of the delegates arising out of the 'Aha. The total: $7,037,005.51. Additionally, the Office of Hawaiian Affairs spent $902,955.48 for legal services to defend the case of Akina v. State of Hawai'i, for a grand total of $7,939,960.99.[12]

Political crosscurrents

The process that culminated in the Na'i Aupuni congregation suffered from crosscurrents of political waters in Hawai'i. One current flows in the direction of democratic participation of Native Hawaiians, the aboriginal people of Hawai'i, to determine their future. This process of "self-determination," while under the yoke of colonization since 1893, is aspirational but leaves much to question about whether self-determination can truly be attained within the limitations of the US Constitution and Act 195.

A second current calls for historical accuracy, noting that Hawaiians who lost their continuing right of self-determination by US aggression had the genetic makeup of many ethnicities, including Caucasians, Chinese, Japanese, Filipinos, etc. Was this to be a national movement for decolonization, or a US-defined, native people's exercise in limited "sovereignty"? The call for Hawaiian "sovereignty" was used in both attempts, creating a continuing confusion of purpose.

A third current is the resisting of colonial US laws. One example is the Voting Rights Act, interpreted as restricting those very Native Hawaiian people who lost their right of self-determination due to the US invasion in 1893, and who are now prohibited from engaging in a democratic process of voting among themselves for their representatives to take the first step to self-determination. A lawsuit attempting to stop an election from taking place among the Native Hawaiian people was defeated at the District Court and the Circuit Court level, finally reaching the US Supreme Court. The Supreme Court issued a temporary restraining order, holding up the count of the ballots, to allow the Supreme Court time to consider if the process violates US law of voter discrimination—in other words, whether all US settlers now residing in Hawaiʻi should participate in such an election process.

A fourth current is the fear among Native Hawaiians of being victimized in a scam to steal their fundamental human rights, and of being swallowed up by the colonial forces of the United States and its puppet, the State of Hawaiʻi, and its suspect offshoot, the Office of Hawaiian Affairs.

Within these crosscurrents, the Naʻi Aupuni ship set on a journey to glimpse a preferred future and to return with a framing document or "constitution"—all within a limited timeframe, limited funds, and a questionable crew of more than 150 people brought together simply by their submitting their names as nominees, having no predetermined or tested leadership.

The original plan was for a gathering of forty specially chosen (elected) delegates to crew the waʻa, and to take forty days to accomplish its quest. But instead, the election of delegates was scuttled, and the crew ultimately increased to 156—almost four times its original number. The larger crew did not result in a better voyage, especially given that the waʻa was not large enough and the direction and leadership were not well defined. Additionally, the trip was shortened to twenty days to produce a framework envisioning the future of the Hawaiian nation.

Provisioning for the vessel was inadequate. The Royal Hawaiian Golf Course Clubhouse on Auloa Road in Kailua, Oʻahu, became the designated meeting place. There was one large gathering room that could adequately seat participants around banquet tables, plus two side rooms to seat fifteen to twenty people adequately for meeting purposes (but no tables in them), and a dining room of circular tables, serviced by a food-service room for self-service meals. There was limited logistical support: no telephones or copy machines, limited computer communication systems, and no administrative or general office support. There was a new and specially designed electronic polling system, but many participants, especially older members, could not engage in electronic voting and communication due to their lack of familiarity with the system. Also of concern was the lack of timely response by the system.

The meetings were held in private, causing much controversy at the entrance gate to the golf club. The television coverage was mostly adequate, although still unsatisfactory to those who wanted to be in the meeting room and "in the face" of those purportedly designing the future of the Hawaiian nation.

The waʻa started off in choppy waters and unfavorable, windy conditions with all the sniping, accusations, distrust, and other general suspicion, both in and out of the meeting space. And yet, the waʻa was expected to beach within twenty days with documents detailing the future course of the Hawaiian nation!

Sparks of beauty and color along the journey

While faced with these challenges, there were beautiful and colorful aspects along the journey. The participants consisted of a wide mixture of Native Hawaiians, from various ports across the world, from various age groups and levels of academic background, each bringing different experiences and perspectives. Some were familiar with the contending issues of Hawaiian self-determination. Others were at the introductory stage of the subject. All participants brought unique viewpoints, and the majority appeared willing to listen to opposing views.

The all-or-nothing thinking of choosing between independence or integration (federal recognition) was softened; rather than asserting which position was correct or better, conversations seemed to gravitate toward what would be the best approach to raise the nation rather than divide it. The language of the discourse began to shift. One paper that circulated among participants spoke of changing the conjunction from "independence or integration" to "independence *and* integration." The paper argued that we should no longer be divided by the minutia of details over Hawaiian sovereignty but united by the vast agreement over historical injustice imposed on Native Hawaiians and the need for unity over things that we could agree upon now.

Other discussions, while not finding their way into official documentation of the gathering, revolved around building new economic models, examining the nation's deep culture, conceptualizing alternative understandings of constitutional structures and principles.

An "aloha economy" was suggested as an alternative model to conceptualize the preferred economy as a substitute for the formula that revolves around ideas of "gross national product," "gross domestic product," capital accumulation, rates of investment and return, and other Western economic concepts. This "aloha economy" would create space in the Hawai'i economic system for traditional interchange, for new values of environmental protection, for an attitude that in sharing, there is always enough, and for a respect for all our environmental elements, not as resources but as members of our Hawaiian family.

There was discussion of reconstructing a Hawaiian national economy through the eyes of a hungry child rather than through a capitalist lens of ever-expanding markets and resources. Under such an economy, one would approach the development of the national economy with a question—what does a child hunger for?—and build an economy around that question. A child hungers for healthy food, clothing, shelter, family, a pristine environment, education, good health, identity and culture, affection, love and laughter, dreams, goodness, challenge, friendship, safety, and an understanding of continuity from the past to the future. These basic needs should form the building blocks for an economic system.

Another discussion introduced the subject and definition of Hawai'i's deep culture, examining the foundations of the culture that permeates the underlying nature of society. One manifestation of the dominant deep culture can be described as DIE (domination, individualism, and exclusion), which runs today's formal systems in economics, environmental management, education, law, judiciary, health systems, and politics. This deep culture is so pervasive that it can even invade family relationships and one's home life. A second deep culture that operates predominantly in our informal systems is built around values of OLA ('olu'olu, lōkahi, and aloha) and is present where communities and families reside. It is also sometimes found in churches, civic organizations and associations, and solemn or celebratory gatherings. As Hawaiʻi unfolds into its future, what should be the primary deep culture upon which we place our formal and informal systems—DIE or OLA?

Another subject was reframing the understanding of the constitutional history of Hawaiʻi. The general approach has been to understand Hawaiʻi's constitutional history as beginning with the first written constitution of 1840, followed by a series of new constitutions over the years. However, another view presented was that there is, and has been, only one fundamental constitution, which was defined by the pronouncement of the founder of the modern Hawaiian nation, Kamehameha I, who on his deathbed said, "E naʻi wale no ʻoukou, i kuʻu pono ʻaʻole pau."[13] This insistence on pono was later reiterated by his son, Kamehameha III: "Ua mau ke ea o ka ʻāina i ka pono."[14] Pono is the constitution; the written documents that followed were merely different expressions of that fundamental constitution, moving from one based deeply in culture, customs, and ancient laws of proper behavior, to a yielding to this new technology of literacy and new concepts of governance, yet still hanging on to the central constitution of pono. Accepting this approach to Hawaiʻi's constitutional foundation, what are the implications for drafting a constitution that will bring us into the future? Are we obligated to replicate the forms of earlier constitutional drafts, or are we free to design our own expressions and visions of a pono Hawaiʻi, given our contemporary circumstances and hopes for the future?

These important deliberations occurred in small discussion groups, in lunch circles, or in caucuses. The relationships formed at the congregation have carried forward among some of the participants and the general public. One example is the Hawaiʻi National Transitional Authority (HNTA), an unincorporated group of individuals gathering on the internet and in person to unify various positions of Hawaiian self-determination, to continue with discussions on these topics, and to work on specific issues to move Hawaiʻi forward.

The return from the journey

Upon returning from the twenty-day journey, a product dressed as a constitution was displayed by Naʻi Aupuni as the proposed end result of its travel. A ratification vote was to be taken two months following the close of the gathering.[15] A half month after the close of the gathering, Naʻi Aupuni announced it would not pursue the ratification of the document, instead leaving that task to the members to pursue.[16] As of this writing, no ratification vote has been announced.

What Is in the Constitution of the Native Hawaiian Nation?

The Constitution of the Native Hawaiian Nation is to be distinguished from the other document produced by Naʻi Aupuni—the Declaration of the Sovereignty of the Native Hawaiian Nation. The constitution purports to be a continuation of the Hawaiian government following the overthrow in 1893. The document can be discussed as both a process and a product.

The process

The introductory part of this paper summarized the historical context of the Hawaiian sovereignty movement from various perspectives. The February 2016 ʻAha convened by Naʻi Aupuni must be understood as part of that broader process of the sovereignty movement. The procedure followed in "rolling out" this gathering, its methods of operating, its rules of order, and the management of the meeting, are also to be understood in appreciating the product of this gathering.

Media coverage

The plenary sessions (General Assembly) were recorded and broadcast by 'Ōlelo Community Media via television. The committee or caucus meetings were not recorded by 'Ōlelo. Each committee or caucus decided for itself whether to have the TV crew record the proceedings. Individuals were permitted to record, and many people did so, posting such records on a variety of social media. While this congregation was "closed" to the physical presence of the general public, it was also an exceptionally "open" gathering through the combination of TV live coverage and social media. This provided a historical record of various points of view throughout the gathering.

Rules of Order

The congregation adopted *Robert's Rules of Order: Newly Revised, 11th Edition*, and a slate of executive officers were elected. For a time, the inappropriate application of these rules of order discouraged deliberation and debate, resulting in discussions that were shut down once anyone "called the question" from the floor and a mere majority vote was taken to stop such debate. After this practice was protested by an appeal to the decision of the chair, the chair changed his practice to refusing to call for the question unless he saw no one coming to the microphone to engage in debate on a question. He did, however, terminate debate when there were no speakers either on the pro or con side of a question, although there may have been additional speakers still lined up to speak on the opposite side. This had the effect of cutting off debate, without a vote.

On the whole, there was a great divide between those familiar with *Robert's Rules of Order* and those who were not. This divide allowed some to take advantage of their familiarity or ignorance to such a point that the process could, and at times did, become manipulative and abusive. The "crew training" for this journey was not adequate for the intensely deliberative nature of the congregation.

Mediation

This congregation was stuck between a gathering for deliberative purposes and one for negotiation, bargaining, and producing a constitutional document within an abbreviated time frame. The three "professional" mediators would have been well suited for a gathering for mediating or settling disputes or oppositional positions, but not for engaging a deliberative assembly. The mediators tried to facilitate a smooth and friendly conversation among the participants. However, they were neither trained nor experienced in bringing about respectful deliberation of important issues, nor, by their own admission, were they trained in *Robert's Rules of Order*.

There should have been a clear distinction between the nature of deliberation and mediation, with more emphasis on hearing the voices of one another than to take a vote as soon as a popular majority could be obtained, and then move onward. The twenty-day time limit was an inherent obstacle to a deliberative body of this nature.

Caucuses

The congregation was divided into various caucuses spread across various rooms, including the dining areas. Each of the caucuses met simultaneously. If participants wanted to participate in more than one caucus, they were free to do so, but they could only be engaged in one caucus at a time. This made continuity of one's work impossible. For example, many people were interested in the Preamble caucus, the International caucus, and the Rights of Citizen caucus. All were in operation at the same time, along with all other caucuses. Leaving the Preamble caucus after it appeared that certain agreements and directions had been made, and then attending another caucus, could easily result in the agreements and direction in the Preamble caucus changing dramatically as other members attended and changed earlier agreements and directions. Because of this variability, the earlier deliberations in some caucuses were lost or re-threaded. There was no reliable continuity of a particular caucus, nor was there a matching of themes across caucuses.

The only assured continuity was the chair, who headed each caucus and was able to track the discussions and agreements made by a meeting of a caucus, which could still be changed by new participants dropping in to the next meeting without any understanding of prior discussions and agreements. Each chair was to meet with a drafting group for drafting and coordinating the work produced by the caucuses.

Drafting committee

When the drafting committee received the caucuses' reports, they were to apply appropriate "wordsmithing" skills appropriate for coordinating the various reports and to fit within a constitutional framework. At times, the drafting committee itself undertook to make substantive changes to the work, arguing that the changes were made because of their consultation with expert legal advice. The source of said legal advice was never revealed. This practice allowed for too much liberty on the part of the drafting committee.

The drafting committee's meetings were held at the Richardson School of Law at the University of Hawaiʻi at Mānoa campus, a separate venue from the gathering of the congregation in Maunawili, after the convention had adjourned for the day. The drafting committee was open to all members to participate. However, members living in Waiʻanae or Lāʻie and undergoing long travel times, family responsibilities, or other myriad obligations could not attend such meetings and be back in Maunawili in time for the next day's work.

The timing of the release of the constitution draft was poorly managed. When the initial draft was released, it was one day prior to the scheduled end of the congregation's meeting. The final document was not released until the last day of convening, a few hours before the final vote. Consultation on the whole document in a comprehensive manner, by individuals and among members, became impossible. This compressed process made it impossible to make a comparison with the preliminary rules of the Department of Interior. Debate was limited to a few minutes for each member to respond to this document as a whole. Therefore, it cannot be said that this congregation properly and adequately considered this document.

Attention to previous NHC work

The congregation gave inadequate attention to the NHC's previous work toward an independence model and integration frameworks. The work of the NHC was a culmination of ten years of gatherings, a ratification referendum to form the convention, and an election of delegates to attend its convention. It held meetings throughout Hawaiʻi and in various states of the United States. Yet the Naʻi Aupuni congregation allowed only a ten-minute presentation of the NHC product, with five minutes for questions and answers.

Results

At the end of the Naʻi Aupuni congregation, two documents were issued. The first was the Constitution of the Native Hawaiian Nation, which was adopted by a majority of the members by roll call (80 in support, 33 opposed, and a number who refused to dignify the process with a response but whose lack of response was added to the majority, making it 88). The second was the Declaration of the Sovereignty of the Native Hawaiian Nation, adopted by voice vote (see attachments 1 and 2).

The product

The Constitution of the Native Hawaiian Nation is about fifteen single-spaced pages. It begins with a preamble and includes eight chapters. This article deals only with certain sections and concepts of the constitution. Due to space constraints, it does not address the Declaration of the Sovereignty of the Native Hawaiian Nation. Brief comparisons will also be made, as appropriate, with the NHC's proposal for an independence constitution.

The preamble

The first paragraph of the preamble refers to ancient history and deep cultural concepts, using ʻōlelo Hawaiʻi to anchor the document in Hawaiian beliefs. In the second paragraph, the narrative moves from the cultural to the political:

> *Honoring all those who have steadfastly upheld the self-determination of our people against adversity and injustice, we join together to affirm a government of, by, and for Native Hawaiian people to perpetuate a Pono government and promote the well-being of our people and the ʻĀina that sustains us. We reaffirm the National Sovereignty of the Nation. We reserve all rights to Sovereignty and Self-determination, including the pursuit of independence. Our highest aspirations are set upon the promise of our unity and this Constitution.*

In the initial discussions of the Preamble caucus, there was a strong preference to recite the history of the Hawaiian government being overthrown by US forces and the subsequent removal of culture, language, and historical understanding of our nation. However, the prevailing consideration was that we should not open the document with such a negative history but instead lead with a higher statement of strength that reflects our common national elements, positive values, and the connectedness of our generations. The preamble reflects that change.

In the closing days of the convention, there was consternation over the inclusion of the terms *self-determination* and *independence*. However, after long discussion and debate, the Preamble caucus was clear in its desire for the preamble to use self-determination and independence as contemplated in the International Bill of Human Rights and in other international language. It was so declared in the final floor debate, when the Preamble caucus chairperson was specifically asked if those terms were used in the same sense as the language used in those international documents, and the chairperson responded clearly and positively that they were!

Comparing the language with that of NHC's July 2000 proposal for an independence constitution, we see a different approach of the constitutional framework (see attachment 3). It opens with an acknowledgment to the Source of all creation, speaks of a foundation of Aloha, invokes the word sovereignty, and proclaims the right to control our destiny. It next speaks of pono, followed by an expansion of partnership among the host people and of all others under an umbrella of human rights and fundamental freedoms and between the human and the natural elements. It identifies as divine elements of nature, the sun, wind, sky, fresh and salt waters, land, and the people and their representations of life, change, fluidity, stability and humanity. Finally, it speaks of a government of, by, and for the people into the generations yet to come. Intertwined into this preamble are Hawaiian value statements as anchor marks.

Both the Naʻi Aupuni congregation constitution and the NHC draft for an independent Hawaiʻi reflect a common expression of self-determination and a fundamental value of pono.

The people
The Naʻi Aupuni document excludes from the members of this "nation" those people who do not have indigenous Hawaiian blood. As a "continuum" from our overthrown government to the present, this treatment leaves a large hole in our history. In the Hawaiian government, beginning with the reign of Kamehameha I, non-Native Hawaiians were part of the Hawaiian political, cultural, and civic body. Furthermore, one of the fundamental principles of indigenous peoples' rights in developing international standards is the right of self-definition, which includes the right of indigenous peoples to describe, for themselves, who are members of their political group.[17]

In taking a more exclusive approach, the Naʻi Aupuni document is a turn away from Hawaiʻi's history, culture, and the more enlightened view of the rights of the Hawaiian people. It is a concession to the federal recognition standards of US policy, which generally limits the membership of its "recognized" nations to indigenous peoples only. It raises a central question of whether the constitution is written for the people, or to appease the colonial government at the expense of the historical, political, and cultural integrity of the Hawaiian people.

By contrast, the NHC document addresses the distinction between the "host people and culture of this land," while also recognizing the human rights and fundamental freedoms to be accorded to every person of Hawaiʻi, in calling for a partnership. This language is more in line with a continuity of the Hawaiian nation.

The name
The Naʻi Aupuni document contains no name for the nation. One of the requirements of the US DOI proposed and final rules is that the constitution, or formative document, must have a name for the nation.

The NHC document states simply that Hawaiʻi is the name of the nation.

Article 1: Territory and Land
This article follows language that does not clearly set forth whether the subject is one of territorial jurisdiction or of land title. In the first paragraph, it reads as if the subject is territorial jurisdiction, claiming the territory to include "all lands, water, property, airspace, surface and subsurface rights, and other natural resources, belonging to, controlled by, and designated for conveyance to and for the Hawaiian Nation."

This present-day outlook is a one-dimensional statement of time and lacks a "looking back" claim of the territory of the Hawaiian government. It asserts no claim over Maunakea, Haleakalā, and other land areas of recent controversy. It makes no claim of waters, including the twelve miles beyond the shores of the islands, or the 200-mile exclusive economic zone. All the fisheries are left out, as are the subsurface minerals and the deep ocean waters used for heat transfer, energy creation, potential for cage culture in the harvesting of fish, etc.

The next paragraph in the Na'i Aupuni document deals with title and the Native Hawaiian people, stating:

> *The Native Hawaiian people have never relinquished their claims to their national lands. To the maximum extent possible, the Government shall pursue the repatriation and return of the national lands, together with all rights, resources, and appurtenances associated with or appertaining to those lands, or other just compensation for lands lost.*

The language here is unclear regarding the claims of the Native Hawaiian people to their national lands. If this is a reference to the pre-overthrow Hawaiian government, it should have stated clearly that the Hawaiian monarchy never relinquished its national lands. The people owned no such lands as a group but only through its government. This paragraph skirts the fact that the monarchy's Government lands and Crown lands were taken and maintains a pretense that there were lands set aside for the Native Hawaiian people en masse. In fact, the people owned *rights in* the land to have access for purposes of traditional, cultural, and sustenance purposes, but these rights were never seen as *title to* the lands.

Both paragraphs of Article 1 reference a superior entity. The first references "belonging to, controlled by, and designated for conveyance to and for the Hawaiian Nation." The second makes a more oblique reference by stating, "To the maximum extent possible, the government shall pursue the repatriation and return of . . ." Both paragraphs suggest, but refuse to simply state, that the lands and territories belonging to Native Hawaiians are now in the hands of the US government through theft, and all of the lands should be given back.

The language in the NHC document for independence (Article II) is much clearer with regard to territory:

> *The <u>national</u> territory [of Hawai'i][18] consists of the Hawaiian archipelago, stretching from Kure Atoll in the North to Hawai'i in the South and all of those lands, atolls and other territories whose jurisdiction have been assumed by the United States of America previously claimed by Hawai'i prior to the US 1893 invasion. Those territories previously part of the constitutional Hawaiian monarchy but which have subsequently been declared the territory or possession of a state other than the United States of America may be included within the territorial jurisdiction of Hawai'i upon concluding negotiation with that claiming state and Hawai'i.*

> *The territorial waters of Hawai'i shall include the waters twelve (12) miles from the shores of all lands of Hawai'i. The exclusive economic zone defined by the 1982 Convention on the Law of the Sea is adopted as applying to Hawai'i.*

Casting a wide net, the NHC document takes in all of the Hawaiian territory, including the 200-mile exclusive economic zone, all of the lands including Kalama (Johnston) Atoll, Palmyra Island, Sinkiang Island among the Solomon group, and lands to the northernmost island in the Hawaiian Archipelago. It addresses territorial jurisdiction and deals with the return of private lands taken in a separate section regarding post-colonization outstanding claims.

Article 2: Citizenship

This article deals with two subjects: who are the citizens, and who has the right to vote. It declares a citizen as being "any descendant of the aboriginal and indigenous people who, prior to 1778, occupied and exercised sovereignty in the Hawaiian Islands and is enrolled in the nation." Later in the document (Article 9, Section 2) it states, "The Nation has the inherent power to establish the requirements for citizenship in the Nation. The Nation reserves the right to modify or change citizenship requirements solely through a constitutional amendment."

Section 2 of the document says citizenship in the United States is not to be affected by citizenship in the Native Hawaiian Nation. This is an interesting incursion into the domestic laws of the United States and how it treats its citizenry. It is also a curious statement in terms of what is left out, i.e., citizenship in a place other than the United States. This oddity becomes understandable when one appreciates that the purpose of Section 2 is to act as a "wink" to the reader to alleviate any concern about losing US citizenship—this is all part of a plan to fit within the US framework.

Section 3 declares that all citizens who have attained the age of eighteen years are eligible to vote. This is effective as a protection against laws that deprive citizens from voting because of criminal convictions, declaration of mental status, etc.

The NHC independence document (Article VI) treats Citizenship as follows:

> Citizenship shall consist of three general classes:
> - all Kanaka Maoli throughout the world _who elect to be citizens;_
> - descendants of subjects of the Hawaiian Kingdom prior to July 4, 1894 _who elect to be citizens;_ and
> - _all persons born in Hawaiʻi, and_ other individuals _who have been a resident of Hawaiʻi for a continuous period of five years prior to this constitution coming into force and effect, and who choose willfully to pledge their allegiance to Hawaiʻi._

The major difference here is that citizenship is not limited only to those of Native Hawaiian ancestry, but also includes those of other ancestries. To fully appreciate this arrangement, one must understand that the NHC document creates two primary bodies: one restricted to Native Hawaiians only, and the second encompassing people of all racial extraction, with agreed-upon separation and limited powers for each body.

Article 3: National and Official Language
ʻŌlelo Hawaiʻi is the national language. ʻŌlelo Hawaiʻi, along with English, are official languages. The document does not distinguish between a national and an official language.

In referencing official languages, the NHC document states:

> ʻŌlelo Hawaiʻi and English shall be the official languages of Hawaiʻi in which any and all official proceedings and legal transactions may be conducted.
>
> The Education Department of the General government shall be required to incorporate the teaching of ʻŌlelo Hawaiʻi coextensive with the teaching of English.
>
> _Within ten years after the formation of the general government,_ all public employees _shall be_ proficient in both languages as working languages.

Article 4: National Right to Self-Determination.
The Naʻi Aupuni congregation document makes a bold statement in declaring, "The Nation has the right to self-determination, including but not limited to, the

101

right to determine the political status of the Nation and freely pursue economic, social, cultural, and other endeavors."

This language is aligned with that of international law, found in the "International Covenant on Economic, Social and Cultural Rights"[19] and the "International Covenant on Civil and Political Rights,"[20] where each states in its respective Article 1: "All peoples have the right of self-determination. By virtue of that right they freely determine their political status and freely pursue their economic, social and cultural development."

When considering the national context, the DOI final rule stipulates at 50.13(j) that the document "Not contain provisions contrary to Federal law." Other than that general reference to federal law, the rule points to no specific federal law. It can be argued that the Naʻi Aupuni document's claim to the right of self-determination is part of the body of federal law by virtue of the US participation in forming the foundational principle of the Charter of the United Nations, with the said charter being subsequently ratified by the United States and thus becoming part of the "law of the land" under Article VI of the US Constitution. It could also be argued that the principle of self-determination is founded on none other than the US Declaration of Independence, which is seen as a sacred document and as part of the unwritten constitution of the United States of America. Finally, it can also be argued that the United States has signed both of the aforementioned International Covenants, and the US Senate ratified the International Civil and Political Rights document in 1992. It has not yet ratified the Economic, Social and Cultural Rights document as of 2017.

The NHC document uses different language but with the same outcome as to proclaim self-determination: "We proclaim *our right to control our destiny*, to nurture

the integrity of our people and culture, and to preserve the quality of life that we desire."

Article 5: Collective Rights

This article effectively declares the right of traditional and customary practice, recovery of bones and funerary objects, the protection of rights of Native Hawaiian tenants (thus excluding the rights of non-Native Hawaiians), and a claim for intellectual properties. However, it ignores the claim of self-definition, i.e., the right to determine its membership in the Hawaiian nation. This is a fundamental right fought for and won in the international development of indigenous peoples' rights[21] and should have been added to the Naʻi Aupuni document.

Article 6: Rights of the Individual

This article is effective in protecting individual rights. However, Section 5 contains serious flaws in stating that the right to counsel is to be paid for at the defendant's own expense.

Another flaw is found in Section 9, where no imprisonment for debt is assured, unless such debt had been incurred as a result of fraud. Section 11 is also problematic; it provides every citizen the right to bear arms, which, as written, would allow children to carry weapons as well as those with a history of violent criminal and noncriminal behavior.

Section 14 is an attempt to protect the people's right to a healthy environment. It states, "All persons have the right to be free from exposure from harmful substances used in warfare, nuclear power plants, and waste materials." This statement would benefit from a rewriting to be more broad and inclusive.[22]

In comparison, NHC's proposed independence document has a much more expanded listing of rights, which delineates such rights over thirty sections in Article 4 (Peoples' Rights and Protections).

Article 7: Customary Rights

Article 7 of the Naʻi Aupuni document addresses four specific customary rights: to protect subsistence, cultural, medicinal, and religious purposes; to manifest, practice, develop and teach spiritual and religious traditions, customs, and ceremonies; to be stewards of water under its jurisdiction; and to sustain the ʻāina.

These are important rights that should be specifically set forth. However, there may be some confusion in the wording of the Naʻi Aupuni document, as the Native Hawaiian people have the first three rights, but the Nation has the fourth right (to sustain the ʻāina), leaving the reader to question why this distinction exists.

Also important is what is omitted from these rights for Native Hawaiians. If one speaks of self-determination, it is necessary to set forth control or participation over population expansion and transfers, foreign investments and trade, visa for foreign travels into Hawaiʻi, domestic taxing authority and tariff levies, Hawaiʻi national security and defense, and control over foreign and domestic military use of Hawaiian territories.

Article 9: Reservation of Rights and Privileges

This article specifically protects the Hawaiian Homes Commission Act from "this Constitution or the laws of the Nation." However, it does not protect the Hawaiian Homes Land Recovery Act,[23] which protection is required by the preliminary and final rule of the DOI. As a result, this article fails to meet the minimum requirement of the final rule.

Article 10: Kuleana

This article seems to restate and expand the first paragraph of the preamble—dedicating the government to prioritize Hawaiian culture, to steward Hawaiʻi's environment, to protect the rights of its citizens, to support home rule, to provide for the general welfare, to pursue repatriation of national lands, to ensure reasonable traditional and customary access to water on national lands, etc. With nineteen specific items, it seems to be the "catchall" article—perhaps a listing of favorite projects for participants not patient enough to await a legislative assembly to work out these projects and directions—that appears out of place in a constitutive document that sets forth the broad principles of a nation and its general operation.

Article 14: Sovereign Immunity

Article 14 declares, "The Nation and its Government possess sovereign immunity, which can only be waived in accordance with the law."

This statement may have various readings. It may be considered a position of independence from the United States, and that in having sovereign immunity, its citizens and territories may be beyond the jurisdiction of the United States, including its powers of taxation, judicial authority, police, etc. The statement could also be interpreted as having a subservient sovereign immunity, which becomes a concoction of US demotion of such terms under the authority of the United States.

The concept of sovereign immunity is presently in flux, especially given the formation of the International Criminal Court and the setting aside of sovereign immunity, even to heads of states,[24] for crimes defined under that court's jurisdiction.[25] This author does not seek to clarify the extent of sovereign immunity declared in the Naʻi Aupuni document and leaves its full meaning in uncertainty.

Article 16: Oath of Office

This article describes that public officials must take an oath to support and defend the "Constitution of the Nation." However, "no person shall be compelled to take an oath or make an affirmation that is contrary to their religion or belief." This language raises the question of what a belief may consist of such that the oath need not be taken. The exemption for taking an oath of office undermines the call for the taking of an oath. It may have been better to say, "Every public official must carry out the duties of the office faithfully and in compliance with the constitution and laws of the nation."

Article 17: Removal from Office

Members of the judiciary may be impeached when action is initiated by the president, subject to trial and two-thirds majority of the legislative body. The president can be impeached by a trial and a two-thirds majority of the legislative body. No power is given to the impeachment of a member of the legislature. There are no appeals to the lack of due process from any trial and vote. In a highly politicized body, and when no appeal is possible outside of the legislative process, this power of removal can become abusive or a means to remove the president or a member of the judiciary for decisions or actions that are unpopular. This article also omits any question of impeachment of the vice president. In the event of a president's impeachment, Article 39 requires the vice president to undertake the position of the president. This article, in light of the other powers given the vice president, is a political time bomb. The vice president is given oversight of the Office of Citizenship and Elections (Article 23). The vice president is also charged with addressing the unique needs of the Kahiki citizenry

(Article 34)—those who live outside of Hawaiʻi. Given such powers, the vice president is placed in a position of great potential conflict, not only in overseeing his or her own and other's elections but also in creating a special relationship with the Kahiki citizenry that may, itself, outnumber the rest of the citizenry, or at least be large enough to sway an election or impeachment result. As the vice president would automatically assume the position of president in the event of the impeachment of the president, the conflict of interest would be unavoidable.

Article 19: Judicial Autonomy

The judiciary budget is protected from diminishment by the legislature unless it is a government-wide reduction, proportionately applied to the judiciary. Besides budgetary consideration, nothing more is said with regard to judicial autonomy, such as protecting the judicial decisions from political questions, i.e., laws of marriage, divorce, sexual identity, abortion, etc. This idea of budgetary autonomy by the judiciary, or any other agency or branch of government, is an incursion into the legislature's control over the funds of the government and the executive's responsibility to oversee the balanced administration of the government. One might ask, at what point does this diminishment of executive powers end? In the Naʻi Aupuni document, an appointed body of the executive now has independent control over its budget. The judiciary should be autonomous over its judicial duties, but it should be subject to the same budgetary policies and controls prescribed for the legislative body.

Article 23: Elections

This article discusses how voting lists are created and maintained, including giving procedures for voting—such as residency, age, disqualification, and recall requirements—to an Office of Citizenship and Elections. It would seem more appropriate to have the legislative body undertake such procedures and criteria rather than placing such powers in the hands of an appointed body under the control of the vice president.

Article 23 also allows for disqualification for voting but does not give any guidelines or identify the body that may determine disqualification, leaving this matter to the vagary of "unless disqualified by law."

The article attempts to account for controlling campaign financing through the legislature, permitting ceiling limits on public funding by "political" entities, public disclosure of contributions, contribution limits, corporate donation prohibitions, and expenditure limits.

Overall, this article should be reviewed for its delegation of authority. The decision to allow so much power over elections to be placed in the hands of a political officer, the vice president, should be reconsidered for its potential for conflicts of interest. If the vice president should become a candidate for the presidency, that person would oversee his or her own election race and may have the opportunity to disqualify opponents or manipulate the voting rolls to make it difficult to allow voting by a constituency in favor of the opposition.

The earlier stipulation in Hawaiʻi regarding the placement of state elections in the office of the lieutenant governor, a political office itself subject to election, was proven unwise and was subsequently removed.

Article 30: Legislative Elections

Voters in the respective districts may vote for representatives. This seems clear. However, problems in applying this provision arise when considering the representative count (below).

Article 31: Representative Count

This article provides for forty-three representatives, twenty-two of whom are to be elected based on population and distributed as follows:

Hawaiʻi – 2
Maui -1
Molokaʻi – 1
Lānaʻi – 1
Kahoʻolawe – 1
Oʻahu – 6
Kauaʻi – 1
Niʻihau – 1
Kahiki (outside of Hawaiʻi) – 8

Another twenty-one representatives are to be elected based on the land of each district, as follows:

Hawaiʻi – 4
Maui – 4
Molokaʻi – 2
Lānaʻi – 1
Kahoʻolawe – 1
Oʻahu – 4
Kauaʻi – 4
Niʻihau – 1
Kahiki – 0

This approach poses a major challenge to the concept of a representative form of government. The general understanding is that representation should be of people, not space or geography. The reason representation is based on the population is to bring a sense of equality among people who form the citizenry. For example, a citizen who comes from Oʻahu would have the equivalent weight of representation as one who comes from Maui. However, the model articulated in the Naʻi Aupuni document disregards this logic. For instance, Oʻahu, with the vast majority of Native Hawaiians, would have a total of ten representatives while Kahoʻolawe, which has zero permanent residents, would have two representatives. This model has no semblance of representation based on population.

If the argument is that the land needs a voice, then send a pōhaku from each of these islands to be represented in the legislative sessions, but to pretend that the land has elected individuals is specious. Following this train of thought, would the vast waters that surround our islands also be represented? And the sky, the air, the clouds, the feathered beings, and the creatures that inhabit this space?

Finally, this article violates the prior article, which requires that representatives be elected by those who are residing in the districts. Where will one find residents on Kahoʻolawe to vote for other residents of Kahoʻolawe?

Article 23 makes a special exemption regarding elections for the island of Kahoʻolawe, declaring that for Kahoʻolawe, residency may be established by demonstrating at least four consecutive years of stewardship to the island. It does not define what kind of stewardship, who maintains the record of stewardship, or why this special compensation is being given to Kahoʻolawe. Nor does it address the possibility that a person who has dedicated herself to the protection to the islands for four consecutive years, for example from 1990 to 1993, could now vote twice for representatives: once for Kahoʻolawe and once for the island she resides on!

No explanation is given for this deviation that would allow a special interest group to have an advantage in representation within the legislative body. Other special interest groups could just as easily argue for their interest—to represent Maunakea, Maunaloa, kūpuna, mānaleo, "pure" Hawaiians, practitioners of the ancient Hawaiian religions, and so forth. Giving one island special treatment for electoral representation is a violation of the fundamental concept of a representative democracy, an elevation of special interest above the masses, a movement from an egalitarian society to an elitist society, and a contradiction to the direction of the preamble of the first written constitution of Hawaiʻi, which declares that all men are equal before the law.

The idea that land masses should have a separate category of representatives should be removed from the document. The representation of Kahoʻolawe should be taken out until the situation changes and the island has a population of Native Hawaiians residing there over a reasonable period of time. The representative legislature should be properly apportioned to the population of the people it represents within a reasonable deviation of 1 to 1.25 points.

The current proposal for twenty-two representatives elected by the human population and twenty-one representatives based on island geography runs counter to representative democracy.

Article 33: Legislative Calendar

The legislature shall convene on January 17 of each year and shall establish a calendar in coordination with cultural protocols. The Naʻi Aupuni document does not identify which cultural protocols, whether or not they would include the various phases of the moon and, if so, what moon calendar should be followed. This nonspecificity gives rise to certain questions. For example, is an oli in the English language considered cultural protocol? Would an oli or mele in honor of Jesus Christ be appropriate? To call for cultural protocols without providing clarification leads only to uncertainty. An example of the confusion and disarray that can come about with the call for cultural protocol in the constitution is what happened among the members of the Naʻi Aupuni congregation prior to its first meeting. There were very passionate voices for and against "cultural protocols," the selection of the protocols, the person to lead or guide such protocols, and the religious expression to be contained in such protocols. Even in what appeared to be protocols that come from a particular expression of religion, there was not agreement about which specific entity, deity, or representation would be used. Would it be appropriate to use the leaves and nuts of the kukui tree in the decorations or in the ceremony? Would the Christian members of the legislature agree to such a display of the kinolau of a Native Hawaiian religious deity? Which deity is to be called? Who is to settle the matter?

The document should say nothing about the protocols in opening the legislature.

Article 44 (Judicial Power) to Article 48 (Term of Office for Justices and Judges)

A judicial branch is to be established consisting of a chief justice, three justices with lifetime appointments, and judges who shall serve no less than ten-year terms. Article 15 calls for appointment of the judiciary by the president, subject to the approval of the legislature's simple majority. The chief justice is elected by a majority of the justices. The chief justice presides over the courts, may establish courts, tribunals, offices, and forums of general or exclusive jurisdiction as prescribed by law, and "may account for customary practices of the Native Hawaiian people." Although the meaning of that last phrase is not explained, it is an appropriate addition that liberates rather than restricts the judiciary.

On the whole, the judicial authority kuleana in Chapter 6 does not adequately describe the scope of jurisdiction of the courts. It calls for its judicial powers over all cases arising under this "constitution, the laws of the Nation, treaties, compacts, and agreements made, or which shall be made, under the Nation's authority." Where does this leave cases regarding the aliʻi trusts, the Department of Hawaiian Home Lands, noncitizens' violation of law upon territories under the jurisdiction of the nation, contract disputes between citizens or between citizens and noncitizens, land disputes between citizens over lands outside of the territorial boundaries of the nation, disputes over Hawaiian customs and traditions between Hawaiian and non-Hawaiian citizens, child welfare disputes, etc.?

Article 46 states that the judiciary's primary focus is "restorative justice." It gives no guidelines or explanation of what is meant by restorative justice. In the current practice of law, restorative justice applies generally to criminal cases in which justice should focus on repairing the harm, allowing the people most affected by the crime the ability to participate in the resolution of the crime while the government tries to maintain order and keep the peace. While this practice has its merits, it cannot be applied unilaterally. For example, a woman habitually abused by a family member, who finally brings a complaint to the courts, may not want to participate in "repairing the harm"—other than distancing herself from her abuser. In this example, it is uncertain to what extent the judiciary would call upon the abused woman to participate in counseling sessions or mediation to achieve restorative justice. Yet, restorative justice is a constitutional priority per the Naʻi Aupuni document. By creating such a priority, the judiciary is mandated to operate in this way to follow the constitution. A better approach would be for the constitution to allow the judiciary to consider restorative justice but not make it a primary focus.

Article 51: Ratification

This constitution is subject to a ratification vote, and a ratification election is to be held. The constitution becomes effective upon approval of a majority vote of individuals who are eligible to be citizens, have attained the age of eighteen, and have cast a ballot in the ratification election.

Summary Critique

How do the Na'i Aupuni process and document measure up to international law standards of self-determination?

Both the process and the constitutional document produced by Na'i Aupuni fail to meet the requirements of self-determination. The question of who is entitled to the right to self-determination should not be determined by the colonial government. In the case of Hawai'i, all people who lost the continuing right to exercise self-determination following the aggression of the United States, depriving them of their right to determine their futures, should continue to possess that right. The US government's redefining of Hawaiian nationals as only those with Native Hawaiian blood is not consonant with Hawaiian law, Hawaiian history, the UN Charter respecting non-self-governing territories, or the general laws of nations. Those who identified as Hawaiian nationals prior to the US government's aggression in 1893 were of many different racial ancestries. To follow that aggressive government's redefinition of the nationals of the nation it attacked is tantamount to foolishness.

Hawai'i was placed on the list of non-self-governing territories in 1946 (UN General Assembly, 1946).[26] Self-determination, in the context of non-self-governing territories, should afford a people three options: independence, free association, or integration. The present document produced by Na'i Aupuni, styling itself a "constitution," fails to clearly set out a path for any of these options. Instead, it attempts to put these options under a single document. This constitution was supposed to go through a process of ratification, but it is unclear what is to be ratified. The document merely adds to the confusion.

As we watch the events occurring at the United Nations regarding the Indigenous Peoples' Forum and the application of the Declaration of Rights of Indigenous Peoples, we are seeing member states of the United Nations attempting to transition the right of self-determination for indigenous peoples to the domestic jurisdictions of the states, thereby avoiding the scrutiny of the international community. The United States has followed this tack from the early meetings of the UN Working Group on Indigenous Populations meetings in Geneva Switzerland as well as the Indigenous Peoples' Forum at the UN office in New York. Considerations of indigenous peoples' rights across the world are multifaceted, and there may indeed be cases where it may be appropriate for states to treat these rights as internal or domestic matters.

But for Hawai'i, such treatment is inappropriate. Hawai'i's case is distinguished by the fact that Hawai'i was recognized as a nation under international law prior to the US takeover in 1893. There is clear evidence of aggression by the United States against that Hawaiian nation, as referenced in the 1993 Apology Resolution, in the 1946 submittal to the United Nations naming

Hawaiʻi as a non-self-governing territory, and in the December 1893 address to the joint houses of Congress by US President Cleveland.[27] Hawaiʻi's unique historical and contemporary backdrop cannot be equated to that of only indigenous peoples' rights. Hawaiʻi's rights include the full panoply of self-determination, without any limitations of US domestic laws or any claims of US exceptionalism from the general rules of international conduct.

The United Nations, dissatisfied with the poor record of decolonization of its member states, adopted its Declaration on the Granting of Independence to Colonial Countries and Peoples. In it, the UN General Assembly (1960) declared:

> All peoples have the right to self-determination; by virtue of that right they freely determine their political status and freely pursue their economic, social and cultural development. . . .
>
> Immediate steps shall be taken, in Trust and Non-Self-Governing Territories or all other territories which have not yet attained independence, to transfer all powers to the peoples of those territories, without any conditions or reservations, in accordance with their freely expressed will and desire, without any distinction as to race, creed or color, in order to enable them to enjoy complete independence and freedom.

That 1960 declaration is directly applicable to Hawaiʻi. As a non-self-governing territory, we have not yet attained independence and are entitled to those immediate steps to transfer all powers to the people of Hawaiʻi without any conditions or reservations, to enable us to enjoy complete independence and freedom.

The twisting of the use of the term Native Hawaiians—thus limiting the exercise of self-determination to only a limited group of people, while still denying a wider body who can be called Hawaiian nationals, or those entitled to claim such nationality—should not be allowed as an escape from its international obligation to accord self-determination to such nationals by the US colonial government. The question of Hawaiian self-determination is indeed a right of the Native Hawaiian people. But it is far more than that. Hawaiʻi's rights of self-determination encompass a far larger expanse of people beyond one's native blood!

How do the Naʻi Aupuni process and document measure up to the US DOI final rule for federal recognition?

Prior to and during the congregation, only the proposed rule adopted by the DOI was available. In that rule, there were eight criteria to be met before the DOI would consider the governing document to have been properly ratified (Office of the Secretary, Department of the Interior, 2015).[28]

Seven and a half months after the Naʻi Aupuni congregation adjourned, the DOI's final rule was adopted.[29] The following analysis references the final rule to examine to what extent the Naʻi Aupuni document that emerged from the congregation would meet the requirements for federal recognition. All further reference to the "rule" will indicate the final rule unless otherwise noted.

The rule's first criterion (§50.11) calls for a narrative with supporting documentation describing how the Native Hawaiian community drafted the document, including how the document was based on meaningful input from representative segments of the Native Hawaiian community and reflects the will of the community.

Whether the document reflects the will of the community could be assessed if the document were to be ratified. Whether those who drafted the Naʻi Aupuni document were "representative segments" of the Native Hawaiian community may be questioned. The fact that there were 156 participants at the congregation from all parts of the world could be used to indicate the representative segments. The fact that the drafters were not elected may be excused by the fact that the Supreme Court ordered a temporary restraining order not to count the votes and announce the result. However, that excuse remains merely an excuse and will not adequately substitute as support for the representativeness of the members of the congregation. Whatever the reason for the selection of these participants, the fact that they were nominated by a minimum of ten others does not seem to be an adequate foundation to the claim that this was a representative segment of the community. On this criterion the Naʻi Aupuni congregation's document fails.

For a Native Hawaiian government to reestablish a formal government-to-government relationship with the United States, the rule (§50.12) requires that the Native Hawaiian government have a constitution or other governing document ratified both by a majority vote of Native Hawaiians and by a majority vote of those Native Hawaiians who qualify as HHCA Native Hawaiians. "Native Hawaiians" are defined as individuals who are descendants of the aboriginal people who, prior to 1778, occupied and exercised sovereignty in the area that now constitutes the state of Hawaiʻi. An "HHCA eligible Native Hawaiian" is a person who meets the definition of "Native Hawaiian" in the Hawaiian Homes Commission Act, regardless of whether the individual resides on Hawaiian home lands, is an HHCA lessee, is on a wait list, or receives benefits under the act.[30] The final rule uses the term HHCA Native Hawaiian as simply "a Native Hawaiian individual who meets the definition of 'Native Hawaiian' in HHCA sec. 201(a)(7)."[31] To ensure an objective measure so that the vote represents the views of the Native Hawaiian community as a whole, the rule requires a minimum of thirty thousand affirmative votes from Native Hawaiian voters, including a minimum of nine thousand affirmative votes from HHCA Native Hawaiians.

The ratification provision of the Naʻi Aupuni constitution fails to meet the final rule in that it simply calls for a majority vote of eligible citizens ages eighteen and older to adopt the constitution. The final rule does provide that a second vote may be taken once a first vote adopting the document as its constitution has been accomplished. In that second vote, however, separate vote tallies for HHCA Native Hawaiians and for all Native Hawaiian voters must be kept. As of this writing, nothing has happened to advance the document. The second criterion calls for verifying that participants were appropriate Native Hawaiians. DHHL records, or another state commission or agency that verifies descent, could be used for this purpose.

In the DOI's proposed rule, there was a specific requirement that Native Hawaiians, in order to qualify under the federal guideline, must be US citizens (Office of the Secretary, Department of the Interior, 2015).[32] The final rule made a significant revision by excluding that citizenship requirement.[33]

Many advocates for Hawaiian independence have been kept out of Hawaiʻi's political life because of their insistence that they are not US citizens, claiming instead their Hawaiian nationality. As a result, such advocates are not permitted to vote in US and state elections, including elections for the Office of Hawaiian Affairs.

They cannot hold political office in the state government. These advocates also run into difficulty when applying for employment, not being able or willing to claim US citizenship or to "produce papers" to show they are lawfully in the United States and able to obtain employment. They are not able to meet the driver's license requirements, as well as the federal security requirement for flying interisland. The change in citizenship requirements in the DOI's final rule sheds new light on the necessity of US citizenship for Native Hawaiians and may indicate a turn away from this continued marginalization of such Hawaiian nationals from the centers of Hawaiʻi society.

The third criterion of the final rule, found at §50.13, is not met by the Naʻi Aupuni document. Table 1 (pp. 112–13) summarizes how the Naʻi Aupuni document aligns with §50.13.

This initial analysis demonstrates that the proposed Constitution of the Native Hawaiian Nation contains significant contradictions to and violations of the DOI final rule. It is therefore fair to conclude that the Naʻi Aupuni congregation did not produce a document that would meet the test of the DOI for US federal recognition.

Not only did the Constitution of the Native Hawaiian Nation fail to meet the final rule of the DOI for federal recognition, it also failed to meet the standards under international law for self-determination. In short, the Act 195 process—which was passed by the state legislature and financed by the Office of Hawaiian Affairs for almost eight million dollars—has failed to bring the Native Hawaiian people closer to federal recognition by the US government.

Lessons Learned

The Act 195 experience can teach us a number of lessons. First, one should not try to rush to a preferred solution for the sake of political expediency, especially when the problem is so deep and has persisted over such a long period of time. The fact that there was a president in the White House who appeared to be supportive of federal recognition of a Hawaiian nation, and whose term of office was soon to expire, was a poor rationale for pushing aside the prior work taken to bring the Hawaiian community together in a deliberate process of consulting, elections, and preparing a broad-based plan for a comprehensive solution. The process previously taken—which was recognized by the legislature and included the Sovereignty Advisory Council, the Hawaiian Sovereignty Advisory Commission, the Hawaiian Sovereignty Elections Council, the plebiscite by which an election of leaders from the Hawaiian community would meet in a convention to propose suggestions for a Hawaiian form of government, a subsequent election of such leaders, and the convening of the Native Hawaiian Convention—was a deliberate process that should be honored and allowed to reach its conclusion. Starting up a separate process to favor federal recognition via the Office of Hawaiian Affairs was a mistake.

Second, the trustees of the Office of Hawaiian Affairs should never again breach their trustee obligation and bend to the legislature's will, thus taking the Hawaiian community through a wasteful and painful experience. The Kanaʻiolowalu efforts came out of Act 195 of the 2011 state legislature as part of a process for resolving a Native Hawaiian matter of federal recognition. That legislature ransomed a real property transfer of Kakaʻako and other lands to finance Kanaʻiolowalu. The Office of Hawaiian Affairs was willing to be manipulated by

Table 1. Alignment of the Naʻi Aupuni document with §50.13 of the DOI's final rule on governing documents

REQUIREMENT OF DOI'S FINAL RULE	CRITERION MET?	COMMENTS
State the government's official name	No	There is no name in the Naʻi Aupuni document for the government.
Prescribe the manner in which the government exercises its sovereign powers	Yes	This concept is explained throughout the document.
Establish the institutions and structure of the government, and of its political subdivisions (if any) that are defined in a fair and reasonable manner	Uncertain	The method of selecting members of the legislative authority may be questioned, and the manner of selecting representatives could be considered unfair and unreasonable. The representative count (per Article 31) is not fair and reasonable in several ways: It fails to meet the one-person, one-vote standard, it allows for representation by land mass, and it makes exception for representation from Kahoʻolawe.
Authorize the government to negotiate with governments of the United States, the State of Hawaiʻi, and political subdivisions of the State of Hawaiʻi, and with nongovernmental entities	Yes, but introduces other concerns	While this criterion is met under Article 13 of the Naʻi Aupuni document, the article exceeds the requirement with the addition of "other sovereign." This appears contrary to federal policy, under which only the federal government is entitled to engage with other sovereigns, as in foreign countries.
Provide for periodic elections for government offices identified in the governing document	Partially	This requirement is met by Article 29 for the legislative body and Article 38 for the executive officers, but fails in the design of the judiciary.
Describe the criteria for membership: 1. Permit HHCA-eligible Native Hawaiians to enroll 2. Permit Native Hawaiians who are not HHCA-eligible Native Hawaiians, or some defined subset of that group that is not contrary to Federal law, to enroll 3. Exclude persons who are not Native Hawaiians 4. Establish that membership is voluntary and may be relinquished voluntarily 5. Exclude persons who voluntarily relinquished membership	Partially	Most criteria are met; however, provisions for (4) are not included in the the Naʻi Aupuni document, and provisions for (5) are not specified.

REQUIREMENT OF DOI'S FINAL RULE	CRITERION MET?	COMMENTS
Protect and preserve Native Hawaiians' rights, protections, and benefits under the HHCA and the HHLRA (Hawaiian Homes Land Recovery Act)	No	The HHLRA protection is not included in the Na'i Aupuni document.
Protect and preserve the liberties, rights, and privileges of all persons affected by the government's exercise of its powers	No	The Na'i Aupuni document violates the requirement to provide free counsel for a criminal defendant and permits imprisonment for debt in cases of fraud (Article 6).
Describe the procedures for proposing and ratifying amendments to the governing document	Yes	Criterion is met.
Not contain provisions contrary to federal law	No	The Na'i Aupuni document fails on numerous counts, such as the right to self-determination; imprisonment for debt (fraud cases); engagement in treaties, compacts, and other arrangements with other sovereigns; and violation of the one-person, one-vote standard.

the legislature and ended up financing the process for almost eight million dollars.

Third, a convention of Naitve Hawaiians should be formed around processes of deliberation, not merely counting votes or trading favors—especially when attempting to resolve long-standing issues such as human rights, fundamental freedoms, historical injustice, future planning, and the choice of remaining part of the United States, taking an independence route, or examining other possibilities of political relationships. Such deliberation requires adequate time and patience, taking in the voices from both within the convention and from the affected and interested public. Time is the greatest resource that must be made available to the convention process. Twenty days of deliberation for the February 2016 congregation was inadequate and seemed to reflect a rushed and inexperienced agenda and perhaps a predetermined outcome. For a successful convention, there must be liberal opportunities for recess and consultation with the community because it will eventually be the community that will have to approve of the deliberative results.

Fourth, any future convention must provide participants with appropriate staffing resources, necessary equipment for communication (among the convention members and with the public), adequate space, and the ability to coordinate various caucuses so that the discussion and final document will cover all matters consistently and effectively. All members—representing a range of backgrounds, sophistication, ages, and experience—must be given adequate time for input and for deliberation. Technologies must be appropriately adapted for this purpose.

Fifth, prior work products and processes, including the Kanaʻiolowalu experience, must be given due consideration, as representative of past voices and experiences. Furthermore, a deliberate effort must be made to include perspectives from the wider community. Presently, favor seems to be shown to elites from professions such as academia, law, politics, and business to serve in such conventions. A more egalitarian approach must be undertaken so that kuaʻāina views will also be represented. The challenge remains for such representation; there are no secret formulae to encourage a broader base of people to serve. And when such representation is achieved within a convention, special efforts must be made to include full opportunity and active participation by that representation. The rules of procedure, the use of technology, and the meeting places and times must be taken into consideration for the purpose of inclusiveness and participation, not just for expediency.

Conclusion

The failure of the Kanaʻiolowalu process is an opportunity for us to consider fundamental questions of self-determination: Who is the "self," and what is the full range of choices that "determination" should represent? Are we seeking a government of, for, and by the people? Or do we aspire for a government of an elite class of aliʻi, or a monarchial family? Who is the Hawaiian political self?

Should the self be able to trace ancestry to Hawaiian nationals of any racial extraction who descend from those of the Hawaiian nation, pre-US aggression, in 1893? Should the self include all persons who have lived in Hawaiʻi pre-"statehood" and have continued to maintain constant contact with Hawaiʻi? Should the measure of a Hawaiian self be only those who have maintained a Hawaiian political, cultural, spiritual, and language lifestyle? Should the self exclude those who identify as US citizens? Should the self include only those who affirm that they would select a Hawaiian citizenship rather than a US citizenship when the opportunity to do so arises?

If we are to be inclusively defined in the Hawaiian state, should we encourage special treatment for the Native Hawaiians? Should the question of indigenous peoples' rights have particular regard for our indigenous peoples? How can we be explicit in a formative document to protect indigenous Hawaiians while protecting the human rights and fundamental freedoms of all in Hawaiʻi?

For the question of "determination," there must be a broad, public discussion of the full range of choices along the spectrum of determination. The usual choices are independence or integration, including "statehood" and federal recognition of the Native Hawaiian people. A third option of free association, such as a "commonwealth" status, has not been talked about much in discussions of Hawaiian determination. The question of independence or integration is usually treated as an immediate and final decision. However, new voices are questioning the use of the *or* conjunction, arguing that *and* is just as viable. For example, why can't the decision be made to select both independence in the eventual future *and* the interim status of integration—*and*, especially for the Native Hawaiians, a degree of federal recognition? For the sake of national unity, can we agree to aspire to both approaches, unify the national body first, and resolve to answer the and/or question as we work toward both goals through an inclusive approach?

A consideration of the future status of Hawaiʻi, including independence, must account for a wide assortment of issues usually left out of public discussions because of what may appear to be an anti-United States policy. But discussing such issues is crucial for a fair review of the options. What are the positive and the negative aspects of Hawaiian independence for the Hawaiian nation? That question must be opened particularly wide, without shying away from the limitations that appear to be imposed upon us by US constitutional, congressional, or presidential mandate. Rather, we should be mindful of historical injustices and remember the voice of Liliʻuokalani as contained in her "pule" (Queen's Prayer) of forgiveness. We should also be cognizant of the resounding call for pono as the foundation of "ke ea o ka ʻāina," of international law, and of the propensity toward independence in recent decades, given that a majority of the world's independent countries far outnumber those that had existed before the 1945 formation of the United Nations.

Life today is far more complicated than it was 120-plus years ago. Our conditions have changed under years of colonization under the United States. Its military occupation has done major ecological damage to our lands. Its control over our education system has erased fundamental aspects of our national consciousness, our native language, our cultural practices, and our intellectual treasures. Its monetary system has changed our economic, social, and business climate and has had a profound effect on the foundations of our deep culture. Its policy of population transmigration has changed much of the face of these islands' people, resulting in many of our native peoples being strangers and homeless in our own homelands.

The constitutional document that emerges from these discussions must meet the high principle of pono. It must be realistic and address the needs of the people of Hawaiʻi. The constitution need not replicate one of the earlier amendments in our history. Hawaiʻi's history should not be a chain that pulls us back to replicate the past, but rather a springboard propelling us into our future.

These are all matters that should be part of the grand discourses in Hawaiʻi before we attempt to craft a document that defines the constitution of our Hawaiian nation. Let us raise the nation—but not from a checklist given to us by the US colonial administrator intending to maintain its control over us, and not even from the lofty perspective of the principles and processes of international law. Instead, let us turn to our own examination of pono in all of its meanings for Hawaiʻi nei, and let this be the guiding principle we live by and take into our future, following the path of aloha.

ATTACHMENT 1

CONSTITUTION OF THE NATIVE HAWAIIAN NATION

Proposed constitution, produced by the Naʻi Aupuni gathering, March 2016

PREAMBLE

We, the indigenous peoples of Hawaiʻi, descendants of our ancestral lands from time immemorial, share a common national identity, culture, language, traditions, history, and ancestry. We are a people who Aloha Akua, Aloha ʻĀina, and Aloha each other. We mālama all generations, from keiki to kupuna, including those who have passed on and those yet to come. We mālama our ʻĀina and affirm our ancestral rights and Kuleana to all lands, waters, and resources of our islands and surrounding seas. We are united in our desire to cultivate the full expression of our traditions, customs, innovations, and beliefs of our living culture, while fostering the revitalization of ʻŌlelo Hawaiʻi, for we are a Nation that seeks Pono.

Honoring all those who have steadfastly upheld the self-determination of our people against adversity and injustice, we join together to affirm a government of, by, and for Native Hawaiian people to perpetuate a Pono government and promote the well-being of our people and the ʻĀina that sustains us. We reaffirm the National Sovereignty of the Nation. We reserve all rights to Sovereignty and Self-determination, including the pursuit of independence. Our highest aspirations are set upon the promise of our unity and this Constitution.

UA MAU KE EA O KA ʻĀINA I KA PONO.

CHAPTER I - OF THE NATION

Article 1 - Territory and Land

1. The territory of the Native Hawaiian Nation is all lands, water, property, airspace, surface and subsurface rights, and other natural resources, belonging to, controlled by, and designated for conveyance to and for the Hawaiian Nation.

2. The Native Hawaiian people have never relinquished their claims to their national lands. To the maximum extent possible, the Government shall pursue the repatriation and return of the national lands, together with all rights, resources, and appurtenances associated with or appertaining to those lands, or other just compensation for lands lost.

Article 2 - <u>Citizenship</u>

1. A citizen of the Native Hawaiian Nation is any descendant of the aboriginal and indigenous people who, prior to 1778, occupied and exercised sovereignty in the Hawaiian Islands and is enrolled in the nation.

2. Citizenship in the Native Hawaiian Nation shall not affect one's citizenship in the United States.

3. All citizens that have attained the age of eighteen years are eligible to vote.

Article 3 - <u>National and Official Languages</u>

1. ʻŌlelo Hawaiʻi is the National language.

2. ʻŌlelo Hawaiʻi and English shall be official languages.

3. The Government shall respect the right of its citizenry to understand the actions and decisions of its Government, and endeavor to communicate effectively with the citizenry while supporting the national language.

CHAPTER II - DECLARATION OF RIGHTS

Article 4 - <u>National Right to Self-Determination</u>

The Nation has the right to self-determination, including but not limited to, the right to determine the political status of the Nation and freely pursue economic, social, cultural, and other endeavors.

Article 5 - <u>Collective Rights</u>

1. The Native Hawaiian people shall have the right to honor our ancestors; maintain, protect, and repatriate iwi kūpuna, funerary, and cultural objects; protect sacred places; and protect the knowledge and wisdom from traditional and customary sources.

2. The rights of Native Hawaiian tenants in the ʻĀina (land, water, air, ancestor) and ahupuaʻa, shall not be abridged.

3. The Native Hawaiian people have the right to maintain, control, protect, and develop

their intellectual property over cultural heritage, traditional knowledge, and traditional cultural expressions.

Article 6 - <u>Rights of the Individual</u>

1. No person shall be deprived of life, liberty, or property without due process of law.

2. All people shall be guaranteed equal protection of the law.

3. The right of the people to be secure in their persons, houses, papers, and effects, against unreasonable searches and seizures shall not be violated and no warrants shall issue except upon probable cause, supported by oath and affirmation, and particularly describing the place to be searched and the persons or things to be seized.

4. No person shall be twice put in jeopardy for the same offense, nor be compelled to be a witness in a criminal case against himself or herself.

5. In all criminal prosecutions, the accused shall have the right to a speedy and public trial, by an impartial jury of not less than 12 jurors of his or her peers; to be informed of the nature and cause of the charges against him or her; to be confronted with the witnesses against him or her; to have a compulsory process for obtaining witnesses in his or her favor; to have assistance of counsel for defense at his or her own expense.

6. Every person is presumed innocent until proven guilty by law.

7. Bail shall be set by the judicial authorities and shall be available to all defendants, except where the granting of bail would constitute a danger to the community. Excessive bail shall not be required, nor excessive fines imposed, nor cruel and unusual punishment inflicted.

8. The writ of habeas corpus (of the body) shall be granted without delay and free of cost. The privilege of the writ of habeas corpus shall not be suspended.

9. There shall be no imprisonment for debt, except in cases of fraud.

10. No ex post facto law, nor any law impairing the obligation of contracts, shall be imposed.

11. Every citizen shall have the right to bear arms.

12. Citizens have a right to traditional medicines and to maintain their health practices,

including the conservation of their vital medicinal and cultural plants, animals, and minerals.

13. Every child citizen has the right to parental care, or to family or appropriate alternative care, when removed from the family environment; to basic nutrition, shelter, basic health care services, and social services; and, to be protected from maltreatment, neglect, abuse, or degradation.

14. All persons have the right to be free from exposure from harmful substances used in warfare, nuclear power plants, and waste materials.

Article 7 - <u>Customary Rights</u>

1. The Native Hawaiian people reserve all rights and responsibilities customarily and traditionally exercised for subsistence, cultural, medicinal, and religious purposes.

2. The Native Hawaiian people have the right to manifest, practice, develop, and teach their spiritual and religious traditions, customs, and ceremonies.

3. Ola i ka wai, water is life; and the Native Hawaiian people shall exercise traditional and customary stewardship of water. The Nation shall protect, control, and regulate the use of water resources under its jurisdiction for the benefit of its people.

4. The Nation has a right, duty, and kuleana, both individually and collectively, to sustain the ʻĀina (land, kai, wai, air) as an ancestor, source of mana, and source of life and well-being for present and future generations.

Article 8 - <u>Government Prohibitions</u>

The Government shall not:

1. Pass any law that abridges a citizen's right to make end of life decisions, be treated with dignity, and a humane death;

2. Take private property for public use without just compensation;

3. Make any law respecting the establishment of religion or prohibiting the free exercise thereof, or abridging the freedom of speech or of the press, or the right of the people to peaceably assemble; or

4. Make any law with the intent to suppress traditional Native Hawaiian religion or beliefs.

Article 9 - <u>Reservation of Rights & Privileges</u>

1. All rights, privileges, and powers not articulated in or pursuant to this Constitution shall be reserved in common to the citizens.

2. The Nation has the inherent power to establish the requirements for citizenship in the Nation. The Nation reserves the right to modify or change citizenship requirements solely through a constitutional amendment.

3. Any benefits accorded to the citizenry, by virtue of their status as citizens of the United States, shall not be diminished or impaired by the provisions of this Constitution or the laws of the Nation.

4. The rights of beneficiaries of private and other trusts, programs, or services shall not be diminished or impaired by the provisions of this Constitution or the laws of the Nation.

5. The rights of beneficiaries of the Hawaiian Homes Commission Act, 1920, as amended, shall not be diminished or impaired by the provisions of this Constitution or the laws of the Nation. The kuleana toward these beneficiaries is affirmed.

CHAPTER III - PURPOSE AND PRINCIPLES OF GOVERNMENT

Article 10 - <u>Kuleana</u>

1. The kuleana (right; responsibility; jurisdiction) of Government is to ʻĀina (land; water; air; ancestor); citizens; and Ke Ao Hawaiʻi (All things Hawaiian).

2. The Government shall provide for the prudent stewardship of the ʻĀina as the source of life and well-being, as expressed through the values reflected in the ʻŌlelo Noʻeau: He aliʻi ka ʻĀina, he kauā ke kanaka.

3. The Government shall provide for the prudent stewardship of water resources, as expressed through the values reflected in the ʻŌlelo Noʻeau: Ola i ka wai.

4. The primary purpose of Government is to meet the needs and priorities of its citizens, protect their rights, and care for the ʻĀina.

5. The Government shall ensure the liberty of the citizens and groups of citizens to mālama kuleana and pursue happiness.

6. The National Government shall empower kuleana-based governance, and support home rule and local governance.

7. The Government shall provide support to the citizens for housing, healthcare, food, and education.

8. The Government shall prioritize Hawaiian culture, history, language, traditions, customs, knowledge, and ancestral wisdom.

9. The Government shall pursue the repatriation and return of the national lands, together with all rights, resources, and appurtenances associated with or appertaining to those lands, or other just compensation for lands lost.

10. The Government shall ensure reasonable traditional and customary access to water on National lands.

11. The Government shall manage the Nation's assets in a fiscally responsible manner, balancing the needs of today with the needs of future generations.

12. The Government shall enact laws, create policies, and act in such a way that is resonant with and honors the traditions, customs, usage, and practices of the nation.

13. The Government shall protect and seek repatriation of iwi kūpuna, cultural objects, sacred places, and knowledge and wisdom from traditional and customary sources.

14. The Government shall seek repatriation of iwi kūpuna and cultural objects.

15. National Government shall advocate for Native Hawaiian rights, services, trusts, and programs with other sovereigns, institutions, and organizations.

16. The Government shall focus on restorative justice principles that follow on the traditions of puʻuhonua, mālama, and hoʻoponopono.

17. The Government recognizes the rights of traditional and customary units of Native Hawaiian society, especially that of ʻohana.

18. The Government shall provide for a certification process to enable a group of citizens to assert their collective kuleana in service of the nation.

19. Consistent with the first right articulated by Ka Mōʻī Kamehameha in the Kānāwai Māmalahoe, the Government shall promote the safety and security of all citizens and the Nation.

Kānāwai Māmalahoe - The Law of the Splintered Paddle:

E nā kānaka,
To my people,

E mālama ʻoukou i ke akua
honor the divine

A e mālama hoʻi ke kanaka nui a me kanaka iki;
And respect all people, great and humble

E hele ka ʻelemakule, ka luahine, a me ke kama a moe i ke ala
Let the elderly and the child lie down by the roadside

ʻAʻohe mea nāna e hoʻopilikia.
And let no one cause them harm.

Article 11 - Seat of Government

The Seat of Government shall be located in the Hawaiian Islands.

Article 12 - Rule of Law

The Government shall be bound by the Constitution, laws of the Nation, the customs of the Native Hawaiian people, and the rule of law.

Article 13 - Foreign Relations

1. The President shall have the power to conduct negotiations and enter into treaties, compacts, and other agreements with other sovereigns, political sub-divisions of such sovereigns, or other organizations and entities for the benefit of the Nation.

2.   Treaties and compacts shall be subject to a two-thirds ratification by the Legislative Authority.

Article 14 - <u>Sovereign Immunity</u>

The Nation and its Government possess sovereign immunity, which can only be waived in accordance with the law.

Article 15 - <u>Appointments</u>

1.   Judicial Authority appointments by the President are subject to confirmation by simple majority of the Legislative Authority.

2.   The President may appoint members of the Legislative Authority in the event of a vacancy; except that where more than two (2) years remain in the term, an election shall be held to fill the vacant seat.

Article 16 - <u>Oath of Office</u>

1.   Every public official, before entering upon the kuleana of their respective office, shall take and subscribe to the following oath in either ʻŌlelo Hawaiʻi or English language: I do solemnly swear that I will faithfully support and defend the Constitution of the Nation, and conscientiously and impartially discharge my duties as _____ to the best of my abilities.

2.   No person shall be compelled to take an oath or make an affirmation that is contrary to their religion or belief.

Article 17 - <u>Removal From Office</u>

1.   Impeachment proceedings and removal of judicial appointments may be initiated by the President subject to a trial conducted by the Legislative Authority and two-thirds majority vote of the body.

2.   The Legislative Authority may, following a trial to determine cause, impeach the President through two-thirds majority vote of the body.

Article 18 - <u>Office Limitation</u>

1.   Public officials may not hold any other position within any branch of the Government, or within any other government, while holding an elected office.

Article 19 - <u>Judicial Autonomy</u>

Legislative Authority may not diminish the Judicial budget, without the consent of the Judicial Authority, except where proportionate government-wide reductions are in effect.

Article 20 - <u>Special Session</u>

The President may call a special session of the Legislative Authority.

Article 21 - <u>Moku Council</u>

1.   Within four (4) years of ratification of the Constitution, there shall be established within the Office of the President, a Moku Council with no less than nine (9) members.

2.   The Moku Council shall advise the President on the needs of its respective districts, the delivery of relevant services to its districts, and on other decision-making that would benefit from the Moku Council's place-based expertise.

3.   The President shall appoint one (1) representative from each district, until such time as the Moku Council shall recommend a statutory process of determining council membership.

4.   The Moku Council shall elect, from among its members, a representative to serve in the Executive Cabinet.

Article 22 - <u>Local Government</u>

1.   The Legislative Authority may create political subdivisions within the Nation and provide for the government thereof.

2.   Each political subdivision shall have and exercise such powers as conferred under general laws.

3. Each political subdivision shall have the power to frame and adopt a charter for its own self-government within such limits and under such procedures as may be provided by general law.

Article 23 - <u>Elections</u>

1. The Vice President shall establish an Office of Citizenship and Elections whose responsibilities shall include, but are not limited to, the following: (1) Enroll, manage, and maintain the list of citizens of the Hawaiian Nation; and (2) establish procedures for voting that includes residency, age, disqualification, and recall requirements.

2. The Office will establish and execute a process to enroll, create, and maintain a list of Nation citizens.

3. Office will administer elections for the Legislative Authority and President and Vice President, including procedures to demonstrate residency.

4. All citizens who have attained the age of eighteen (18) shall be allowed to vote for the seats associated with their permanent residency, where citizens may provide only one permanent residency. Kaho'olawe residency may be established by demonstrating at least four (4) consecutive years of stewardship to the island.

5. Citizens shall be automatically registered to vote upon reaching the age of eighteen (18), unless disqualified by law.

6. The Legislative Authority shall enact campaign finance laws on the financing of political candidates seeking public office. These laws shall include, but are not limited to: (1) ceiling limits on public funding by political entities; (2) public disclosure of contributions; (3) contribution limits; (4) corporate donation prohibitions; and (5) expenditure limits.

Article 24 - <u>Recall of Elected Officials</u>

All elected officials are subject to recall for cause, which may be initiated by signature of twenty-five (25) percent of the votes cast in the last election for that office. Any recall is subject to the majority vote of eligible votes cast for the respective office.

Article 25 - <u>Statutory Initiative and Referendum</u>

1. The Legislature may vote by two-thirds of the body to send questions directly to the citizenry through a ballot referendum.

2. The citizenry may, by petition signed by at least ten (10) percent of the number of voters in the last Executive election, place a statutory amendment on the ballot for direct vote.

Article 26 - <u>Law Enactment</u>

Bills passed by the Legislative Authority are subject to the veto of the President. In the case of a veto, the Legislative Authority may override the veto with two-thirds vote of the body.

CHAPTER IV - LEGISLATIVE AUTHORITY KULEANA

Article 27 - <u>Legislative Power</u>

1. The legislative power shall be vested in the Legislative Authority, which shall be unicameral and consist of Representatives.

2. Legislative Authority shall have the power to pass legislation with regard to any matter.

Article 28 - <u>Legislative Qualifications</u>

1. Any person who is a citizen and has reached the age of eighteen (18) may be elected.

2. Representatives shall be citizens, eighteen (18) years of age, and reside in the district at the time of election, and for the duration of their time in office.

Article 29 - Term of Office for Representatives

Representatives shall be elected for four years; no Representative shall serve more than a total of twelve (12) years.

Article 30 - <u>Legislative Elections</u>

Representatives shall be elected by voters who have established residency in the respective district.

Article 31 - <u>Representatives Count</u>

1. The initial Legislative Authority shall be comprised of forty-three (43) land-based and population-based Representatives to be elected at-large from the legislative districts.

2. Following the first election, the individual districts shall create sub-districts for their district seats and stagger the terms of office.

3. Reapportionment may be done through constitutional amendment or convention.

4. Each Legislative district shall have the following number of Representatives based on the population of each district:

    > Hawaiʻi - 2;
    > Maui - 1;
    > Molokai - 1;
    > Lānaʻi - 1;
    > Kahoʻolawe - 1;
    > Oʻahu - 6;
    > Kauaʻi 1;
    > Niʻihau - 1;
    > Kahiki - 8.

5. Each legislative district shall also have the following number of Representatives based on the land for each district:

    > Hawaiʻi - 4;
    > Maui - 4;
    > Molokai - 2;
    > Lānaʻi - 1;
    > Kahoʻolawe - 1;
    > Oʻahu - 4;
    > Kauaʻi - 4;
    > Niʻihau - 1;
    > Kahiki - 0.

Article 32 - Representative Privilege

Members of the Legislative Authority shall be privileged from suit for any speech or debate spoken during assembly or in execution of their duties.

Article 33 - Legislative Calendar

The Legislative Authority shall establish a calendar in coordination with cultural protocols, which shall convene on January 17 of each year.

CHAPTER V - EXECUTIVE AUTHORITY KULEANA

Article 34 - Executive Power

1. The executive power shall be vested in the President, who shall execute the laws of the Nation.

2. The President may: Issue executive orders; prepare the national budget; receive resources, assets, or gifts on behalf of the Nation; recommend legislation; grant reprieves and pardons, except in cases of impeachment; and contract to effectuate the law.

3. The President shall have the authority to appoint all executive officials of the Nation, except elected officials or as otherwise provided by law.

4. The President shall pursue the acquisition of lands for the Nation to meet the needs and aspirations of the citizenry.

5. The President may establish Executive Departments that meet the needs of the Nation, with the priority to deliver services addressing disparate needs in the community.

Article 35 - Executive Elections

The President and Vice-President shall be elected in an election.

Article 36 - Qualifications of Executives

No person shall be eligible to hold the office of the President and Vice-President unless they have attained the age of thirty (30) years and have resided in the Hawaiian Islands for not less than ten (10) years immediately preceding the election.

Article 37 - Responsibility of the Vice-President

There shall be a Vice-President to serve in the Executive Cabinet who shall have the kuleana for the unique needs of the Kahiki citizenry and other responsibilities as assigned by the President.

Article 38 - Term of Office for Executives

The President and Vice-President shall be elected for a term of four years.

Article 39 - Line of Succession

In the event of vacancy, impeachment, death, resignation, or the absence of the President from the Nation, the Vice President will assume office of the President followed by other officials as prescribed by law.

Article 40 - Continuity of Governance

The President will maintain the immediate past President as a counselor to ensure continuity of governance.

Article 41 - The Executive Cabinet

1. The President shall convene an Executive Cabinet comprised of the Vice-President, one (1) representative from the [Cultural, Spiritual Hui], one (1) representative from the [Hui of the Royal Organizations], one (1) representative from the Moku Council, and the Heads of Executive Departments.

2. Heads of Executive Departments shall be nominated by the President, then presented to the Legislative Authority for confirmation or rejection by a simple majority.

Article 42 - The [Cultural, Spiritual Hui]

There shall be a [Cultural, Spiritual Hui], which shall elect within ninety (90) days of the election of a new President, by its own internal processes, a representative to serve in the Executive Cabinet.

Article 43 - The [Hui of Royal Organizations]

There shall be a [Hui of the Royal Organizations], which shall elect within ninety (90) days of the election of a new President, by its own internal processes, a representative to serve in the Executive Cabinet.

CHAPTER VI - JUDICIAL AUTHORITY KULEANA

Article 44 - Judicial Power

The judicial power shall be vested in the Judicial Authority.

Article 45 - Judicial Authority Qualifications

The President shall establish qualifications with the consent of the Legislative Authority for Justices and Judges.

Article 46 - Judicial Authority Primary Focus

The primary focus of the Judicial Authority shall be restorative justice.

Article 47 - Judicial Authority Structure

1. The Chief Justice is the head of the Judicial Authority and presides over the courts. The Chief Justice may establish courts, tribunals, offices, and forums of general or exclusive jurisdiction as prescribed by law, and may account for customary practices of the Native Hawaiian people.

2. The scope of judicial power shall encompass all cases, in law and equity, arising under this Constitution, the laws of the Nation, treaties, compacts, and agreements made, or which shall be made, under the Nation's authority.

Article 48 - Term of Office for Justices and Judges

1. The Judicial Authority shall consist of:

    a. Not less than three (3) Justices with life-time appointments; and

    b. Judges serving a term of no less than ten (10) years.

2.   The Chief Justice is elected by an absolute majority of Justices.

CHAPTER VII - AMENDMENTS AND CONSTITUTIONAL CONVENTION

Article 49 - Amendments

1.   Proposed amendments to this Constitution may be initiated by any of the following methods:

    a. A resolution of the Legislative Authority adopted by two-thirds affirmative votes;

    b. A valid petition submitted to the Legislative Authority signed by not less than fifteen (15) percent of the registered voters of the Nation in the last executive election; or

    c. A constitutional convention.

2.   The Legislative Authority shall establish the format and rules for adopting amendments.

Article 50 - Constitutional Convention

1.   A Constitutional Convention shall be held within four (4) years of the establishment of the Moku Council and appear as a ballot question for citizenry at least every ten (10) years after the Government's formation. The citizenry may, through a constitutional initiative, call for such a convention earlier.

2.   The Legislative Authority shall establish the format and rules for convention participation with elected delegates from each legislative district.

CHAPTER VIII - RATIFICATION

Article 51 - Ratification

The present Constitution is subject to a ratification vote.

1.   A ratification election shall be held for the purpose of ratifying this Constitution.

2.   The Constitution shall become effective upon approval by a majority vote of individuals who are eligible to be citizens, have attained the age of eighteen (18), and cast a ballot in the ratification election.

ATTACHMENT 2

Declaration of the Sovereignty of the Native Hawaiian Nation
An Offering of the ʻAha

Proposed declaration, produced by the Naʻi Aupuni gathering, March 2016

Mai ka pō a ke ao (from the darkness to the dawn), the origin of all life, our ancestral lines emerged from this ʻāina. Our genealogical cosmology intertwined our very existence to the symbiotic kinship of our people and this ʻāina. The ancients rooted themselves here in comprehensive communal family systems inseparable from this ʻāina. The skillfully navigated migrations of subsequent ancestral lines brought forth the complex kapu system of divine aliʻi (lineal chiefs) to enforce the structure and kuleana (responsibility) of our population to cultivate and maintain the health and bounty of this ʻāina.

Our society evolved into three kuleana: nā aliʻi (chiefs) led and protected our lāhui (nation); nā makaʻāinana (common people) nurtured and fed our lāhui; and nā kaula and kāhuna (experts) maintained and perpetuated our ʻike (wisdom). While the traditional structure has shifted over time, these three essential kuleana continue to exist today.

As we find our way forward as a lāhui, we will forever aloha our aliʻi of old for their example and dedication to purpose and to our people. Their resilience and adaptability in a changing world enabled them to mālama (care for) their kuleana to protect our people's ability to mālama their kuleana to nurture, feed and perpetuate our ʻike in accordance with our traditions and our ʻāina.

In the spirit of pono and aloha, we the ʻAha gathered in February 2016, bring forward the following Historical Facts as some of the basis of the enduring Sovereignty of our nation, and our dedication to the present and future needs of our lāhui.

The arrival of the first Westerners brought the realities of a larger foreign world beyond to our shores. As King Kamehameha I unified the Hawaiian archipelago under one rule in the Kingdom of Hawaiʻi, the aliʻi became increasingly aware of a threat to our ʻāina, our lāhui, and way of life.

King Kamehameha III, Kauikeaouli, established the Kingdom of Hawaiʻi as a constitutional monarchy, as a strategy to protect our lāhui from efforts to colonize our beloved ʻāina under the disastrous policies of Imperialism and Manifest Destiny. Kamehameha III fulfilled his kuleana to the lāhui and secured recognition in the world of the Kingdom of Hawaiʻi, as an independent, legitimate and Sovereign State. The treaties of our Kingdom are a testament to how the world, including the United States, viewed us as an equal sovereign in the family of nation-states.

Under the leadership of King Kamehameha III, our people flourished in education and achieved an unparalleled literacy rate. Kamehameha IV, and his Queen Emma, dedicated themselves to advancing education and providing for the expanding health needs of the lāhui, as leprosy and other foreign diseases decimated our population. Kamehameha V began a revival of traditional practices, and repealed laws banning the kāhuna. During his reign, he facilitated the recognition and use of laʻau lapaʻau.

King Lunalilo led our lāhui to more democratic institutions, and was the first aliʻi to be elected King. King Kalākaua led us to further affirm our place in the world by joining the Universal Postal Union in 1885, and building our first royal palace. Our beloved Queen Liliʻuokalani will forever be revered for her personal sacrifice and dedication to protecting the rights of our lāhui.

In our efforts to move forward as one lāhui, and recognizing our long and glorious history in Hawaiʻi since time immemorial, our lāhui continues to struggle to reconcile our present from a past where our Kingdom of Hawaiʻi was illegally overthrown. We endeavor to share our true history so the world may know and come to understand our cause towards self-determination through self-governance.

As foreigners came to our shores, a group representing business interests came to be known as the Hawaiian League. They organized to gain control of our lands for commercial purposes, and sought annexation of our islands to the United States.

In 1887, members of the Hawaiian League, backed by the Honolulu Rifles forced King Kalākaua to sign a new constitution, known as The Bayonet Constitution, stripping executive authority and imposing property and income requirements that reduced the electoral power of the native population while extending suffrage to European and American foreigners.

In 1893, Queen Liliʻuokalani sought to restore what was lost to our lāhui through the promulgation of a new constitution. An agent of the United States conspired with local insurgents to the overthrow the lawful government of our Kingdom.

In 1893, the United States government played a fundamental role in our loss of control in our islands, when 162 troops from the U.S.S. Boston marched on ʻIolani Palace in support of the overthrow of the Hawaiian Kingdom government. It also subsequently recognized the dominion of the provisional government.

133

Upon investigation by his special commissioner, Senator James Blount, on December 18, 1893, U.S. President Grover Cleveland, condemned the overthrow of the Hawaiian Kingdom as "an Act of War" and recommended restoration of Queen Liliʻuokalani to the U.S. Congress.

On July 4, 1894, the Republic of Hawaiʻi was proclaimed, over the objections of Queen Liliʻuokalani and the Native Hawaiian people. Soon after, foreign powers that once recognized the Kingdom of Hawaiʻi, recognized the legitimacy of the Republic.

On June 16, 1897, with Secretary of State John Sherman, the Hawaiian Annexation Commissioners of the Republic of Hawaiʻi signed a Treaty for Annexation with the United States. Led by the Hui Aloha ʻĀina and Hui Kalaiʻāina, our people rallied against ratification of the Treaty and restoration of our Queen by signing the Kūʻe petitions. Because of that effort, the Treaty of Annexation failed to be ratified by the U.S. Senate.

In 1898, Hawaiʻi was unilaterally annexed to the United States without a Treaty, and against the expressed will of the Native Hawaiian people and others, through a Joint-Resolution. In 1900, the United States passed the Organic Act, creating the territorial government, and restoring to the lāhui the power to vote in the elections of local offices. Our lāhui was kanalua (of two minds) on whether to exercise that right to vote. True to our culture, we once again looked to our Queen Liliʻuokalani for guidance. On June 9, 1900, she said,

"Aloha to all of you: I did not think that you, the lāhui, were still remembering me, since ten years has passed since I became a Mother for you, the lāhui, and now the United States sits in power over me and over you, my dear nation. What has befallen you is very painful to me but it could not be prevented. My mind has been opened (hoʻohamama ia) because of what the United States has now given to the lāhui Hawaii.

Here is what I advise - that the people should look to the nation's leaders, Mr Kaulia and Mr Kalauokalani. A great responsibility has fallen upon them to look out for the welfare of the lāhui in accordance with the laws that the United States has handed down, to ensure that the people will receive rights and benefits for our and future generations, and I will also derive that one benefit (ie, the welfare of the people). We have no other direction left, except this unrestricted right (to vote), given by the United States to you the people.

Grasp it and hold on to it; it is up to you to make things right for all of us in the future." (as reported in the Ke Aloha ʻĀina newspaper, and translated and printed in the Oiwi Journal Vol. 2, page 127.)

Our lāhui followed our beloved Queen's words, and controlled territorial politics for the first 30 years. We elected Robert Wilcox and Prince Jonah Kūhio Kalanianaʻole to serve as our first and second elected delegates to represent Hawaii in the United States Congress. Prince Kūhio sponsored the first bill for statehood in the Congress in 1919.

Over time, the United States supported a mass in-migration of American settlers to our island home, primarily through the expansion of a military presence in Hawaii.

In 1946, Hawaiʻi was included on the UN's list of non-self-governing territories scheduled for decolonization. In 1959, Congress enacted the Hawaiʻi Admissions Act, and allowed all voters, including military personnel, to consider the question of statehood. The State of Hawaiʻi was ratified, and Hawaiʻi was removed from the UN list. The next year, the UN adopted the Declaration on Decolonization, requiring that full independence be an option for peoples to consider.

The United States military's actions have caused irreparable harms to our natural and social environment including: 49 years of bombing runs on our island of Kahoʻolawe; ongoing use of vast areas of our limited land for military purposes, including Mākua Valley and Pōhakuloa: ongoing devastation to our marine ecosystems from biennial RIMPAC exercises in our Hawaiian waters; and ongoing economic and social impacts of United States and government subsidized housing, for nearly 49,000 United States military personnel in Hawaiʻi.

On Nov. 3, 1993, the United States Congress officially apologized for its role in the overthrow of the Kingdom of Hawaiʻi, and committed to a process of reconciliation with the Native Hawaiian people. Public Law 103-150 was signed into law by President William Clinton.

We declare that these are but a few of the truths about the injustices our people and lands have endured, including the banning of our Native tongue, since foreigners came to our islands. Yet, in the triumph of our resilience, we have pressed for justice through more than a century of nonviolent resistance to oppression, guided by the example of our great Queen Liliʻuokalani who, faced with the overthrow of her government, chose the path of non-violence "to avoid bloodshed."

Today, we welcome the unfolding of time, the recovery of our language, and with it, the uncovering of our true history and cultural roots. We press forward to bring the ʻike of our ancestors to mālama ʻāina and mālama kuleana. We welcome our renewed commitment to one another, and to our national sovereignty as a capable nation pressing forward for social, cultural and economic independence and self-sufficiency in Hawaiʻi.

We recognize that under federal and international law, all indigenous peoples have the right to self-determination; and by virtue of that right, are free to determine our political status and pursue our economic, social and cultural development.

As the world moves toward justice, equality and self-determination for indigenous peoples, we acknowledge the unconquerable forces of pono and aloha, and stand for justice for ourselves as a collective, as a people, as a nation, as Hawai'i. We reaffirm our commitment and understanding that in order to form our government, all Kānaka Maoli (indigenous Native Hawaiians) are free to choose whether to exercise their right to vote in a future ratification and election.

We support the development and implementation of educational and outreach plan to support the lahui's ability to make an informed decision regarding any adopted documents, and the decisions we made together.

We mahalo our lāhui for allowing us to 'auamo kuleana to work together. In the immortal words of our great warrior King Kamehameha I, "Imua e nā poki'i a inu i ka wai 'awa'awa, 'a'ohe hope e ho'i mai ai." *[Translation: Forward my young brothers (and sisters) and drink of the bitter waters (of battle), there is no turning back (until victory is secured).]*

ATTACHMENT 3

Constitution of Hawai'i

Proposed constitution (updated), produced by the Native Hawaiian Convention, 2000

The following is the updated proposed constitution for independence from the Native Hawaiian Convention. It is the latest document from the convention and has not been formally ratified by the convention. The refusal of the State Legislature and the Office of Hawaiian Affairs to continue the funding of the convention to completion has prevented the further consideration by the convention. The underlined portions of this document, except for headings, are added materials which have been part of the process of the continued update and review of the document. The rest of the document had been approved by the convention for distribution and feedback from the Hawaiian population. Pōkā Laenui, Chairperson, Native Hawaiian Convention

Constitution of Hawai'i
(Independence)

Preamble

Hawai'i, bequeathed to us from the Source of all creation since time immemorial, nurtures our bodies, minds and spirits upon a foundation of Aloha.

We rise in a unified cry to our devotion for Hawaiian sovereignty. We proclaim our right to control our destiny, to nurture the integrity of our people and culture, and to preserve the quality of life that we desire.

We recognize that wisdom from the past forms the spring board into our future. Ua mau ke ea o ka 'āina i ka pono. Only in Pono are we able to build a society worthy of the dignity of our past and the hope for our future. Thus, Pono forms the guiding principle upon which Hawai'i today must stand. In Pono we have partnership, mutual respect and cooperation with all that abounds and surrounds us.

We build this government upon partnership, recognizing the integrity of the distinct host people and culture of this land and the special place to be established within the government for their protection and perpetuation. We recognize equally the human rights and fundamental freedoms to be accorded every person of Hawai'i and commit to the protection and perpetuation of such rights and freedoms within the governmental framework. All people are free and equal, and endowed with inalienable rights and the responsible vigil of freedom. He pono kēia.

We recognize all the Divine elements of Hawai'i – of life, of change, of fluidity, of stability, of humanity, and all of the nature elements which give physical representation to those elemental forces – the sun, the wind, the sky; the fresh water, the salt water, the land, including the mountains and the forests, and the people who populate Hawai'i. He pono kēia.

We reaffirm our belief in a government of the people and by the people; for the generations who were, are and is yet to come. We understand our relationship to the land, the kinship responsibility that unites us as a people with those around the globe. We recognize the harm caused by our past abrogation of this kinship responsibility and avow to vigilantly guard against such a wrong again. We acknowledge our commitment to each other and to the land; to our kūpuna and to our mo'opuna yet to come. He ali'i ka 'āina; he kaua ke kanaka.

E mau ke ea o ka 'āina i ka pono.

Article I, Name

Hawai'i.

Article II, Territory

The <u>national</u> territory consists of the Hawaiian archipelago, stretching from Kure Atoll in the North to Hawai'i in the South and all of those lands, atolls and other territories whose jurisdiction have been assumed by the United States of America previously claimed by Hawai'i prior to the US 1893 invasion. Those territories previously part of the constitutional Hawaiian monarchy but which have subsequently been declared the territory or possession of a state other than the United States of America may be included within the territorial jurisdiction of Hawai'i upon concluding negotiation with that claiming state and Hawai'i.

The territorial waters of Hawai'i shall include the waters twelve (12) miles from the shores of all lands of Hawai'i. The exclusive economic zone defined by the 1982 Convention on the Law of the Sea is adopted as applying to Hawai'i.

Article III, Supremacy

This Constitution shall be the supreme authority of the government of Hawai'i.

Article IV, Peoples Rights & Protections

<u>Principle I</u>
<u>All human beings are born free and equal in dignity and rights. They are endowed with reason and conscience and should act towards one another in a spirit of Aloha.</u>

<u>Principle 2</u>
<u>The fundamental rights and freedoms set forth to all citizens are to apply without distinction of any kind, such as race, color, sex, language, religion, political or other opinion, national or social origin, property, birth or other status.</u>

<u>Principle 3</u>
<u>Everyone has the right to life, liberty and security of person.</u>

Principle 4
No one shall be held in slavery or servitude.

Principle 5
No one shall be subjected to torture or to cruel, inhuman or degrading treatment or punishment.

Principle 6
Everyone has the right to recognition everywhere as a person before the law.

Principle 7
All are equal before the law and are entitled without any discrimination to equal protection of the law. All are entitled to equal protection against any prohibited discrimination and against any incitement to such discrimination.

Principle 8
Everyone has the right to an effective remedy by the competent national tribunals for acts violating the fundamental rights granted him by this constitution or by law.

Principle 9
No one shall be subjected to arbitrary arrest, detention or exile.

Principle 10
Everyone is entitled in full equality to a fair and public hearing by an independent and impartial tribunal, in the determination of his rights and obligations and of any criminal charge against him.

Principle 11
  1.Everyone charged with a penal offense has the right to be presumed innocent until proven guilty according to law in a public trial at which he has had all the guarantees necessary for his defense.
  2.No one shall be held guilty of any penal offense on account of any act or omission which did not constitute a penal offence, under national or international law, at the time when it was committed. Nor shall a heavier penalty be imposed than the one that was applicable at the time the penal offence was committed.

Principle 12
No one shall be subjected to arbitrary interference with his privacy, family, home or

correspondence, nor to attacks upon his honor and reputation. Everyone has the right to the protection of the law against such interference or attacks.

Principle 13
1.All citizens have the right to freedom of movement and residence within the borders of Hawai'i consistent with this constitution, and the laws established by the national congress.
2.All citizens have the right to leave the country, and to return to the country.

Principle 14
1.Everyone meeting the requirements of this constitution and of law has the right to a nationality.
2.No one shall be arbitrarily deprived of his nationality nor denied the right to change his nationality.

Principle 15
1.Men and women of full age, without any limitation due to race, nationality or religion, have the right to marry and to found a family. They are entitled to equal rights as to marriage, during marriage and at its dissolution.
2.Marriage shall be entered into only with the free and full consent of the intending spouses.
3.The family is the natural and fundamental group unit of society and is entitled to protection by society and subject to regulation by the State.

Principle 16
1.All citizens have the right to own property alone as well as in association with others. The State shall have the right to regulate and register ownership of all property.
2.No one shall be arbitrarily deprived of his property.

Principle 17
Everyone has the right to freedom of thought, conscience and religion; this right includes freedom to change his religion or belief, and freedom, either alone or in community with others and in public or private, to manifest his religion or belief in teaching, practice, worship and observance. The government shall make no law establishing a religion or religious practice.

Principle 18
Everyone has the right to freedom of opinion and expression; this right includes freedom to hold opinions without interference and to seek, receive and impart information and ideas through any media and regardless of frontiers.

Principle 19

 1.Everyone has the right to freedom of peaceful assembly and association.
 2.No one may be compelled to belong to an association.

Principle 20

The people shall have the right to privacy and to be secure in their persons, houses, papers, conversations, ideas and effects. This right shall not be infringed upon through unreasonable searches and seizures. No Warrants shall issue, but upon probable cause, supported by oath or affirmation particularly describing the place to be searched, and the persons or things to be seized.

Principle 21

No person shall be held for a felony unless on a presentment or indictment of a grand jury, unless in the military service of the government in time of war or public danger. No person shall be subject for the same offense to be twice put in jeopardy, to be compelled in any criminal proceeding to be a witness against himself, nor be deprived of liberty or property without due process of law. In all criminal prosecutions, the accused shall enjoy the right to a speedy and public trial by an impartial jury of his peers within the district wherein the crime shall have been committed, to be informed of the accusation, to be confronted with the witnesses against him, to have compulsory process for obtaining witnesses in his favor, and to have the assistance of counsel.

Principle 22

 1.Every citizen has the right to take part in the government, directly or through freely chosen representatives.
 2.Every citizen has the right to equal access to public service.
 3.The will of the citizens shall be the basis of the authority of government; this will shall be expressed in periodic and genuine elections which shall be by universal and equal suffrage and shall be held by secret vote or by equivalent free voting procedures. Every elector shall be free from arrest on election days, during his attendance at election and in going to and returning therefrom, except in cases of treason, felony, or breach of the peace. No elector shall be obliged to perform military duty on the day of election as to prevent his voting, except in time of war or public danger.

Principle 23

All citizens have the right to social security and is entitled to realization of the economic, social and cultural rights indispensable for his dignity and the free development of his personality. All citizens have the responsibility for the contributions to society necessary to effectuate the social security and economic, social and cultural rights accorded to its citizens.

Principle 24

  1.All citizens have the right to work, to free choice of employment, to just and favorable conditions of work and to protection against unemployment.

  2.Everyone, without any discrimination, has the right to equal pay for equal work.

  3.Everyone who works has the right to just and favorable remuneration ensuring for himself and his family an existence worthy of human dignity, and supplemented, if necessary, by other means of social protection.

  4.Everyone has the right to form and to join trade unions for the protection of his interests.

Principle 25

  1.Everyone has the right to a standard of living adequate for the health and well-being of himself and of his family, including food, clothing, housing and medical care and necessary social services, and the right to security in the event of unemployment, sickness, disability, widowhood, old age or other lack of livelihood in circumstances beyond his control. 2.Motherhood and childhood are entitled to special care and assistance. All children, whether born in or out of wedlock, shall enjoy the same social protection.

Principle 26

  1.Everyone has the right to education. Education shall be free, at least in the elementary and fundamental stages. Elementary education shall be compulsory. Technical and professional education shall be made generally available and higher education shall be equally accessible to all on the basis of merit.

  2.Education shall be directed to the full development of the human personality and to the strengthening of respect for human rights and fundamental freedoms. It shall promote understanding, tolerance and friendship among all nations, racial or religious groups, and shall further the activities for peace in the world.

  3.Parents have a prior right to choose the kind of education that shall be given to their children.

Principle 27

  1.Everyone has the right freely to participate in the cultural life of the community, to enjoy the arts and to share in scientific advancement and its benefits.

  2.Everyone has the right to the protection of the moral and material interests resulting from any scientific, literary or artistic production of which he is the author.

Principle 28

  1.Everyone has duties to the community.

  2.In the exercise of his rights and freedoms, everyone shall be subject only to such limitations as are determined by law solely for the purpose of securing due recognition and respect for the rights and freedoms of others and of meeting the just requirements of morality, public, peace, safety, and the general welfare in a democratic society.

3.These rights and freedoms may in no case be exercised contrary to the purposes and principles of this constitution and of pono.

Principle 29

Nothing in this Bill of Rights may be interpreted as implying for the government, any group or person any right to engage in any activity or to perform any act aimed at the destruction of any of the rights and freedoms set forth herein.

The rights of the people established by this constitution shall not be abridged unless as set forth in this constitution or by the process established herein and in no other manner.

Article V, Aboriginal/Hawaiian Fundamental Rights

Right of Self-Definition: The Kanaka Hawaiʻi Maoli are the aboriginal people of the islands of the Hawaiian archipelago and those people whom they shall define within their system of self-governance. Individuals so defined as Kanaka Hawaiʻi Maoli shall have the opportunity to decline such attribution to themselves individually.

Right of Self-Governance: The Kanaka Hawaiʻi Maoli shall have the right to decide their own priorities in the process of development, as it affects their lives, beliefs, institutions and spiritual well-being and the territories (including land and sea) under their jurisdiction, as further defined by this constitution. They shall also have control over their own economic, social and cultural development, including management and policy control over vocational training, health services, and education. The administration of justice and the power to retain or create social institutions to address the needs of the Kanaka Hawaiʻi Maoli are also reserved to them.

Territorial Rights: There shall be set aside lands, waters, and other natural resources for the exclusive control of the Kumu Hawaiʻi established in this constitution at Article VII. Such areas shall be limited to undeveloped or minimally developed lands which were previously in the inventory of the Crown and Government lands of Hawaiʻi prior to July 4, 1894. Such resources shall be sufficient for the maintenance of the Kanaka Hawaiʻi Maoli in their traditional system of living. These include the rights to hunt, fish, trap and gather, and to control mineral and sub-surface resources for the purpose of religious, cultural, and subsistence purposes.

143

Cultural Rights: The right to maintain the cultural traditions of the Kanaka Hawai'i Maoli shall not be impaired. Included in this right shall be the right to maintain contact with other indigenous and tribal peoples across oceans to pursue shared economic, social, cultural, spiritual and environmental development, the right to educate their children in their own native language, the right to practice their own traditional health and healing practices, and the right to express their own sense of spirituality in their own form. All of these rights shall remain subject to the limitations that they are not to be destructive to the protected rights of all other individuals in the society.

Custom and Protocol: Reserved to the Kanaka Hawai'i Maoli, as expressed through the Kumu Hawai'i, shall be all of the official state customs and protocols, including ceremonies of international import with other states.

Immigration & Population: The Kumu Hawai'i shall have the control over immigration, determining the criteria for further transfer of population into Hawai'i, the conditions of visa awards, and treaties and executive agreements touching on the temporary and permanent residents of non-Hawaiian citizens.

Crown and Government Lands and Natural Resources: The Kumu Hawai'i shall have the exclusive right of management over the lands and natural resources whose titles were previously part of the inventory of the Crown and Government lands of the Hawaiian nation prior to July 4, 1894 or lands which have subsequently been exchanged for such lands. With the exception for the lands set aside under territorial rights described above, all net proceeds from the management of the former Crown and Government lands and natural resources under this provision shall be allocated 20% to the Kumu Hawai'i and 80% to the general Hawai'i public.

Participation in the Kumu Hawai`i: Initially, any Kanaka Hawai'i Maoli, 16 years and older, shall be permitted the privilege of participating, including voting, in all activities of the Kumu Hawai'i.

Limitations of Rights: All of the kuleana set aside for the Kumu Hawai'i and the Kanaka Hawai'i Maoli shall be limited by the constitutional guarantees of human rights as well as other constitutional limitations or powers specifically set forth therein.

Article VI, Citizenship

Citizenship shall consist of three general classes:

-all Kanaka Maoli throughout the world <u>who elect to be citizens</u>;
-descendants of subjects of the Hawaiian Kingdom prior to July 4, 1894 <u>who elect to be citizens</u>; and
-<u>all persons born in Hawai'i, and </u>other individuals who <u>have been a resident
of Hawai'i for a continuous period of five years prior to this constitution coming into force and
effect, and who</u> choose willfully to pledge their allegiance to Hawai'i.

Article VII, Government Structure

The nation shall have two primary governing bodies operating in partnership for the Kanaka Hawai'i Maoli public and the general Hawai'i public.

1) The Kumu Hawai'i, comprised of Kanaka <u>Hawai'i</u> Maoli, <u>whether citizen or not,</u> shall have exclusive management rights over crown and government lands and natural resources; the right to self-definition; the right to self-governance; control over immigration and population <u>transfer</u>; indigenous education and health care; and international protocol<u> all as set forth above in Article V</u>. All other powers not specifically reserved to the Kumu Hawai'i shall accrue to the General Government.

2) The General Government, comprised of all citizens, shall have all powers not reserved to <u>the</u> Kumu Hawai'i.

Either or both of these bodies<u>, the Kumu Hawai'i or the General Government,</u> may permit appropriate political subdivisions within their realm of responsibilities, such as counties, ahupua'a, townships, etc. <u>These bodies may also create other branches of government, including an executive and judicial branch, for the nation.</u>

An advisory conflict resolution office shall be established to which disputes not readily resolvable between the two bodies shall be submitted. This office shall consist of five members, two of whom shall be appointed by each <u>government</u> partner and the fifth appointed by the members appointed by the partners. Should it not be able to resolve any dispute of a non-constitutional nature, this office shall be empowered to put the question of controversy before all the citizens of Hawai'i for a vote <u>and require a mere majority of the votes cast to decide the matter</u>. If a dispute of a constitutional nature should arise calling for an amendment to this constitution <u>resulting in</u>

a detraction of the rights and powers of the Kumu Hawai'i or of the Kanaka Hawai'i Maoli citizen, both government partners would have to ratify said amendment. Otherwise, only a majority of the votes cast would be required to amend the constitution. The advisory conflict resolution office shall be empowered to determine the definition of any controversy, whether constituting a dispute of a non-constitutional nature, or a constitutional nature detracting from the rights and powers of the Kumu Hawai'i or of the kanaka Hawai'i Maoli citizen.

Article VIII, General Provisions

Private Real Property Ownership

I. Assurances to Private Ownership:

Hawaiian citizens and non-citizen residents may own their residence in their own name.

II. Forfeiture for Non-residents

Non-citizen, non-residents: Non-citizen non-resident ownership of land may be subject to termination within ten (10) years following their continuous non-residence of Hawai'i. If terminated, said land ownership will be included in the inventory of the general government.

Citizen, non-resident: Citizen, non-resident ownership of land may be subject to termination within twenty (20) years following their continuous non-residence of Hawai'i. If terminated, said land ownership will be included in the inventory of the general government.

III. Prohibition of Sale of Real Property to Non-residents
Transfer of real property title to non-resident, non-citizens shall be prohibited.

There shall be no transfer of real property to non-residents with the exception of citizens who establish residence in Hawai'i within five years from date of transfer.

Official Languages

'Ōlelo Hawai'i and English shall be the official languages of Hawai'i in which any and all official proceedings and legal transactions may be conducted.

The Education Department of the General government shall be required to incorporate the teaching of 'Ōlelo Hawai'i co-extensive with the teaching of English.

Within ten years after the formation of the general government, all public employees shall be proficient in both languages as working languages.

Flag

A national flag design shall be chosen by agreement of the two governing partners.

Motto

A national motto shall be chosen by agreement of the two governing partners.

Anthem

A national anthem shall be chosen by agreement of the two governing partners.

National Security Board
A National Security Board shall be established to advise on the nation's security from domestic or external influences. This board shall consist of 15 members from among whom shall be individuals with education, training and experience in the fields of economics, agriculture, international affairs, public health, military defense, and local cultures. Members of the board shall be appointed, 8 by the general governing body and 7 by the Kumu Hawai'i. The members shall appoint their leadership from among themselves and may otherwise organize their work as they deem appropriate. None of these members may hold any elective office nor any rank within any military force, and shall resign from office and remain out of office for a period of two years prior to undertaking any public office or military post.

Taxation

The government shall have the power to impose taxes.

Article IX, Amendments

Any amendment to this Constitution must be approved by a majority of the citizens of Hawai'i.

However, any amendment to this constitution which would alter the defined rights of the Kumu Hawai'i or of the Kanaka Hawai'i Maoli would require the approval of the Kumu Hawai'i.

147

Article X, Ratification & Transition Process

Upon approval of this constitution by the Aha Hawai'i 'Ōiwi, it shall be presented to the Kanaka Hawai'i Maoli population throughout the world for ratification. If ratified by a majority of the votes cast, an election for 51 members of the Kumu Hawai'i shall be held.

Upon election of said members of the Kumu Hawai'i, this constitution shall be presented to the eligible citizens of Hawai'i for ratification. If ratified by a majority of the votes cast, an election of 51 delegates constituting the general governing body shall be held.

Upon election of said members of the general governing body, the Kumu Hawai'i and the general governing body shall collaborate in the review of this constitution, determine their on-going structure of governance, and establish the mechanism for the safe and smooth transition of authority in Hawai'i from the United States of America.

REFERENCES

Act to amend the Alaska Native Claims Settlement Act, and for other purposes, Pub. L. 104-42, 48 U.S.C. 109 Stat. 357, 360 (1995).

Akina v. State of Hawaiʻi. US Dist. HI, Aug. 13, 2015.

Apo, P. (2015). Minutes from Asset and Resource Management meeting, Office of Hawaiian Affairs. Retrieved from http://190f32x2yl33s804xzaogfi4.wpengine.netdna-cdn.com/wp-content/uploads/ARMminJan_27_2015.pdf

Elbert, S. H., & Mahoe, N. K. (1975). *Nā mele o Hawaiʻi nei: 101 Hawaiian songs.* Honolulu, HI: University of Hawaiʻi Press.

Judicial Watch, Inc. v. Namuʻo et al. Case No: 1SP151000059, Hawaiʻi 1st Circuit Court, 2015.

International Labour Organization. (1989). Indigenous and tribal peoples convention, C169. Retrieved from www.refworld.org/docid/3ddb6d514.html

Naʻi Aupuni. (2015a). Retrieved from www.naiaupuni.org/about.html

Naʻi Aupuni. (2015b). Grant Agreement between the Akamai Foundation and the Office of Hawaiian Affairs. Retrieved from http://www.naiaupuni.org/docs/FundingAgreementFINAL.pdf

Native Hawaiian Roll Commission. (May 9, 2014). Kanaʻiolowalu, Frequently Asked Questions. Retrieved from http://kokua.kanaiolowalu.org/support/solutions/45716

Office of the Secretary, Department of the Interior. (2015). Procedures for reestablishing a formal government-to-government relationship with the Native Hawaiian community, 80 Fed. Reg. 59113 (proposed Oct. 1, 2015), 43 C.F.R. 50, 59113–59132. Retrieved from www.federalregister.gov/documents/2015/10/01/2015-24712/procedures-for-reestablishing-a-formal-government-to-government-relationship-with-the-native

Pukui, M. K. (1983). *ʻŌlelo noʻeau: Hawaiian proverbs and poetical sayings.* Honolulu, HI: Bishop Museum Press.

S. J. Res. 19, 103rd Cong. (1993). A joint resolution to acknowledge the 100th anniversary of the January 17, 1893 overthrow of the Kingdom of Hawaiʻi, and to offer an apology to Native Hawaiians on behalf of the United States for the overthrow of the Kingdom of Hawaiʻi. Retrieved from www.congress.gov/bill/103rd-congress/senate-joint-resolution/19/text

State of Hawai'i v. Nae'ole, Pihana, Alana et al. Wai'anae District Court of the 1st Circuit, 1982; full citation currently unavailable due to age and location of files.

State of Hawai'i v. Walter Paulo et al. 1PC000053875, 1st Circuit Court, 1980.

State of Hawai'i v. Wilford Pulawa, CR 46476, 1st Circuit Court, 1974.

UN General Assembly. (1946). Information from non-self-governing territories transmitted under Article 73e of the charter, A/RES/218. Retrieved from www.refworld.org/docid/3b-00f1ea34.html

UN General Assembly. (1960). Declaration on the granting of independence to colonial countries and peoples, A/RES/1514(XV). Retrieved from www.refworld.org/docid/3b00f06e2f.html

UN General Assembly. (1998). Rome statute of the International Criminal Court (last amended 2010). Retrieved from http://www.refworld.org/docid/3ae6b3a84.html

UN General Assembly. (2007). United Nations declaration on the rights of indigenous peoples, A/RES/61/295. Retrieved from www.refworld.org/docid/471355a82.html

United States. (1894). Hawaiian Islands: Report of the committee on foreign relations, United States Senate, with accompanying testimony and executive documents transmitted to Congress from January 1, 1893, to March 10, 1894. S. Rep. 227. Washington, DC: Government Printing Office. Retrieved from https://catalog.hathitrust.org/Record/001261378

ABOUT THE AUTHOR

Pōkā Laenui (a.k.a. Hayden Burgess) graduated from the University of Hawaiʻi William S. Richardson School of Law and has been an advocate for Hawaiʻi's self-determination since 1971. He served as trustee of the Office of Hawaiian Affairs (1982–86), vice president and international spokesperson for the World Council of Indigenous Peoples (1983–90), indigenous expert for the International Labour Organization (1989), and speaker at the UN General Assembly (1991), where he was named one of five pioneers of indigenous rights. He also served as chairperson of the Native Hawaiian Convention, convenor of the Hawaiʻi National Transitional Authority, and director of the Hawaiian National Broadcast Corporation. He is a primary contributor to the website www.hawaiianperspectives.org, which contains many of his writings, radio programs, lectures, and videos. His wife is Puanani Burgess, his children are PuaʻEna, Pohaokalani, and Laʻameaomaunaʻala, with daughter-in-law Christianna and moʻopuna Layla Ahonuialanakila.

NOTES

1. Personal interview in May 2018 with Coline Aiu, kumu hula and daughter of Margaret Aiu and heir to her hālau.

2. Story related to author from unnamed confidential informants in preparation for a 1978 double murder/kidnap trial in Hawaiʻi.

3. President Cleveland's joint message to Congress, December 1893.

4. *Territory of Hawaiʻi v. Grace Fortescue et al.*, 1931.

5. The purpose statement of Hui Naʻauao includes the following, taken from its original By Laws:

   a. To promote an awareness and understanding of Hawaiian sovereignty and self-determination;

   b. To promote and increase an awareness of Hawaiian cultural values, heritage, history and current events;

   c. To enable Native Hawaiian descendants to understand and exercise their explicit and implicit rights;

d. To develop expertise and leadership skills amongst Hawaiian people;

e. To provide training and technical assistance to Hawaiians in areas of concern to the Hawaiian community;

f. To gather historic and current information regarding Hawaiian concerns for public dissemination;

g. To promote continuity of consciousness of the people of Hawai'i in all of its many aspects.

6. Names for such a list were obtained through a number of sources, including the OHA election list and the Kamehameha Schools list, as well as names obtained by registration using forms circulated by telephone books. Registrants were required to certify their qualification to vote. Upon returning the mail, in ballots, materials were checked to see if the accompanying certification was completed before the ballots were counted.

7. Section 2, Act 195, Hawai'i Legislative Session 2011.

8. Section 2, Act 195, Hawai'i Legislative Session 2011 at §-5, "Native Hawaiian convention." *Honolulu Star-Advertiser*, December 15, 2015.

9. Rather than using the term *convention*, I have chosen the term congregation to denote a more generic gathering without necessarily any official authority, as this gathering seemed to be. A convention would suggest that members were elected as delegates to this gathering.

10. This was formalized by Senate Joint Resolution 19, 103rd Congress (1993).

11. N. Ota, records specialist, OHA, email communication to author, August 24, 2017.

12. Traditional recitation of Kamehameha I's last words spoken on his deathbed in Kailua, Kona. Reported in Pukui's *ʻŌlelo Noʻeau* (1983).

13. Preamble to the Constitution of the State of Hawai'i (1978). The words are from the acceptance speech of King Kamehameha III on July 31, 1843, on the occasion of the restoration of the Hawaiian Kingdom, as recorded in the song and notes to "Nā Aliʻi," in *Nā Mele o Hawaiʻi Nei*, by Elbert and Mahoe (1975).

14. *Honolulu Star-Advertiser*, July 15, 2015.

15. Press release by Na'i Aupuni, March 16, 2016.

16. UN Declaration of Rights of Indigenous Peoples at Article 33 and the International Labour Organization's Indigenous and Tribal Peoples Convention (ILO 169) (1989) at Article 1, Section 2. "Self-identification as indigenous or tribal shall be regarded as a fundamental criterion for determining the groups to which the provisions of this Convention apply."

17. The NHC independence document has not been finalized. The latest draft is used for comparison in this paper. The underlines and brackets from that document reflect the latest editing updates for the document.

18. Annex to G.A. Res. 2200 (XXI) of 16 December 1966.

19. Annex to G.A. Res. 2200 (XXI) of 16 December 1966.

20. See Articles 2 and 3 of the UN Declaration on the Rights of Indigenous Peoples (UN General Assembly, 2007); see also Article 1, Section 2 of the ILO Convention 169.

21. A possible inclusive statement might be, "Hawaiʻi shall be free from all atomic, biological and chemical weapons and weapons residue, from nuclear power plants, from waste materials used as weapons such as depleted uranium, from weaponized drone planes, and from any weapon, whether considered offensive or defensive, with capability of reaching beyond 200 miles off the archipelagic line of the Hawaiian Islands."

22. 43 C.F.R. Part 50, at 50.42 (e)(2), at 171. The Act (Act to amend the Alaska Native Claims Settlement Act, and for other purposes, 1995) can be found at Public Law 104-42, 48 U.S.C. Note Prec. 491, 109 Stat. 357, 360.

23. Article 27 of the Rome Statute (UN General Assembly, 1998), establishing the International Criminal Court, states:

Irrelevance of official capacity

1. This Statute shall apply equally to all persons without any distinction based on official capacity. In particular, official capacity as a Head of State or Government, a member of a Government or parliament, an elected representative or a government official shall in no case exempt a person from criminal responsibility under this Statute, nor shall it, in and of itself, constitute a ground for reduction of sentence.

2. Immunities or special procedural rules which may attach to the official capacity of a person, whether under national or international law, shall not bar the Court from exercising its jurisdiction over such a person.

The absolute immunity for heads of state in customary international law is now in flux as we consider relevant UN Security Resolutions (see Security Council Resolution 1593), in combination with the Rome Statute, and/or the Genocide Convention that had removed the immunity of heads of state.

24. Article 5 of the Rome Statute defines Crimes within the jurisdiction of the court:

1. The jurisdiction of the Court shall be limited to the most serious crimes of concern to the international community as a whole. The Court has jurisdiction in accordance with this Statute with respect to the following crimes:

(a) The crime of genocide;

(b) Crimes against humanity;

(c) War crimes;

(d) The crime of aggression.

25. Hawai'i was placed on the list of non-self-governing territories via UNGA Resolution 66, by the United States.

26. A record of President Cleveland's address (United States, 1894) is available at https://catalog.hathitrust.org/Record/001261378

27. These criteria are found at www.federalregister.gov/documents/2015/10/01/2015-24712/procedures-for-reestablishing-a-formal-government-to-government-relationship-with-the-native

28. Press release, US Department of the Interior, September 23, 2016. Available at www.doi.gov/hawaiian, 43 C.F.R. Part 50.

29. Federal Register/Vol. 80, No. 190/Thursday, October 1, 2015, Proposed Rules, p. 59129 at §50.4.

30. P. 157, 43 C.F.R. Part 50, [Docket No. DOI–2015-005]; Final Rule.

31. Federal Register/Vol. 80, No. 190/Thursday, October 1, 2015, Proposed Rules, p. 59129 at §50.4. "*Native Hawaiian* means any individual who is a: (1) Citizen of the United States.

32. See page 49 (B) Major Changes, citing the elimination of US citizenship requirement (50.4; 50.12), Final Rules, 43 C.F.R. Part 50.

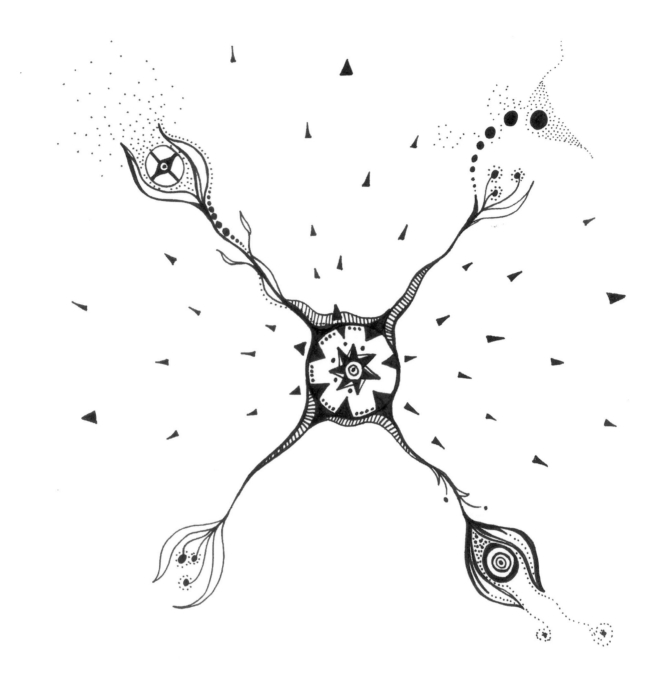

Losing Our Heads

GREGORY PŌMAIKA'I GUSHIKEN

This piece is a critical reflection that discusses the ways my Kanaka Maoli grandfather passed in a car accident in the 1980s. I rewrite the autopsy that reported his cause of death, showing that it was more than just a single, tragic moment. By reflecting on his death, I attempt to construct an understanding of the ways in which colonialism interpellates Hawaiians into the role of the "bad" Hawaiian and how we enact these interpellations—not because we choose to, but because we are forced.

Date & Time: Monday, April 14th, 1980 at approximately 8:33 PM

Location: Nānākuli, Oʻahu approximately 1500 feet past the Kahe Power Plant, immediately before Nānākuli Town.

Description: Driving Westbound on Farrington Highway, the victim, due to intoxication as indicated by posthumous assessment, lost consciousness while operating the vehicle causing it to break through the guardrail and collide with the adjacent rock wall. The speed at which the vehicle struck the wall, in addition to the angle at which it struck, caused the victim to be thrown out of the vehicle through the driver-side window. Autopsy has determined that the ultimate cause of death was internal decapitation. The victim was not wearing a seatbelt.

CORRESPONDENCE MAY BE SENT TO:
Gregory Pōmaika'i Gushiken
1 Miramar Street #929321, La Jolla, California, 92092
Email: ggushike@ucsd.edu

Hūlili: Multidisciplinary Research on Hawaiian Well-Being, Vol. 11, No. 1
Copyright © 2019 by Kamehameha Schools

I used to think about it, the idea of decapitation, a lot. At the time I didn't know why, but when my grandmother would scold me about wearing my seat belt, the topic would always come up. "Eh, Pōmaikaʻi, you goin lose your head!" she would scold in her deep pidgin, from the driver's seat of her Ford Bronco, as I spiritedly squirmed out of the snug embrace of my seat belt. I always thought that the malihi ghosts of the polyester safety belt, which had this rigid way of locking itself in place if you pulled too hard, would strangle me, but my grandmother, like all Hawaiʻi mothers, was staunch in her instruction, so I obediently buckled the strap firmly across my chest, securing myself in the embrace of the rattling iron carriage, knowing that my fear of strangulation would be better than the loss of my body.

I understood the consequences of car safety well because of these scoldings, especially the importance of a poʻo, but it wasn't until much later that I understood the idea of *"internal decapitation"*—that there didn't need to be a guillotine and executioner for someone to lose their head, that familiar feeling of self and life and all that comes from it—and why it was such a concern to my grandma. Likewise, the strangling feeling I often feared in the back seat of my grandma's clanking wheels haunted my head with questions as the space between my chest and my eyes grew larger. After all, strangulation is just the deprivation of air to the body, which, like decapitation, can sever the ties between our heads ripe with resurgent conviction, hearts full with aspirations, and the histories buried between them that make us whole. For one reason or another, the idea fascinated me. When you gaze upon the body of someone who has died due to internal decapitation or strangulation, you don't see sutures or cloth or surgical tape; you see the solemn face of death itself, beautiful in the most frustrating of ways, or at least that's how my mother would

have seen it at her father's funeral. You would have no idea that this person's death certificate reads, "cause of death was internal decapitation," or "cause of death was strangulation."

Internal decapitation is known as "atlanto-occipital dislocation" in the discourses of doctors whose skin does not strike contrast against the maddening whiteness of their coats. Their reports detail the microbiology of loss and the anthropology of accidents with such detail that words become just significations of forgotten paths to breathe. They told my grandma that her husband died that evening because the oxygen that passed between his palms and to his dark-brown corneas had ceased to do so, and that his head had ceased to be a part of his body. But between the tears, a lāhui knows that the internal decapitation of my grandfather occurred long before that chilled April night. And the more I read and reread his death certificate, the less this government-certified document makes sense. Again and again, I am torn back to the final scene of the crash as the Waiʻanae mountains stared down in resignation at the lifeless body of yet another Kanaka cut off from its nurturing embrace, another Kanaka destroyed by the vicious cycle of colonial capital and capitalist colonialism. They said that he died that night because his head was removed from his body, but none of the coroners who examined him could have even known that there are those whose heads are taken from their unsuspecting bodies long before they lie lifeless on an iron table under synthetic lights. We call ourselves Kānaka Maoli.

James MacShane Hanakahi, Jr. was my grandfather, and he could have been described as any or all the following: one of "da boys," a hard worker, an alcoholic, a workaholic, a father, a Christian, an abuser, an athlete, a victim, a homeowner, a welfare recipient, a Hawaiian. Spending his childhood torn from one place to the next, from the now-demolished Damon Tract to Waiʻanae to Waipahu, his life as a Kanaka in an island paradise, betrayed by the world he grew up in, was wrought with incensing images of lazy, perverted, savage Hawaiians.

He could not escape this image, even in the grand hall of mirrors ride at the 50th State Fair. His family could not afford the fair. I'm not saying that they couldn't afford the greasy, smoldering hot dogs and the sugar-laden, deep-fried distractions. I'm saying that the price of humanity, the price of being present, the price of being able to embrace the true meaning of aloha, was too high a price. By aloha, I don't mean the touristy gimmicks that I'm forced to regurgitate at part-time jobs to survive in a system that doesn't even understand what "aloha" means. What I'm saying is, the price of looking into the eyes of our kūpuna and finding something—anything, really—to hint at our legitimacy, our history, our validity, was just too damn high for Kānaka like my grandfather to even dream of.

But this story isn't about him. It isn't about me, either. This is about how the system cuts off our heads before we can even become another tragedy for KHON to report on the nine o'clock news, just so the media can talk more about the "war on drugs," which is really a war on Hawaiians.

Date & Time: Monday, April 14th, 1980 at approximately 8:33 PM

Location: Nānākuli, Oʻahu ~~approximately 1500 feet past the Kahe Power Plant, immediately before Nānākuli Town~~ *at the intersection of pulsating blue badges, silent scarlet sirens, and the scent of snow-white dread, approximately 1,500 feet past the black smoke of Kahe Power Plant that softly strangles the surrounding ocean.*

Description: Driving Westbound on Farrington Highway, the victim, due to ~~to intoxication~~ *colonization* as indicated by posthumous assessment, lost consciousness while operating the vehicle causing it to break through the guardrail and collide with the adjacent rock wall. The speed at which the vehicle struck the wall, in addition to the angle at which it struck, caused the victim to be thrown out of the vehicle through the driver-side window. Autopsy has determined that the ultimate cause of death was ~~internal decapitation~~. *a burning need in the back of the victim's palms to be validated and affirmed by a system that would do neither.* The victim was not wearing a seatbelt.

With unbearable pressure from his haole bosses, along with the unending pile of bills on the linoleum kitchen counter, it seemed that anything could put my grandfather over the edge. With threats of being fired and criticism of him by his father, every entrance to James's home was adorned with cracks to the head and, if it was a particularly bad day, threats with a gun.

However, this was nothing compared to his sister's reality. Their father had raped James's sister just days after my great-grandmother had left. I often assume, when trying to make sense of the very same beatings my grandfather delivered to my mother and grandmother, that James was haunted by his early memories of abuse and betrayal at home. But I digress. Making sense out of madness never seems to work, and there's no way to really know what my papa James had experienced.

In any case, on April 13, 1980, the day before his last, my grandfather received and then delivered his obligatory beatings like on any other day—first, from his haole bosses; second, to his wife and daughters. With pressure from the US military, the construction company

159

demanded longer hours, harder work and, sometimes, less pay. It seems evident that when the US military is involved, the reasonable becomes the impossible, and I guess the same happens in the domestic sphere of those workers whose lives are lived through time cards and paychecks.

For my grandfather, even the smallest speck of the previous night's rice stuck on his fork at breakfast would prompt a violent beating of anything that could be beaten. That day was one of those times. He raised his fists again and again, maddeningly increasing the pressure at which he struck. My mother curled into a ball on ground that was almost as cold and hard as the hole in her father's heart. The cold pierced through generations, into mine. Transitioning from blows by fists to the bluntness of a frying pan, he swung and swung until crimson red waterfalls came gushing out of my mother's nose and mouth, rivers that would flow through my wounds years later. When he stormed out of the house, it was as though a hurricane had come and passed. For now, the family was safe, and that was all that mattered.

THE THING ABOUT THESE CYCLES OF VIOLENCE IS THAT THEY DON'T STOP.

Most of what happened to my grandfather between this point and the moment of his death is unknown to me, but I would learn years later from my mother—as she lay broken on the kitchen floor after being beaten by her second husband—that the last thing she thought of her father before his death was, "I hope he dies. I hope he just leaves. I hope this just stops."

The thing about these cycles of violence is that they don't stop. They just keep spinning around and around until somebody breaks into a million little pieces. They say that daughters seek out lovers who are like their fathers, and I guess that explains everything that needs to be said about me, my mother, and him—James MacShane Hanakahi, Jr.

As I scan the death certificate over and over, jet black text becomes incomprehensible markings on blank space. In the back of my mind, I reimagine the moments leading up to the accident. Covered in that film of sweat that accumulates after laboring relentlessly for hours in the piercing hot sun, James paces the outskirts of the construction site, awaiting the signal from his haole supervisor to finally leave. He was supposed to be done several hours ago.

His contracts to build housing on US military bases that strike the ʻāina of his ancestors burn. Frustrated, but too fearful and too weary to protest, he stares into the gold-orange glow of the setting sun, imagining the fantastic sight of a green flash, much different from the green flashes of cash that would appear in his checking account. The boss okays him to leave the already pitch-black construction site. He gets into his truck. Not knowing it's his last, he gulps down one of the beers from the six-pack he just bought at 7-11.

Buzzed but not drunk, tired but not dead, grandfather makes a trek that would be his last. Speeding past the bleak emptiness of what would later become Kapolei town, and scraping past the turn that would someday become Koʻolina, he accelerates past Kahe Power Plant in an effort to get home just a little faster so he can get just a bit more sleep, before he loses just a little more of his dignity when he goes back to work the next morning. Then it hits him. No, it's not an epiphany, because epiphanies are only for men of a certain variety: White, wealthy, and educated. What hits James is a wall, the stone cold wall he had driven by every day of his working life. The wall that the bus, packed with young, "industrious" Hawaiian men, grazed as they were whisked away to fight for a country not their own. He had just driven past the very same wall this morning, and it would become the one thing that meant he could never pass anything ever again.

This is where it gets gruesome. I imagine my grandfather in his last moments, his two hands grasping the wheel, his toes curling as he attempts, pathetically, to exert enough force on the brake to stop the car. Then he realizes it is too late. The wall is right there. His seat belt is off, and his window wide open. I wonder: Was he afraid? Was he relieved? Was he happy? It eats at me, but there is no way I can ever know. His body is thrown out of the vehicle as it collides with the wall, and with the snap of his neck, his life is over, just like that. It's over.

But I still ask myself, "Is it really over?"

It can't be, because the suffering isn't even close to being over. What if every strike, every abuse, every evil word that left his mouth wasn't his? What if there were just some way to explain it all? This suffering cannot be without cause. It lives on, even to this day. It lives in the angry fists met by impoverished Hawaiian children, and in the cycles of abuse that spin through generations. It lives on in its original form, its first sin. It lives on through a legacy of colonialism in the islands.

The truth is that each abuse, each incensed fit that he threw, was caused by something greater. When we, as Hawaiians, live in a world where we are not allowed to connect with our land and determine, for ourselves, how and why we live on this earth, we cannot find peace and harmony in the chaos of loss. The truth is, no matter how hard I try to conduct this posthumous reflection on my grandfather, these unheard liturgies will never reach him. So, what can come of them? Perhaps, I muse, these quiet reflections on my grandfather's abuse and death will mollify that unspeakable trauma each Kanaka carries on their back. For it is not until we recognize the construct of colonialism and the way it turns Hawaiians—who must be connected to our 'āina—into agents

EACH ABUSE, EACH INCENSED FIT THAT HE THREW, WAS CAUSED BY SOMETHING GREATER.

of capitalist production and radically self-destructive consumption, that we can finally say the word "ea" and know that it means not just sovereignty or saliently silencing logics but also breath, filling our strangled lungs and severed esophaguses with life.

James MacShane Hanakahi is my grandfather. He had no obituary, but I often try to write one in my head. He lived his life with honest intentions, faltered by the economic and political dominance of White supremacy. In an irrational world, people do irrational things to survive. Succumbing to alcoholism, drug addiction, inhumane working conditions, and the loss of love and mercy, he was one of those people. Like another statistic in a campaign to quantify, to classify, and to deconstruct our bodies, his death, and my death, and all of our deaths may be just another cog in the campaign's argumentative machines, whose sole purpose is to snap the iwikuamo'o that binds our cosmic heads to our earthly bodies. I know this imperialist tale is carried by cold, wet feet as they trace the maddeningly modular drainage canals that pass through Moihihi, meeting their abrupt end at the gaze of Nānāikapono Elementary

School where innocence, too, is not spared. I hear its colonial call as clearly as the words "unexploded ordnance" leaving a haole military officer's mouth on the shores of Kahoʻolawe. Still, senseless death in my settled bones reeks with the sickening smell of discomfort and disillusion. Blinded by the blaring lights, and muted by echoing red sirens that tell of Kanaka ʻŌiwi failure, I picked apart each bone, begging for some semblance of sense in the chaos, only to find in this dissection the continued decapitation of my identity, my understanding, and my intellect.

WE ARE BORN DISJOINTED, DISCONNECTED FROM OUR HISTORIES AND OUR MOʻOKŪʻAUHAU

And, yet, in this vindictive blame, I realize that these searing brutalities do not die with the ending of a single life. No, these scarred histories of violence and fear, perpetuated by this systematic cycle of colonizing and corrupting, are not exclusive to a certain type of Hawaiian, a certain type of man, a certain mode of being. No, it is not that we are "bad," or that we are "dirty," or that we are "savage"; it is because when we are born, with the cutting of our umbilical cords, so too are our heads severed by the Western stamps on English-only birth certificates. Dangling from the warm embrace of our mothers, our ʻāina momona, we are born disjointed, disconnected from our histories and our moʻokūʻauhau that cradle us in their knowledge.

But losing our heads does not mean losing our lives. No, it means so much more and so much less than that. In this carnivorous channel of colonization, we are fed lies as truths and told to be the ideal, "good" and "industrious" young men and women in homage to the Western imperialist memories placed in our minds. We are headless, obediently following each name they brand us with, stumbling through foreign halls, speaking tongues unknown to our still dangling heads. We are left with a body without a soul, a heart without a beat. And, yet, in this dismal discord, there is still hope for us, as a Kanaka Maoli collective, to understand and overcome these vast fears and this deep dread.

Only in radical acts of recognition can we begin to undo these egregious acts of decapitation and displacement. Embracing and encapsulating this persistent fear of the petty performativity of "bad" in our native bones compels us to fight back and find our way to an oceanic pathway where our earthbound bodies can finally meet the lost celestial constellations of our heads. In sorrows as deep as the channels that separate and subjugate our island horizons, there lies a truth more profound than the senseless transgressions against Hawaiians by Hawaiians—it is called colonization. As a child, I often blamed my papa for his actions, believing that such egregious acts could be understood only through the lens of a Christian construct of evil. What I did not realize is that true evil comes with each utterance of culture, "knowledge," and "progress" that this foreign force buries into the soil of our chests. This colonial construction of failure and of fear shaped me into its subject—good, industrious and, most importantly, obedient to its ideals.

And in this wild and weary conglomerate of conflicted feelings, I realize that this recognition, this seeing, this feeling, is so much more than just blindly absorbing tales of 2:00 a.m. beatings and 9:00 p.m. car crashes. It is recognizing the trickle of hatred and anger that comes from the beating of our brown bodies into Western submission; it is the act of finally seeing the colonial roots of green bottles and jail cells; it is opening our eyes to the supreme force that colonial forces bear on our people. It is, in short, lāhui—seeing ourselves and seeing each other. And seeing is more than just that—it is writing, it is speaking. I write these words with the intention of posthumously sewing back what was taken from my Papa Jimmy. I write these words to stitch together a broken lāhui. And, above all else, I pull together these ropes of resistance in hopes of remembering and recognizing myself. For, although I am not James MacShane Hanakahi, I am his namesake. I am his moʻopuna, and our moʻokūʻauhau are one. I keep my head in close orbit to my grounded body, slowly repairing and healing these scars and severed veins so that I can at least rewrite this recurring obituary. And if I could finally do that, I guess it would go something like:

Though they say we are gone, we are never forgotten, and we carry with us the scars of our ancestors, and we carry with us the hope that they had for us, and in this immense weight we recognize that we are not perfect and that our kūpuna have hurt us in ways unspeakable and that they have beat us and raped us and ruined us but we also recognize that the world inflicts these same pains upon those that came before us and we realize and reconcile these differences and we know that although our kūpuna lost their heads, we will not lose ours.

ABOUT THE AUTHOR

Gregory Pōmaikaʻi Gushiken is a Kanaka Maoli writer and PhD student in ethnic studies at the University of California–San Diego, where he writes about the Kanaka Maoli diaspora in Las Vegas and Southern California. He is an alumnus of the English and political science departments at the University of Hawaiʻi at Mānoa.

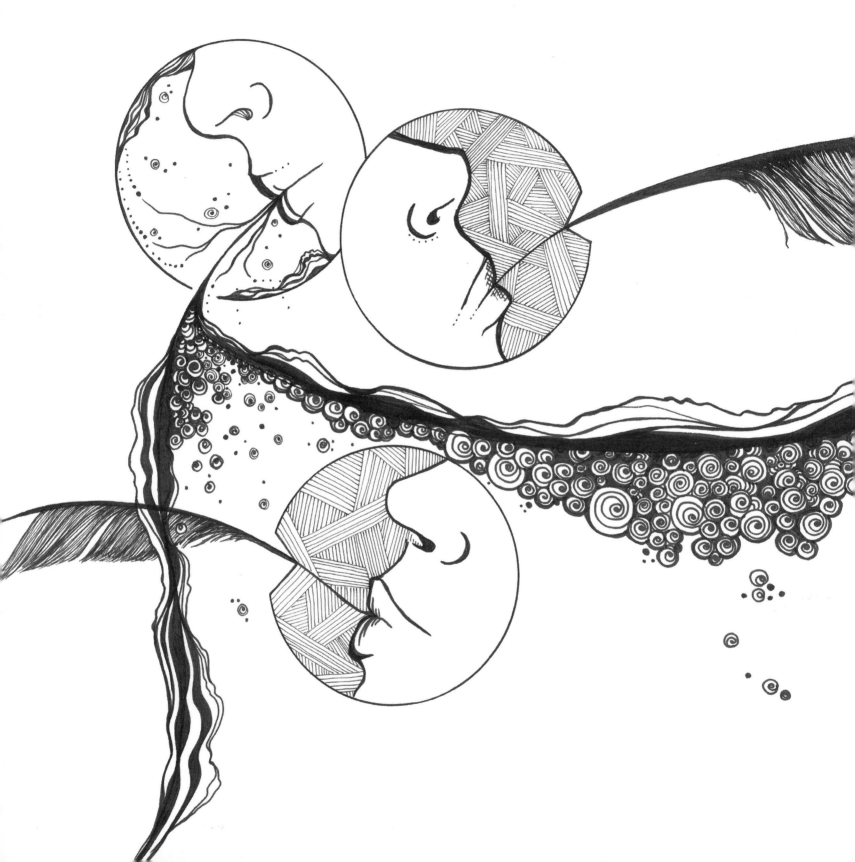

Muliwai FUTURES

Interdisciplinary Research through a Shared Lexicon: Merging 'Ike Kupuna and Western Science to Examine Characteristics of Water

FLORYBETH FLORES LA VALLE, DONNA A. K. CAMVEL, FLORENCE I. M. THOMAS, HŌKŪLANI K. AIKAU, AND JUDITH D. LEMUS

Traditional knowledge and Western science are two distinct disciplines that differ in methodological, substantive, epistemological, and contextual grounds. While there is increasing agreement among scholars that integrating traditional or Indigenous and Western approaches is key to solving complex environmental problems, there is also agreement that there are structural and epistemological barriers to full integration. The authors have collaborated to bridge these gaps. This article describes our attempt to integrate Indigenous knowledge and Western science through a summer research project where two of the authors, one from the biological sciences and one from political science, were asked to identify how their individual research agendas might inform the other and then identify a shared outcome that integrated both knowledge systems. Our discussions, during and after the project, revealed that the knowledge-sharing process, which resulted in the creation of a shared lexicon, was the most valuable outcome. The shared lexicon is a first step toward creating common ground between disciplines and in moving from an interdisciplinary approach toward a transdisciplinary approach to research, teaching, and learning.

CORRESPONDENCE MAY BE SENT TO:
Florybeth Flores La Valle
College of Natural Resources, UC Berkeley
Environmental Science, Policy, and Management
410 O'Brien Hall, Berkeley, CA 94720-3112
Email: lavallef@berkeley.edu

167

Hūlili: Multidisciplinary Research on Hawaiian Well-Being, Vol. 11, No. 1

Bridging Western Science and Traditional Knowledge: Values and Limitations

The bridging of Western science and traditional knowledge to improve our understanding of ecosystems and natural phenomena is not a new concept (Kealiikanakaoleohaililani & Giardina, 2016; Mistry & Berardi, 2016; Ledward, 2013; Gagnon & Berteaux, 2009; Drew & Henne, 2006; Barnhardt & Kawagley, 2005; Agrawal, 1995). For more than fifteen years, ecological and biological sciences have acknowledged that traditional/Indigenous ecological knowledge, produced from many generations of observation of and adaptation to specific environments, is necessary for managing and sustaining the resources in particular places. However, solving emerging environmental issues, often the result of unsustainable historic and contemporary practices, requires a transformative and integrative approach to fuse multiple knowledge systems to achieve success.

Conventional hierarchical constructs of knowledge systems (Evering, 2012) can impede the ability of communities to identify and implement sustainable solutions to complex environmental issues that require transdisciplinary approaches (Mistry & Berardi, 2016; Fortuin & van Koppen, 2016; Lang et al., 2012). Evering (2012) specifically warns against a hierarchical form of knowledge integration in which Western science tends to "harvest" or "validate" Indigenous knowledge (p. 358), a practice that Mistry and Berardi (2016) similarly refer to as "a tendency among the scientific community to assimilate local ecological knowledge within Western worldviews of managing nature" (p. 1274). Lang and colleagues (2012) have argued the need for guidelines leading to a third epistemic way, which transcends approaches that favor any one epistemology in sustainability science. Indeed, case studies indicate that successful community-based conservation efforts are built upon equitable sharing and synergistic relationships between Indigenous knowledge and Western science (Shultis & Heffner, 2016; Walter & Hamilton, 2014; Shukla, 2004; Kellert, Mehta, Ebbin, & Lichtenfeld, 2000).

Traditional ecological knowledge (TEK) has been recognized as important in conservation biology (Gadgil, Berkes, & Folke, 1993; Berkes, 2004), sustainable resource use (Schmink, Redford, & Padoch, 1992), and ecosystem management (Jokiel, Rodgers, Walsh, Polhemus, & Wilhelm, 2011), to name a few. Several collaborations have been attempted by researchers to merge the knowledge domains of science with traditional customary and contemporary practices, with various degrees of success (Johannes, 1989; Simpson, 2004). The project described here is an outgrowth of attempts by the coauthors of this article to bridge the gap between Indigenous and Western knowledge systems.

From 2012 to 2014, Thomas and Aikau, along with several graduate research assistants, collaborated with Kākoʻo ʻŌiwi, a Native Hawaiian nonprofit organization working to restore wetland taro farming in the ahupuaʻa of Heʻeʻia on the island of Oʻahu, to document the impacts of restoration on water quality and the management strategies used to make decisions.[1] This project, funded by Hawaiʻi Sea Grant, was successful in many ways: We were successful at working collaboratively with the community group—the research questions were determined by the needs of the nonprofit organization, we communicated our findings back to the community group, who used the data to make informed management decisions, we trained Kākoʻo ʻŌiwi staff in water quality testing techniques, we completed an assessment of water availability for the restoration, and we provided an interdisciplinary research experience that required graduate students to translate the project's findings for a nonexpert audience. Over the course of our collaboration, we have continued to adapt our thinking, teaching, and research practices to get closer to fully realizing our goal of doing responsive, relevant, and interdisciplinary work that takes full advantage of Western and Indigenous knowledge systems. However, we were unable to fully integrate all aspects of Indigenous knowledge and Western science in the project.

Indeed, the challenges we encountered were similar to those documented by others who have made similar efforts. The scholarly research suggests that despite attempts to bridge the epistemological gap between these knowledge systems, the Western academy appears able and willing to integrate only those aspects of TEK that are most similar to the data generated by the scientific method and that can be readily applied to those environmental problems defined by the scientific community (Simpson, 2002). What is much more difficult for the Western academy to attend to are the spiritual and ontological foundations of Indigenous knowledge systems and, as Simpson (2004) argues, the failure to account for how the impact of land and language loss due to colonization continues to impede progress. Indeed, Indigenous scholars have repeatedly noted that when Indigenous resource management strategies are effective, it is often because they were developed in conjunction with the spiritual beliefs, ceremonial cycles, place-specific practices, and worldviews that combine to inform the genealogical relationships between Indigenous peoples and their territories (Pilgrim, Samson, & Pretty, 2010; Kimmerer, 2015; Simpson, 2004; Nelson, 2008). The result is a vast imbalance and, sometimes, misrepresentations of partnerships between scientists and those who hold Indigenous knowledge (Simpson, 2001).

In an attempt to foster healthy interdisciplinary collaborations for future generations, many educators have called for the need to incorporate traditional ecological knowledge into college science courses (Bang, Medin, & Atran, 2007; Palmer, Elmore, Watson, Kloesel, & Palmer, 2009; Van Eijck & Roth, 2007; Riggs, 2005; Semken, 2005; Kimmerer, 2002; Aikenhead, 2001). Unfortunately, even with widespread acknowledgment of the complementarity between Indigenous and scientific ways of knowing, training students in multiple epistemologies to address complex issues is not a commonly adopted practice in higher education, and the general tendency is still to "enculturate all students into the value system of Western science" (Aikenhead, 2001, p. 337). This rings true based on our experiences as well. The cultural disconnect continues into postgraduate studies, where departmental stovepipes can further compartmentalize thought and critical inquiry, potentially limiting interdisciplinarity between academic units traditionally divided into sciences and liberal arts. Calls for more interdisciplinary graduate education in the sciences have been proposed, but these are often focused on integrating disciplines within a broad branch of science, such as biology (Bronson, Verderame, & Keil, 2011; Lorsch & Nichols, 2011).

Recent proposals for more transdisciplinary approaches to graduate education in conservation and environmental sciences highlight the importance of skills that will help early career scholars successfully navigate and address complex socio-ecological questions (Fortuin & van Koppen, 2016; Courter, 2012), but many graduate programs, particularly in the sciences, remain highly specialized and segregated. Unfortunately, this lack of opportunity for collaboration among early professionals of different disciplines can perpetuate misunderstanding, misappropriation, devaluation, and marginalization of knowledge systems considered to be "other" (Simpson, 2001; 2004).

At the University of Hawai'i at Mānoa, where the coauthors have all worked, Native Hawaiian scholars have consistently argued that moʻolelo (stories/history), oli (chant), mele (song), as well as thousands of pages of nūpepa (Hawaiian newspaper) articles on topics ranging from plant names to moon phases, hold 'ike kupuna (ancestral knowledge) that is relevant to current and future researchers (Silva & Basham, 2004; Goodyear-Kaʻōpua, 2009; Wiener, 2015). However, these kinds of sources are not readily taught in college classes outside courses designated as Hawaiian or Indigenous studies. Even at a university where Hawaiian knowledge is considered to be central to its mission, 'ike kupuna continues to be relegated to those places marked as Indigenous, Native, or Hawaiian.

A pessimistic interpretation of this reality could be that this knowledge is not seen as an authoritative source equal in status to published, peer-reviewed articles. Another explanation is that because most of this archive is written in the Hawaiian language, even if these sources were seen as having value beyond providing historical baseline data, accessing this information is possible only to those scholars and researchers who have the linguistic and cultural expertise to read and accurately interpret these sources. Indeed, it is still difficult to "translate" the highly technical language of the academy into a form that is meaningful for nonexperts, and it is equally difficult to explain how moʻolelo, oli, mele, and nūpepa may hold the kinds of expert 'ike kupuna needed to solve current and future environmental crises. This being said, scholars are actively working to make this archive more accessible to the larger scholarly community. For example, Dr. Puakea Nogelmeier

and the staff of Hoʻolaupaʻi's Hawaiian Language Newspaper Translation project, funded by a Preserve America Initiative grant from the National Oceanic and Atmospheric Administration, seek to make these invaluable resources available and accessible to the general public. Hawai'i Sea Grant developed a website (http://seagrant.soest.hawaii.edu/institute-of-hawaiian-language-research-and-translation/) that displays original Hawaiian newspaper articles along with the English language transcription.

Mālama Wai: An Exploratory Project

Over the summer of 2015, our team came together again to try to integrate science and Indigenous knowledge. The Collaborative Graduate Fellowships program, offered by the Center for Ocean Science Education Excellence Island Earth (COSEE Island Earth), was designed to foster interdisciplinary learning between graduate students of Western science and Hawaiian knowledge. A primary inspiration for COSEE Island Earth is the 'ōlelo noʻeau, "'Aʻohe pau ka 'ike i ka hālau hoʻokahi" (All knowledge is not taught in one school). Moreover, one of the key goals of COSEE Island Earth is to bridge Western and Hawaiian knowledge and epistemologies to more holistically realize ocean literacy and conservation in Hawai'i (Lemus, Seraphin, Coopersmith, & Correa, 2014). Accordingly, as Collaborative Graduate Fellows, La Valle and Camvel were encouraged to design an interdisciplinary collaboration on some aspect of ocean-related research that integrated traditional Hawaiian knowledge and Western science. The Mālama Wai (caring for water) project set out to engage in collaborative, interdisciplinary research that could inform the research of both La Valle and Camvel, doctoral students in marine biology and political science, respectively. The remainder of this article describes the process we undertook to create an interdisciplinary project that equally valued marine science and ʻike kupuna. We learned that before there could be any integration of knowledge systems, we first needed to create a shared language to talk about wai (water). Below is a brief overview of the common lexicon created for this project, which established common ground and goals.

The critical element of interest shared by both students was water; however, the ways in which inquiry, analysis, and hypotheses were carried out were grounded in very different approaches. Additionally, the kinds of sources and data considered to be legitimate for answering their respective research questions required different methods and objectives. When we embarked on this endeavor, the goal for this project was to integrate the practices of Western science with ʻike kupuna as part of an interdisciplinary effort to make conversant the language of science with that of Native Hawaiian moʻolelo as they relate to water.

In its most basic form, bridging science and ʻike kupuna usually follows this model: Western scientists gather Hawaiian traditional ecological knowledge and use it as a qualitative baseline or apply it to their methods, while Hawaiian cultural practitioners use modern scientific tools to help them understand their environment in contemporary times, while keeping future generations in mind. This approach might be characterized as a negotiation of knowledges within a hierarchy (Evering, 2012). Another approach is to leverage both of these different knowledge systems to help solve complex problems. These emerging issues often result from protracted contemporary practices that are unsustainable, which require transformative approaches that combine ancestral knowledge with scientific methods to

achieve success. For example, the Laulima a ʻIke Pono community internship program created opportunities for community members to explore both scientific research and Indigenous moʻolelo and practices at a Hawaiian fishpond alongside scientists and Hawaiian practitioners to better understand current fishpond biogeochemistry and opportunities for restoration (Lemus, 2018).

Initially, we defaulted to the "business as usual" model and used Western scientific knowledge to authenticate place-specific, water-related moʻolelo and used traditional knowledge to inform historical land use. This work was done for three field sites on Oʻahu; however, the one site we refer to as ʻIolekaʻa is the focus of this article. ʻIolekaʻa is an undeveloped kuleana (land that was awarded to Camvel's family in the 1850s as part of the larger process of land reform called the Māhele) and is located in ʻIolekaʻa Valley, in the Heʻeʻia ahupuaʻa (watershed/land division), lying at the base of the Koʻolau Mountains, on the Windward side of Oʻahu island (see fig. 1A–B). Water quality sampling at ʻIolekaʻa was conducted on freshwater streams and on fresh water within taro fields found on the property (see fig. 1C). We were interested in comparing the site-specific moʻolelo with the "unobservable" (with the naked eye) characteristics of water such as salinity, pH, dissolved oxygen, and inorganic nutrient concentrations in areas of biological and cultural interest within the site. We also analyzed the place-based associative values pertaining to the akua (gods). Our analysis sought to locate points of overlap and synergy between the water quality data and the ʻike found in the moʻolelo.

According to a Hawaiian worldview, akua take material form (kinolau) including elements, such as rain, clouds, soil, water, and plant forms. The Hawaiian gods, in their

171

various capacities and forms, function as critical environmental elements whose properties are contained within the complex whole of the earth and are constituent to environmental harmony, or what the Hawaiian worldview refers to as achieving a state of pono (balance, rightness). Kūpuna constantly strived for this state of pono, and when it was maintained, the 'āina (land, that which feeds), ali'i nui (ruling chiefs), and the maka'āinana (commoners) benefitted. A state of pono is not unlike sustainable, holistic approaches to resource use that meet present needs without sacrificing the needs of future generations.

'Ioleka'a and the Akua of He'e'ia

The story of 'Ioleka'a is about 'āina where the gods operate as elements in their micro and macro environments (Camvel, 2012). It is about the relationships between the 'āina, humans, and the gods that surround human and nonhuman persons. The place name 'Ioleka'a is often translated as rolling rat and, while some mo'olelo place the 'iole (rats) who roll (ka'a) to their deaths as central in both historical and contemporary narratives of 'Ioleka'a, it is, by no means, the only possibility. What follows is an example of the process of Papakū Makawalu, a methodology by which Native Hawaiian words are taken apart and each component is purposefully studied in order to rethink how individual components function, to understand the relationship between their meanings and that of other terms and concepts, and to see how they fit back together, producing new knowledge or understandings. The goal is to identify deeper meanings or kaona (hidden meanings) for terms and to explore other associations with places, practices, or objects (Kanahele, 2009).

The prevailing mo'olelo of 'Ioleka'a centers on a feud between the He'e'ia rats, whose feet were red, and the 'Ewa, Honolulu, and Waialua rats, whose feet were any color

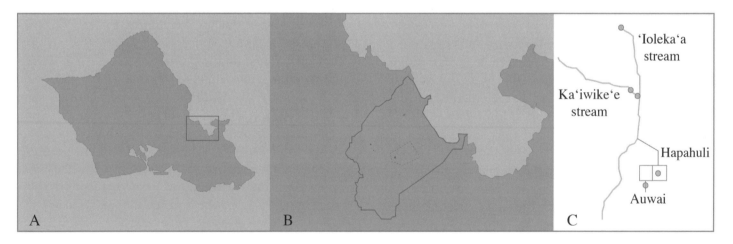

Figure 1. Map of 'Ioleka'a sampling site. (A) Map of O'ahu. The box delineates the location of the He'e'ia ahupua'a. (B) Close-up map of the He'e'ia ahupua'a. The dashed line shows 'Ioleka'a Valley. The dot indicates Camvel's kuleana location. (C) Conceptual map of the streams located in 'Ioleka'a. The circles show sampling locations for water quality testing. The boxes delineate the hapahuli (taro ponds). The straight line labeled 'auwai refers to the taro pond outflow.

but red. The malihini (stranger, outsider) rats came over the ridge and were led to their deaths by the He'e'ia rats, who guided them down the steep, perpendicular cliff path, leading them halfway to a moss-covered pōhaku (stone or rock), from which the malihini rats were encouraged to step and jump. Following the He'e'ia rats, the malihini rats, not familiar with the area, slip and fall into the pool below to their deaths (Kamakau, 1993). One interpretation of the mo'olelo is an example of how place-based knowledge, or being familiar and accustomed to the 'āina, can be a matter of life or death. The figurative meaning for 'iole—to steal, cheat, or lie in wait in order to assail (Pukui & Elbert, 1971)—might imply that there was something of value or significance that motivated the 'iole malihini to traverse the ridge and be tricked into falling from such a treacherous trail. Thus, one moral of the story can be a cautionary tale about the consequences of malihini taking the resources of another ahupua'a. 'Iole also refers to the name of the sinker of a he'e (octopus) lure. Given that the 'ili (land section) of 'Ioleka'a resides within the He'e'ia ahupua'a, this could be another associative meaning for this place name.

Ka'a means to roll, turn, twist, wallow, wind, braid, revolve; to scud or move along, as clouds; rolling, twisting, turning, sloping (Pukui & Elbert, 1971). As a noun, scud refers to Pannus clouds, grey or dark-colored clouds that look like broken layers or sheets of dark frayed clouds, which move quickly across the sky. These clouds are also called messenger clouds because when they take on a dark opaque look, they indicate that rain or snow is on its way. These clouds are common in hilly and mountainous areas and can be found all over the world (World Meteorological Organization, 2017).

When we situate these associations relative to the location of the 'ili, which is at the base of the Ko'olau Mountains on the Windward, often rainy, side of the island of O'ahu, it is not surprising that ka'a could also carry associations with these kinds of clouds and their movement in the sky. Additionally, within a Hawaiian worldview, the akua Lono is associated with long, dark, or black clouds, thundering and accompanying heavy rain, lightning, and rainbows of ho'oilo (rainy season). Ho'oilo occurs from October to January and corresponds to makahiki, a time when all people rested and abstained from work (Malo, 1987). Given how po'e Hawai'i (Hawaiian people) understood these elements to be the kinolau of their beloved akua, it is likely that in giving this place the name ka'a, kūpuna recognized the significance of rain and cloud formations in this 'ili and that these elements are sacred due to their association with the akua Lono.

In addition to the akua Lono, the akua Haumea, Hina, and Kāne are also associated with this ahupua'a. Haumea, a female akua (also referred to as Papa, Laka, Kapo, and Kameha'ikana) is described by Hawaiian historian Lilikalā Kame'eleihiwa (1999) as "most famous on the island of O'ahu, who is the goddess of childbirth, war, and politics" (p. 4). Indeed, it is her mana wahine (female power) that she draws upon to defeat Kumuhonua, "an enemy of her kāne (male lover) Wākea" (Kame'eleihiwa, 1999, p. 4). Portions of this mo'olelo take place in He'e'ia, thus grounding Haumea to various sites in the ahupua'a. As with many akua, Haumea can inhabit plants and is known for taking "possession of certain trees, from which are carved great war gods" (Kame'eleihiwa, 1999, p. 5). She can also transform into mo'o wahine (female lizard deities) who serve as kia'i (guardians) of the wai, muliwai (brackish waters), and kai (sea waters). Ho'omanawanui (2010) describes Haumea as the red earth mother, who births both gods and goddesses, including Hina'aimalama, "the goddess of the moon, who survived domestic abuse to become a powerful goddess of healing and patroness of women's art forms, such as kapa (cloth) production" (pp. 28–29).

Hina, a female akua, is the initiator of the rhythmic cycles of the moon and is associated with growth and reproduction, and her lunar abilities promote growth through the lunar cycles and rhythmic atmospheric forces. The coral reefs are the body of Hina; coral heads (pūkoʻa) are the genitalia of Hina. From them, Hina gives birth to sea urchins, seaweeds, reef creatures, and their cousins of the land—freshwater shrimp, mosses, and small ferns (Kameʻeleihiwa, 1999), all prominent creatures in the Heʻeʻia ahupuaʻa.

The final akua associated with Heʻeʻia is the male akua, Kāne. Kāne is the primary element of fresh water and sunshine, those life-giving components that nourish the ʻāina, the kalo, and the people. This element activates photosynthesis, regulates temperature, and is a critical contributor to the growth of all living things. He is also associated with various cloud formations. As Kāneikaʻōpua, Kāne becomes the billowy white clouds on the horizon, and as Kāneikeao, Kāne becomes the floating cloud (Benson & Roseguo, 2014). Again, when we are familiar with the weather patterns in Heʻeʻia, we come to recognize these akua as ever present. We also come to understand how they work in complementary ways: Lono is the dark clouds that signal rain is approaching, while Kāneikaʻōpua reflects sunny weather. Haumea embodies the trees and plants that thrive in fresh water, while Hina embodies those creatures of the salt and brackish waters. When functioning together in a state of pono, they create an ecological environment where human and nonhuman beings can thrive. In this manner, place-based knowledge is underpinned by moʻolelo, which often reflects the symbiotic

relationship between Kānaka and their environment. A closer examination of the place name, Heʻeʻia, provides an example of this. In this article we use Heʻeʻia because it reflects the geographical, topographical, and cultural significance of this particular place. The word heʻe is commonly known as octopus and also means to slide, surf, slip, or flee (Pukui, 1983). ʻIa is a particle marking passive/imperative, and eia is an idiom that means here, here is, here are, this place. As such, it is understood and known that Heʻeʻia is a place with abundant heʻe and a place that is slippery from the numerous streams and springs.

Creating a Shared Lexicon

As the project developed, some unforeseen challenges arose. Similar to the intricacies involved in translating moʻolelo, we were spending most of our time trying to explain to each other the nuances of the concepts and terms used in our different disciplines. It became clear that before we could develop an interdisciplinary approach to our study about water that combined traditional knowledge with Western approaches, we first needed to understand each other's language. From this technical difficulty in the interdisciplinary process, a new integral goal for this case study emerged:

Create a shared lexicon of Hawaiian language and Western science terms to help in interpreting characteristics of water, both in historical and contemporary times.

The process of coming up with this lexicon involved several hours of talking story about our disciplines. The time committed toward this process allowed for learning about each other's values and principles, for trust to build, and for both disciplines' "voices" to be heard.

Working toward a common goal and a unified product encouraged both fields of knowledge to be involved equally and created a sense of fulfillment for all involved. This revised process addresses Simpson's (2004) critique that Western science can strip Indigenous knowledge of everything that is not valued by Western science and often does not allow for the full participation of knowledge keepers in the process of producing new knowledge.

The objective of the new research focus was to create a lexicon based on existing Hawaiian words rather than generating transliterated terms associated with water. In our unique case, a Hawaiian lexicon created with scientific terms and processes in mind could be used to understand and interpret Hawaiian moʻolelo and historical written accounts about local water bodies. Non-Hawaiian scientists and Native Hawaiian scholars who are not proficient in the Hawaiian language could also use this lexicon to understand how Hawaiian kūpuna might have understood wai.

Wai is sacred and essential to human life and to the production of kalo as a staple food of the Hawaiian people. The value of wai is evidenced by the many oli that refer to and celebrate Kāneikawaiola (the living waters of Kāne), which also refers to fresh water or springs. The lexicon we created includes the hydrological action or function, the Hawaiian concept or term, and a descriptive explanation of how that concept reflects the scientific process. The words wai honua (groundwater), kāʻamaʻai (photosynthesis), and wai kahe (flowing water) were taken from *Māmaka Kaiao*, a dictionary of Hawaiian words used to explain contemporary concepts and material culture unknown in traditional Hawaiʻi (Kōmike Huaʻōlelo, 1998). The remaining words were taken from the *Hawaiian Dictionary* (Pukui & Elbert, 1971). These

two databases were the primary resources used in establishing this lexicon. Based on these dictionaries and the methodology of Papakū Makawalu, we looked for terms and concepts that reflected a Hawaiian epistemological understanding of the scientific process. In this lexicon, we sought to capture the many characteristics and nuances of wai—its flow, volume, depth, location, source, and movement—to bridge our understandings between ʻike kupuna and science (see fig. 2).

Creating a shared lexicon acknowledges the need to share a common language when tackling a common problem. It is also a tool that can be used by researchers working with Kanaka ʻŌiwi communities and by communities working with scientists. A common language is a multidisciplinary tool that can clarify the intersections, universalities, and points of incommensurability between the disciplines. Take, for example, the scientific notion of groundwater. We identified wai honua as an approximation for the meanings associated with this concept—water that resides and moves underground. Our initial search of *Māmaka Kaiao* and other Hawaiian dictionaries did not result in a Hawaiian term for this concept. While the terms wai and honua were found in Hawaiian language newspapers and moʻolelo, the two words were not used together. When combined—wai, defined as fresh water, and honua, defined as land, earth, world—they approximate the meaning and function of groundwater. Additionally, within a Hawaiian worldview, wai is figuratively associated with the circulatory system—the process of blood flowing through the human body, mostly unseen, but sustaining of life. Attention to both literal and figurative meanings of terms allows us to better understand their functions and characteristics.

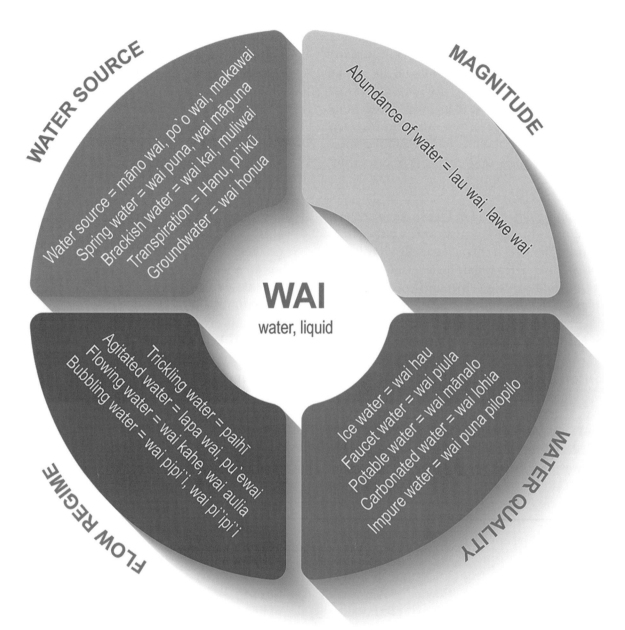

Figure 2. Graphic representation of a shared lexicon bridging Western science and traditional Hawaiian knowledge about water. The panels are divided thematically.

Shared Lexicon: A Step toward Transdisciplinarity

There are several approaches that can be used when people from multiple disciplines work together on a joint project. Figure 3 depicts three of these approaches: multidisciplinary, interdisciplinary, and transdisciplinary. This case study was initially conceived as an interdisciplinary project, where students from separate fields train each other in their discipline's discourse and integrate this knowledge in place-based research. However, as we worked on a shared lexicon, we began to develop what we consider to be transdisciplinary research.

An advantage of moving toward transdisciplinary research is that it allows both parties to become unburdened by the restrictions of a single discipline and not feel like they have to defend their own frameworks. Transdisciplinary research allows for new experiences to take participants with different types of knowledge toward products that go beyond the limits of their own disciplines. In some ways, this was our experience; it was challenging to figure out what kind of product could come out of this research. In Western scientific terms, there was not enough funding to replicate the sampling process at all three sites and at the frequency needed to gather all the data and publish the results in a scientific journal. The same is true of Native Hawaiian studies, which has limited outlets for this kind of transdisciplinary research. Nonetheless, participants in this research project agreed that there was great value in the challenges we faced and in what was accomplished as we worked creatively to address these challenges.

Taking the time to think through a common problem also allows for interpersonal bonds to form and has a transformative effect on the people involved in the collaboration. In some ways, one of the most valuable outcomes of transdisciplinary research is its ability to shape and change individuals' perspectives, actions, and approaches within their own disciplines. All of the participants came away from the project with new insights that changed their behaviors. For example, Camvel, a researcher and co-owner of the ʻIolekaʻa site, learned that when water to the loʻi (taro ponds) is turned off, the pH of the soil drops very quickly, causing a possibly harmful environment for the kalo (taro). Instead, the water flow in the loʻi should be managed and regulated in more careful and cautious ways. Camvel's transformative benefit is the ongoing composition of a modern-day moʻolelo for ʻIolekaʻa that, when completed, will tell the story of this joint research effort from a Kanaka Maoli perspective. In addition, the inclusion of akua, as central to a complex ecosystem found in the Hawaiian ahupuaʻa management system, is being adopted in the creation of the moʻolelo, paying homage to the keen observation skills of the Hawaiian ancestors. La Valle learned that saying oli and pule before field work at her research sites helped to set her intentions and made her open to perceiving and appreciating the unseen elements surrounding her. La Valle also recognized that interacting with poʻe Hawaiʻi has unspoken rules that, when respected, help to build the necessary trust for collaborative work, which is not easily garnered by Western scientists.

Two undergraduate science interns were brought into the project to help with water quality sampling at ʻIolekaʻa. The interns chose to be involved in both science and community outreach work as part of their career goals. The following quotations were taken from their exit interviews.

MULTIDISCIPLINARITY draws on knowledge from different disciplines but stays within the boundaries of those fields (NSERC, 2004).

INTERDISCIPLINARITY is a synthesis of two or more disciplines, establishing a new level of discourse and integration of knowledge (Klein, 1990).

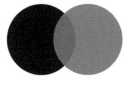

TRANSDISCIPLINARITY involves projects in which researchers from different fields not only work together closely on a common problem over an extended period, but also create a shared conceptual model of the problem that integrates and transcends each of their separate disciplinary perspectives (Rosenfield, 1992).

Figure 3. Definitions and graphic representation of multidisciplinarity, interdisciplinarity, and transdisciplinarity.

"[Camvel] not only taught me a lot about my own culture that I was very ignorant about, but how many Hawaiian stories can be shown to be accurate scientifically."
—Senior, Gonzaga University

"Working in ʻIolekaʻa is what I like to call 'spiritual science.' It's much more than traditional science, there's a mystique that surrounds ʻIolekaʻa. It's not just data and observation; it's something that can't be explained."
—Senior, University of Hawaiʻi at Mānoa

It is challenging to engage in interdisciplinary research between the natural and social sciences, as they draw on different conceptual frameworks with differing epistemologies. The willingness to move beyond theoretical and methodological silos and to explore other possible ways of knowing—though not our sole original intent—is evidence of the strength and uniqueness of this case study. The lexicon was a first step; we then developed a graphic representation of the lexicon that combines themes and can be used as a teaching tool in Hawaiian studies courses and in sciences classes (see fig. 2).

Conclusions and Future Directions

The call for interdisciplinary work is ever increasing at local, institutional, and federal levels (National Science Foundation, 2011). There are times when a single-discipline approach is insufficient. For example, in Hawaiʻi, land management is highly valued but remains a point of contention. Knowing that Hawaiian culture is built on a close-knit patchwork of communities, it is infeasible to think we can improve the health of the ʻāina without several areas of expertise working together. When embarking on an interdisciplinary project, Whitfield and Reid (2004, p. 435) suggest asking the following questions:

- Does the project require various disciplinary experts to work together (instrumental) or to create new theory or method (epistemological)?

- Are there good managers to ensure success of the process, and how?

- Is there an evaluation of success, and how?

This work requires interest on the part of funding agencies, support from institutions, and individuals who are motivated to engage in this work. One of the biggest current hurdles is that goals and products often differ for different disciplines. What is compelling to a scientific audience may not necessarily be the same for audiences interested in a Native Hawaiian perspective. More avenues, such as this journal, need to be made available for interdisciplinary research. When appropriate, these integrated products need to be implemented and institutionalized into career advancement in higher education (e.g., interdisciplinary undergraduate courses as requirements for degrees, and interdisciplinary research requirements for tenure).

Successful transdisciplinary research creates individuals who are conversant in multiple disciplines and therefore can make conceptual frameworks of several subjects more accessible for broader audiences. Even at a small scale, such as this exploratory project, it was evident that collaborating and sharing knowledge had a powerful and transformative effect on all involved.

One of the reasons this was a successful collaboration is because we were willing and excited to learn the content,

values, and approaches within both fields; this type of relationship made it easier to engage in collaborative research. We also came into the project without prior assumptions about each other's disciplines and without unspoken agendas. Maintaining an open mind and showing mutual respect is especially important when dealing with two very different fields of knowledge. Throughout this inter- and transdisciplinary journey, we recognized both the values and limits of each approach and created a shared lexicon that honors Hawaiian and Western knowledge about water.

As technologies advance and global problems bring us together, the borders of disciplinary lines are getting more blurred. In general, when tackling a project or problem, we need to be better at consulting disciplines other than our own, representing all potentially useful knowledge domains and spanning all stakeholders' interests. Additionally, a transdisciplinary approach, such as the shared lexicon in this case study, may be an important way to successfully bridge Western science with 'ike kupuna while creating a useful product that all creators can take pride in.

REFERENCES

Agrawal, A. (1995). Dismantling the divide between indigenous and scientific knowledge. *Development and Change, 26*(3), 413–439.

Aikenhead, G. S. (2001). Integrating Western and Aboriginal sciences: Cross-cultural science teaching. *Research in Science Education, 31*(3), 337–355.

Bang, M., Medin, D. L., & Atran, S. (2007). Cultural mosaics and mental models of nature. *Proceedings of the National Academy of Sciences of the United States of America, 104*(35), 13868–13874.

Barnhardt, R., & Kawagley, A. O. (2005). Indigenous knowledge systems / Alaska Native ways of knowing. *Anthropology and Education Quarterly, 36*(1), 8–23.

Benson, A., & Roseguo, L. (2014). *Nā ao a me nā ua: Clouds and rains (moisture circulation).* Honolulu, HI: Bernice Pauahi Bishop Museum Online Learning Center. Retrieved from http://resources.bishopmuseumeducation.org/resource_type/lesson/LM_Clouds_and_Rain.pdf

Berkes, F. (2004). Rethinking community-based conservation. *Conservation Biology, 18*(3), 621–630.

Bronson, S. K., Verderame, M. F., & Keil, R. L. (2011). Interdisciplinary graduate education: A case study. *Cell, 147*(6), 1207–1208.

Camvel, D. (2012). *Land genealogy of 'Ioleka'a: Mapping an Indigenous identity.* (Doctoral dissertation). University of Hawai'i at Mānoa, Honolulu, HI.

Courter, J. R. (2012). Graduate students in conservation biology: Bridging the research-implementation gap. *Journal for Nature Conservation, 20*(1), 62–64.

Drew, J. A., & Henne, A. P. (2006). Conservation biology and traditional ecological knowledge: Integrating academic disciplines for better conservation practice. *Ecology and Society, 11*(2), 34.

Evering, B. (2012). Relationships between knowledge(s): Implications for "knowledge integration." *Journal of Environmental Studies and Sciences, 2*(4), 357–368.

Fortuin, K. P. J., & van Koppen, C. S. A. (2016). Teaching and learning reflexive skills in inter- and transdisciplinary research: A framework and its application in environmental science education. *Environmental Education Research, 22*(5), 697–716.

Gadgil, M., Berkes, F., & Folke, C. (1993). Indigenous knowledge for biodiversity conservation. *Ambio, 22*(2–3), 151–156.

Gagnon, C. A., & Berteaux, D. (2009). Integrating traditional ecological knowledge and ecological science: A question of scale. *Ecology and Society, 14*(2), 19.

Goodyear-Kaʻōpua, N. (2009). Rebuilding the ʻauwai: Connecting ecology, economy, and education in Hawaiian schools. *AlterNative, 5*(2), 46–77.

hoʻomanawanui, k. (2010). Mana wahine: Feminism and nationalism in Hawaiian literature. *Anglistica, 14*(2), 27–43.

Johannes, R. E. (Ed.). (1989). *Traditional ecological knowledge: A collection of essays.* Gland, Switzerland: The World Conservation Union.

Jokiel, P. L., Rodgers, K. S., Walsh, W. J., Polhemus, D. A., & Wilhelm, T. A. (2011). Marine resource management in the Hawaiian Archipelago: The traditional Hawaiian system in relation to the Western approach. *Journal of Marine Biology*, Article ID 151682, 1–16.

Kamakau, S. M. (1993). *Tales and traditions of the people of old: Nā moʻolelo a ka poʻe kahiko.* Honolulu, HI: Bishop Museum Press.

Kameʻeleihiwa, L. (1999). *Nā wāhine kapu: Divine Hawaiian women.* Honolulu, HI: ʻAi Pōhaku Press.

Kanahele, P. K. (2009). *Kukulu ke ea a Kanaloa: The culture plan for Kanaloa Kahoʻolawe.* Hilo, HI: Edith Kanakaʻole Foundation.

Kealiikanakaoleohaililani, K., & Giardina, C. P. (2016). Embracing the sacred: An indigenous framework for tomorrow's sustainability science. *Sustainability Science, 11*(1), 57–67.

Kellert, S. R., Mehta, J. N., Ebbin, S. A., & Lichtenfeld, L. L. (2000). Community natural resource management: Promise, rhetoric, and reality. *Society & Natural Resources, 13*(8), 705–715.

Kimmerer, R. W. (2002). Weaving traditional ecological knowledge into biological education: A call to action. *BioScience, 52*(5), 432–438.

Kimmerer, R. W. (2015). *Braiding sweetgrass: Indigenous wisdom, scientific knowledge, and the teachings of plants.* Minneapolis, MN: Milkweed Editions.

Klein, J. T. (1990). *Interdisciplinarity: History, theory, and practice.* Detroit, MI: Wayne State University Press.

Kōmike Huaʻōlelo (Hale Kuamoʻo & ʻAha Pūnana Leo). (1998). *Māmaka kaiao: He puke huaʻōlelo Hawaiʻi hou.* Honolulu, HI: Hale ʻO Kikowaena ʻŌlelo Hawaiʻi.

Lang, D. J., Wiek, A., Bergmann, M., Stauffacher, M., Martens, P., Moll, P., . . . Thomas, C. J. (2012). Transdisciplinary research in sustainability science: Practice, principles, and challenges. *Sustainability Science, 7*(Suppl. 1), 25–43.

Ledward, B. C. (2013). ʻĀina-based learning is new old wisdom at work. *Hūlili: Multidisciplinary Research on Hawaiian Well-being, 9*(1), 35–48.

Lemus, J. D. (2018). Impacts of a holistic place-based community internship on participant interest in science and conservation career pathways. *Journal of STEM Outreach, 1*(1), JL1–JL12. ISSN 2576-6767. http://ejournals.library.vanderbilt.edu/index.php/JRLSO/article/view/4436

Lemus, J. D., Seraphin, K. D., Coopersmith, A., & Correa, C. K. V. (2014). Infusing traditional knowledge and ways of knowing into science communication courses at the University of Hawaiʻi. *Journal of Geoscience Education, 62*(1), 5–10.

Lorsch, J. R., & Nichols, D. G. (2011). Organizing graduate life sciences education around nodes and connections. *Cell, 146*(4), 506–509.

Malo, D. (1987). Hawaiian antiquities: *Moʻolelo Hawaiʻi.* (N. B. Emerson, Trans.). Honolulu, HI: Bishop Museum Press.

Mistry, J., & Berardi, A. (2016). Bridging indigenous and scientific knowledge. *Science, 352*(6291), 1274–1275.

National Science Foundation. (2011). Introduction to interdisciplinary research. Retrieved from http://www.nsf.gov/od/oia/additional_resources/interdisciplinary_research/

Natural Sciences and Engineering Research Council of Canada (NSERC). (2004). *Guidelines for the preparation and review of applications in interdisciplinary research.* Ottawa. Retrieved from http://nserc-crsng.gc.ca/NSERC-CRSNG/Policies-Politiques/prepInterdiscip-prepInterdiscip_eng.asp

Nelson, M. K. (2008). *Original instructions: Indigenous teachings for a sustainable future.* Rochester, VT: Bear & Company.

Palmer, M. H., Elmore, R. D., Watson, M. J., Kloesel, K., & Palmer, K. (2009). Xoa:dau to Maunkaui: Integrating indigenous knowledge into an undergraduate earth systems science course. *Journal of Geoscience Education, 57*(2), 137–144.

Pilgrim, S., Samson, C., & Pretty, J. (2010). Ecocultural revitalization: Replenishing community connections to the land. In S. Pilgrim & J. Pretty (Eds.), *Nature and culture: Rebuilding lost connections* (pp. 235–256). Washington, DC: Earthscan.

Pukui, M. K., & Elbert, S. H. (1971). *Hawaiian dictionary.* Honolulu, HI: University of Hawai'i Press.

Riggs, E. M. (2005). Field-based education and indigenous knowledge: Essential components of geoscience education for Native American communities. *Science Education, 89*(2), 296–313.

Rosenfield, P. L. (1992). The potential of transdisciplinary research for sustaining and extending linkages between the health and social sciences. *Social Science & Medicine, 35,* 1343–1357.

Schmink, M., Redford, K. H., & Padoch, C. (1992). Traditional peoples and the biosphere: Framing the issues and defining the terms. In K. H. Redford & C. Padoch (Eds.), *Conservation of neotropical forests: Working from traditional resource use* (pp. 3–13). New York, NY: Columbia University Press.

Semken, S. (2005). Sense of place and place-based introductory geoscience teaching for American Indian and Alaska Native undergraduates. *Journal of Geoscience Education, 53*(2), 149–157.

Shukla, S. (2004). *Strengthening community-based conservation through traditional ecological knowledge.* Natural Resources Institute, University of Manitoba, Canada: Author. Retrieved from http://citeseerx.ist.psu.edu/viewdoc/download?doi=10.1.1.165.98&rep=rep1&type=pdf

Shultis, J., & Heffner, S. (2016). Hegemonic and emerging concepts of conservation: a critical examination of barriers to incorporating Indigenous perspectives in protected area conservation policies and practice. *Journal of Sustainable Tourism, 24*(8–9), 1227–1242.

Simpson, L. (2001). *Traditional ecological knowledge: Marginalization, appropriation and continued disillusion.* Speech presented at the Indigenous Knowledge Conference. Saskatoon, Canada.

Simpson, L. R. (2002). Indigenous environmental education for cultural survival. *Canadian Journal of Environmental Education, 7*(1), 13–25.

Simpson, L. R. (2004). Anticolonial strategies for the recovery and maintenance of Indigenous knowledge. *American Indian Quarterly, 28*(3–4), 373–384.

Silva, N. K., & Basham, J. L. (2004). *I ka 'ōlelo no ke ola: Understanding Indigenous Hawaiian history and politics through Hawaiian language sources.* Pennsylvania State University: Citeseer.

Van Eijck, M., & Roth, W. (2007). Keeping the local local: Recalibrating the status of science and traditional ecological knowledge (TEK) in education. *Science Education, 91*(6), 926–947.

Wiener, C. (Host). (2015, March 17). Looking to our past: Hawai'i's historic Hawaiian language newspapers. MP3. In Center for Ocean Sciences Education Excellence, *All things marine*. Honolulu, HI. Retrieved from http://www.cosee-ie.net/programs/allthingsmarineradioshow/

Walter, R. K., & Hamilton, R. J. (2014). A cultural landscape approach to community-based conservation in Solomon Islands. *Ecology and Society, 19*(4), 41.

Whitfield, K., & Reid, C. (2004). Assumptions, ambiguities, and possibilities in interdisciplinary population health research. *Canadian Journal of Public Health, 95*(6), 434–436.

World Meteorological Organization. (2017). Pannus. In *International cloud atlas*. Retrieved from https://cloudatlas.wmo.int/clouds-accessory-pannus.html

ACKNOWLEDGMENTS

This work would not have been possible without funding from the National Science Foundation Center for Ocean Sciences Education Excellence (COSEE Island Earth), Hawai'i Sea Grant, and UH–Mānoa's Graduate Student Organization. Additionally, we wish to thank the Līhu'e, Kahanu, Paoa, Kea Lono 'ohana, Jesse Boord, and Skyler Tomisato, whose support was essential in being able to conduct water quality testing in 'Ioleka'a.

ABOUT THE AUTHORS

FLORYBETH F. LA VALLE is a postdoctoral researcher working at UC Berkeley on water quality and coastal ecology issues in nearshore environments and in a marine protected area (MPA) in the Philippines. She received her PhD in marine biology at the University of Hawai'i at Mānoa. Her research interests are in nearshore ecology and biogeochemical cycling. Specifically, she studies the effects of land-based pollutants on algal communities in coral reef ecosystems. Her work with Kānaka 'Ōiwi and Hawaiian communities has informed her research and teaching career deeply. She brings what she has learned from all these collaborations in Hawai'i to her current work with communities in the Philippines.

DONNA ANN KAMEHAʻIKŪ CAMVEL teaches Hawaiian studies courses at Windward Community College. She received bachelor's degrees in women's studies and Hawaiian studies, a master's in Hawaiian studies, and is currently a doctoral candidate specializing in Indigenous politics at the University of Hawaiʻi at Mānoa. Her doctoral research on the Heʻeʻia ahupuaʻa employs a multi-faceted lens to observe the ways in which Kānaka ʻŌiwi are restoring land and natural resources that were once degraded, using Indigenous knowledge and science, transforming not only ʻāina and resources, but also Kānaka themselves in the process.

FLORENCE I. M. THOMAS is with the Hawaiʻi Institute of Marine Biology, University of Hawaiʻi. **HŌKŪLANI K. AIKAU** is an associate professor of gender studies and ethnic studies at the University of Utah. **JUDITH D. LEMUS** serves as interim director of the Hawaiʻi Institute of Marine Biology, University of Hawaiʻi.

NOTE

1. In this paper we include contemporary spellings of Hawaiian terms using the ʻokina (glottal stop) and kahakō (macron). We use Native Hawaiian, Kanaka ʻŌiwi, and Kanaka Maoli interchangeably to refer to the Indigenous peoples of Hawaiʻi. We also use Heʻeʻia as the preferred spelling for the ahupuaʻa (land division) on the Windward side of Oʻahu, to reflect the geographical, topographical, and cultural significance of this place.

Kanaka 'Ōiwi Contributions to the Old (K)new Practice of Indigenous Planning

ANTOINETTE KONIA FREITAS

This article discusses the significance of cultural pedagogy among Hawaiian-focused public charter schools and the necessity of 'āina in this educational framework. I argue that Hawaiian-focused public charter schools are a result of the epistemic collisions that occurred in the early 1970s between state notions of land use and Hawaiian ideations around those very lands. The land use struggles at that time, such as the Protect Kaho'olawe movement to stop the US military from bombing the island, served to awaken, among other things, Hawaiian cultural practices. Those practices, coupled with Hawaiian language revival, eventually took root in the project-based activities of many Hawaiian-focused public charter schools. Thus, the cultural pedagogy shared among many Hawaiian-focused public charters is a logical extension of early struggles that heightened awareness about the necessity of land in the production and transfer of knowledge. By discussing Hawaiian-focused education with an eye toward 'āina, I examine larger systems of spatial power and the way in which those systems structurally determine what constitutes legitimate land use.

CORRESPONDENCE MAY BE SENT TO:
Antoinette Konia Freitas
Kamakakūokalani Center for Hawaiian Studies
Hawai'inuiākea School of Hawaiian Knowledge, University of Hawai'i at Mānoa
2645 Dole Street, 209AC, Honolulu, Hawai'i 96822
Email: antoinet@hawaii.edu

Hūlili: Multidisciplinary Research on Hawaiian Well-Being, Vol. 11, No. 1
Copyright © 2019 by Kamehameha Schools

Several years ago, I worked as a planning consultant with a Hawaiian-focused public charter school located in a rural region in Hawai'i. My task was to develop a place-based educational framework that would guide the future site development of the school. This school was located on lands that were abundantly rich with both natural and cultural resources, which seemed well suited to their culture-based educational philosophy and project-based objectives. I have a vivid memory of the environmental studies teacher asking if we could include native and non-native plants that had pleasant smells. She advocated for this so that she could teach outdoors, but more so, that her students (especially the little ones who have short attention spans), while moving from one part of the campus to another, could engage all their senses during the school day.

Working closely with the teachers during several design workshops where they were asked to draw what they considered to be their ideal campus, I was constantly struck at how Hawaiian cultural knowledge informed the rationale for their educational facilities and site layout. It dawned on me that as planners, we miss a great deal of innovation by not being able, or willing perhaps, to incorporate Indigenous vocabulary and local ways of knowing with any degree of consistency—or seeming aptitude—into our planning practices, let alone processes.

As I continued to work with the school, I recognized a complexity to this project that seemed to underscore the ill fit between state land use and Hawaiian ways of knowing. On the one hand, the school seemed to be in a geographic region that fundamentally served its educational philosophy. The site itself was the source of learning; it was the "textbook" and "outdoor classroom," as many of the teachers would say. However, the land use rules seemed to be so heavily weighted in rational and linear processes that they fundamentally shifted, and came to dominate the value, use, and function of that 'āina[1] for that school. The land use system triggered a complicated regulatory environment that the school administrators now had to navigate. Moreover, the regulatory environment was further complicated by the inequality between regular schools and stand-alone charter schools, the most glaring difference being that stand-alone public charters do not receive any fiscal or planning support for facilities. They are expected to build, purchase, renovate, and maintain their facilities with no supplemental funding for those purposes. Basically, this means public charter schools must mount capital campaigns to supplement funding for day-to-day school operations as well as for facilities. By my estimation, the school seemed to reflect the larger struggles facing many Hawaiian communities and families, that is, enduring a land use system that is incongruent with Hawaiian ways of knowing and being.

One strength of place-based education is the adaptation of unique, locally bound characteristics that may serve to overcome the dislocation between school and a child's life (Gruenewald, 2003). That unique adaptation in Hawai'i, I argue, is through 'āina. By framing research questions that explain how 'āina teaches, we can identify Kanaka 'Ōiwi expressions of space and place in ways that inform Indigenous planning. By combining two streams of thought that are rarely brought into the same space with each other, we can address larger theoretical questions that coalesce around how societies might engage in transformative planning by utilizing multiple epistemologies.

In Search of Methodology

One of the difficult issues faced by Indigenous researchers is finding methodologies that are congruent with our social commitments to justice and to our cultural traditions and life experiences (Brown & Strega, 2005; Kovach, 2005; Smith, 1999). All methodologies hold assumptions that shape what constitutes legitimate data, and how those data are collected and analyzed to arrive at findings. The problem in the social sciences is the lingering dominance of positivist methodology, which offers little room for other ways of knowing to enter the field on their own methodological terms. To address these failings, this qualitative inquiry relies on an Indigenous methodology that utilizes the theory-building approach found in grounded theory and the research techniques found in participatory rural appraisal.

Four stand-alone New Century Public Charter Schools agreed to participate in this research project. A total of twenty-nine semi-structured, open-ended interviews and three facilitated workshops were conducted. Three schools identified as Hawaiian-focused public charter schools, with one school identifying as a Hawaiian language immersion school. Importantly, the inquiry drew heavily from the language, worldviews, metaphors, philosophies, and experiences of our Kanaka 'Ōiwi and other Indigenous communities.

Over the years I have enjoyed working with many Hawaiian-focused public charter schools on various planning and facilities projects. While I work in higher education, I have no teaching experience in public charter schools, although I currently serve on a school governance board for a public charter. Sharing the insider role, that is, working within and among Hawaiian educators, affords me unique access to certain data and knowledge not available to an outsider because I come from the same worldview as the participants. This also allows me a "second sight" in those instances where Hawaiian thoughts or ideas emerge that others may disregard as unimportant or miss all together. Moreover, it has been my experience that for some participants in studies such as this, there is a relief in knowing that between the researcher and the participant, we may share common values, philosophies, and worldview, to the degree that the participants do not have to spend time justifying their daily lives and, by extension, their work.

Framing Indigenous Planning

Several scholars have theorized planning as an imperial discipline and colonial practice primarily associated in the West (Jacobs, 1996; Matunga, 2013; Porter, 2010). They describe planning's dominant practice as a linear, rational process in which the fundamental tools and methods, often, have served to displace Indigenous peoples globally. A number of Indigenous political struggles have challenged the dominance of planning systems because of their role in the production of space. Sandercock (2004) observes:

> Since the 1970s, there has been a global movement on the part of Indigenous peoples to reverse injustices and dispossession . . . at the heart of this movement are land claims that are potentially destabilizing of established practices of land use planning, land use management and private property laws . . . the core of planning practice. In the claims of Indigenous peoples for return of, or access to their lands, planners are sometimes confronted with values incommensurable to modernist planning and the modernization project . . .

which privileges development in which exchange value usually triumphs over use value. (p. 119)

Matunga (2013) identifies three epochs of Indigenous planning that provide a periodicity relevant to this discussion. The first epoch, the Classic tradition, covers the precolonial contact phase. This phase is characterized by traditional Indigenous worldviews and their approaches to environmental management. The second epoch, the Resistance tradition, accounts for the immediate postcolonial phase up until the 1970s. The third epoch, the Resurgence tradition, generally considers the period in the 1980s onward, in which Indigenous Peoples move beyond protests of resistance and couple with broader global Indigenous rights movements to assert their worldviews as a means of human rights to land, language, culture, education, health, governance, and resource management, among other things.

The significance of cultural pedagogy among Hawaiian-focused public charter schools straddles the second and third epoch in Matunga's framework. I argue that Hawaiian-focused public charter schools are a result of the epistemic collisions that occurred in the early 1970s between state notions of land use and Hawaiian ideations around those very lands. The land use struggles at that time, such as the Protect Kahoʻolawe movement to stop the US military from bombing the island, served to hoʻāla (awaken), among other things, Hawaiian cultural practices. Those practices, coupled with Hawaiian language, eventually took root in the daily activities of many Hawaiian-focused charter schools. Thus, the cultural pedagogy shared among many Hawaiian-focused charter schools is a logical extension of early struggles that heightened awareness about the necessity of land in the production and transfer of knowledge. By discussing Hawaiian-focused education with an eye toward

ʻāina, we examine significantly larger systems of spatial power[2] and the ways in which such systems structurally determine what constitutes legitimate land use. By privileging Hawaiian land use from a Hawaiian educational point of view, we recast the way in which a "(k)new" old story about planning is told in Hawaiʻi (Edwards & Hunia, 2013).

Public Charter Schools in Hawaiʻi

One of the unique markers of public charter schools in Hawaiʻi is the presence of Hawaiian language and culturally focused schools. The majority of these schools enroll a high percentage of Hawaiian students and have a high percentage of Hawaiian teachers who teach in either their own Indigenous language or through a curriculum taught in English utilizing, among other things, Hawaiian practices. These schools represent a venue for educators to develop curriculum that promotes learning for a range of students whose needs, many would argue, are not met in regular public schools. The state Department of Education (DOE) figures indicate that approximately 180,000 children are enrolled annually in Hawaiʻi public schools. Of this figure, Native Hawaiians represent the largest ethnic group (26.0 percent), followed by Filipinos (22 percent) and white Caucasians (17 percent) (Office of Hawaiian Affairs, 2017). Further, charter school enrollment has risen steadily in recent school years (2014–15 through 2017–18) by about 7 percent (Hawaiʻi Department of Education, 2017). In school year 2015, for example, there were approximately ten thousand students enrolled across thirty-four public charter schools among the five major islands. Moreover, among the seventeen Hawaiian-focused public charter schools, Hawaiian students represented 40.4 percent (or 4,211) of that student population. Based on these figures, one of the seventeen Hawaiian-focused public charter schools has about three times more Hawaiians than non-Hawaiian students. Overall, enrollment in public charter schools is increasing, but why the strong Hawaiian presence in these schools?

Some argue that conventional DOE schools have failed Hawaiian children, and a look at performance indicators may prove these arguments to be valid. Hawaiian educator, Dr. Kū Kahakalau, explains, "I couldn't understand how the students I taught in high school could be articulate, smart and funny in my classes but based on their report cards they were failures" (personal communication, 2013). The overrepresentation of certain demographics in special education courses continues to be a concern in national debates. Locally, 14.6 percent of Native Hawaiian public school students are enrolled in special education courses, compared with 8.3 percent of non-Hawaiian students. Math and reading proficiency scores show that Native Hawaiians score disproportionately lower than non-Hawaiians on standardized tests (Office of Hawaiian Affairs, 2017, p. 6, 8). Hawaiian-focused education can be viewed as one way of resetting the educational foundation through language and culture in ways that benefit Indigenous students. Research conducted by Kanaʻiaupuni, Ledward, & Malone (2017), for example, indicates that "learners thrive with culture-based education (CBE), especially Indigenous students who experience positive socioemotional and other outcomes when teachers are high CBE users and when learning in high-CBE school environments" (p. 311S).

Na Wai Hoʻi e Hele ʻOle ke Ala o nā Kūpuna?

To understand the educational context, it is worthwhile to outline the social and environmental setting that children were generally born into during the time of Kānaka ʻŌiwi wale nō.[3] Approximately twelve to fifteen hundred years ago, the first people to arrive at our pae ʻāina settled and cleared lands for agriculture. On Oʻahu island, Chief Māʻilikūkahi is generally credited for clearly marking and reorganizing land palena; aliʻi on other islands would have implemented similar systems. Beamer (2014) maintains that:

> In the ʻŌiwi system of old, palena created places—spaces of attachment and access to both the metaphysical and physical worlds. They delineated the resource access of makaʻāinana and aliʻi on the ground, literally connecting people to the material and spiritual resources of these places. Palena were cataloged and maintained visually and cognitively, and were passed on orally from generation to generation by inhabitants knowledgeable about the place. (p. 32)

The Hawaiian economy was based on an exchange system that existed within the ahupuaʻa, which provided everything needed in close proximity. Kānaka ʻŌiwi planned kauhale around cultivated field systems and other necessary material resources; thus, their settlement patterns were defined in terms of adjacency, access, and configuration. The ʻohana were generally able to maintain long-term relationships with a specific parcel of land even though the aliʻi might change. Boundary setting established the following land divisions: moku, ahupuaʻa, ʻili kūpono, ʻili ʻāina, and moʻo ʻāina. Ahupuaʻa are "diverse and complex divisions, ranging in size, shape, and geography. Some ahupuaʻa are bounded by mountain ridges and peaks," and since they "defined resource access, they usually extended into the ocean" (Beamer, 2014, pp. 41–42).

191

It was within this setting that Hawaiian methods of teaching and learning were developed. Learning through observation, listening, and repeating are well-known traditional methods of Hawaiian instruction. The idea of education was "practical, skill-oriented, socially useful, in tune with reality, environmentally aware and conserver-cognizant" (Kelly, 1982, p. 13). Reliance on the surrounding environment for basic living meant for our Hawaiian ancestors that "culture furnished the natural and basic content material of their education," and a part of that "curriculum include[ed] attaining an intimate, discriminating knowledge of nature, including names, characteristics and habits of plants, fish, rains, surf spots, just to name a few" (Kahakalau, 2003, p. 38). Learning was acquired through subtle forms of teaching that occurred through everyday living as children observed the daily activities of family and community members. With time, children eventually tried out tasks for themselves or alongside brothers, sisters, and cousins. What is key to this discussion is that a child's relationship with the ʻāina was held in tact during the process of learning and, as such, ʻāina was vital to the subsequent knowledge produced and transferred.

Emergence of the State Land Use System

During the territorial period, Hawaiʻi's government planning was centralized, which resulted in land use being regulated by local boards. In 1937, the territorial legislature established the Territorial Planning Board and, in 1939, the board produced the first comprehensive report that inventoried the physical, social, economic, industrial, and educational resources (Territorial Planning Board, 1939; Downes, 1986). Between 1950 and 1960, Democrats enacted measures intended to bring greater social and economic reforms to the island populous.

They did this through internal state measures and by capitalizing on external factors. They raised taxes on major land owners, made assessment practices more uniform, and gave neighbor island counties zoning power that only Oʻahu had enjoyed since 1939.

The economic situation of Hawaiʻi changed drastically with statehood and jet travel, as outside capital found a way into the islands, affecting tourism, enabling expensive residential development, and increasing military training (Cooper & Daws, 1990; Downes, 1986; McGregor, 2010). Given these economic trends and their impact on land uses, two issues were focusing on public land use policy: the provision of public infrastructure and the preservation of prime agricultural land. Public agencies were becoming increasingly unable to provide public infrastructure due to the costs associated with the spread of urban development. Moreover, the spread of urban development was encroaching on the state's prime agricultural lands—those that were best suited for large-scale pineapple and sugar agriculture and, compared with urban development, had greater potential to buoy the state's economy in the long run.

The State Land Use Law, enacted as Act 187, was adopted in 1961. By creating a system of land uses, it was believed that the state would be able to preserve agricultural lands (as well as preserve its political economic relationships) and produce a mechanism for urban development (for democratic reform purposes) while simultaneously containing development (thus making it cost effective for government). The state land use system classified all lands into one of four land use districts: urban, agriculture, rural, and conservation. By 1963, the democratic governor implemented a "highest and best use" approach to land development. To reinforce this economic policy, the Session Laws of Hawaiʻi (1963) merged the Planning Department with the Department of Economic Development to become the State Department of Planning and Economic Development. Moreover, incentives were created by offering lower tax assessments on buildings rather than land, thus creating an incentive to build. However, the law did not affect the taxes of large land owners, rather, it was their lessees who ended up paying, therefore, by not addressing land ownership:

> Overall and over time, while the Democrats in power did start out down the land reform track in the name of social justice ... [they] opted instead for land development as an essential part of the way to broad social and economic reform. (Cooper & Daws, 1990, p. 7)

Development, it was believed, could create new wealth and increase standards of living for the middle and working class. Therefore, instead of cutting up the "old pie of land wealth, the idea was to make the pie grow rapidly and continually by developing land intensely so that everyone could have more without giving up anything of significance" (p. 7). The land use zoning supported the pro-development ideology, which meant that the few remaining pockets of rural Hawaiian communities and small farmers would begin to feel the pressure to urbanize.

Political Activism Links to Education

With the imposition of statehood in 1959, urban-based economic reforms brought ten years of uncontrolled urban growth. As Hawaiʻi entered the 1970s, public awareness grew increasingly critical of the excessive urban growth, the loss of small-scale family agriculture,

the high cost of living, lagging salaries, and unaffordable housing (McGregor-Alegado, 1980; Trask, 1987). Development threatened the remaining rural pockets of the Hawaiian community, which, for generations, had relied on ʻohana subsistence practices as a way of life. Moreover, the broader issues of education, employment, wages, housing, legal justice, social services, and the concentration of land ownership indicated severe problems facing the Hawaiian community at the beginning of the 1970s (McGregor-Alegado, 1980; Trask, 1987). By 1972, the majority of Hawaiian wage earners received incomes that fell within the low-income level. Among educational indicators for that period, only 50 percent of Hawaiians and part-Hawaiians age twenty-four and older had graduated from high school, and the dropout rate (according to the 1970 Census) was 23 percent, compared with the Hawaiʻi average of 13 percent. The census also showed that only 4 percent of Hawaiians had graduated from college (McGregor-Alegado, 1980, p. 37).

Despite years of large-scale agriculture of the previous century, which erased large swaths of Hawaiian landscape, the remaining wahi pana, or significant Hawaiian places such as heiau, fishponds, and village sites, were now under threat for a second erasure, this time by policy-driven urban development. Influenced in part by similar cultural movements from the late 1960s and early 1970s in the United States and abroad, the Hawaiian movement revived cultural practices and found political voice to articulate a resistance to urban development and the outright destruction of ʻāina and their cultural landscapes. Beginning in the 1970s, intense land struggles erupted, first on Oʻahu, against unbridled urban development of the few remaining Hawaiian communities and small rural pockets (Cooper & Daws, 1990; McGregor-Alegado, 1980; Trask, 1987). Many community-based struggles were occurring across our islands, including, for example, Hālawa

Housing, Kalama Valley, Ota Camp, Waimānalo People's Organization, Old Vineyard Street Residents' Association, Waiāhole-Waikāne Community Association, Heʻeia Kea Residents Association, Mokauea Fisherman's Association, Hale Mōhalu ʻOhana, Niumalu Nāwiliwili Residents, and the Sand Island Residents ʻohana (McGregor-Alegado, 1980, p. 41).

These land struggles catalyzed Hawaiian consciousness around the concepts of Hawaiian rights and the resurgence of Hawaiian language, cultural practices such as hula, and traditional farming methods such as loʻi kalo and loko iʻa. The struggle to stop the US military's bombing of Kahoʻolawe island, perhaps more than any other issues of the day, gave life to the notions of aloha ʻāina and mālama ʻāina. At the beginning of World War II, Kahoʻolawe was taken over by the US Navy for live-fire ordnance exercises and combat training. These exercises grew in scale and intensity. In March 1977, George Helm and Kimo Mitchell lost their lives in the ocean off Kahoʻolawe during a protest of the bombing. The struggle grew into a movement that stopped the military use of the island in 1996, and it also sparked the revitalization and resurgence of Hawaiian culture, music, navigation, arts, agriculture, and aquaculture. McGregor (2007) comments:

> The contemporary rediscovery of Kahoʻolawe as a sacred island dedicated to Kanaloa led to a revival of the traditional Hawaiian value of aloha ʻāina or love and respect for the land. Ancestral memories of the kūpuna focused upon aloha ʻāina as the Hawaiian value at the core of traditional spiritual belief and custom. (p. 264)

McGregor (2007) also notes that recollecting family genealogies inspired contemporary Hawaiians to reestablish or reaffirm family-based kahuna or professions such as navigation, fishing, engineering, healing, and planting. Another significant outcome of the movement to stop the bombing of Kahoʻolawe was the "reestablishment of the Makahiki and other Native Hawaiian cultural and religious ceremonies and practices on Kanaloa . . ." (p. 270). The purpose of one such ceremony was to attract the akua Lono, to Kanaloa, in the form of rain clouds, to soften the earth and to ready it for young plants to revegetate the island (p. 272). These practices reconnected a generation of Hawaiians with their ancestors and with the pragmatic use of ceremony, as in the case of Kahoʻolawe, to call forth rain so that plants could again repopulate and heal the island.

The 1978 Constitutional Convention resulted in the voters of Hawaiʻi ratifying amendments to the state constitution. Three key amendments were significant to the resurgence of Hawaiian language, culture, and education. The first amendment, Article XV, section 4, provides that English and Hawaiian shall be the official languages of Hawaiʻi (Lucas, 2000). The second amendment, Article X, section 4, mandates that the state promote the study of Hawaiian culture, history, and language; the article also requires the state to provide for a Hawaiian education program consisting of language, culture, and history in the public schools. The third amendment, Article XII, section 7, provides that the state reaffirms and shall protect all rights, customarily and traditionally exercised for subsistence, cultural, and religious purposes by ahupuaʻa tenants of Hawaiian ancestry, subject to regulation by the state.

Looking back at the 1960s and 1970s, we see the confluence of two significant events in Hawaiʻi. The first was the establishment of Hawaiʻi's land use law, which advanced a pro-development ideology by the Democratic

Party. The second significant event was an organized Hawaiian activist movement against the deplorable conditions of Kānaka Maoli and their homelands. The alignment of other key events continued between 1970 and 1990 to create fertile ground for a Hawaiian charter school movement to take root in Hawaiʻi—the resistance to development in rural areas; the resurgence of Hawaiian cultural practices and language revival prompted by the Protect Kahoʻolawe movement; the enactment of key state amendments that affirmed Hawaiian language as an official language of Hawaiʻi; the study of Hawaiian culture, language, and history through Hawaiian education programming; the protection of customary and traditional rights of ahupuaʻa tenants; and the articulation of aloha ʻāina as a viable principle and management standard for land use. By the close of the twentieth century, the role of Hawaiian activism, coupled with the revival of Hawaiian practices, heavily influenced a Hawaiian charter school movement focused on ʻāina as a viable way to produce and transmit Hawaiian knowledge.

ʻĀina as a Source of Knowledge Production and Transmission

To understand how Hawaiian epistemology unfolds in an ʻāina-based educational context, I question *how* ʻāina teaches. This is distinct from asking what we learn as a result of ʻāina-based education. Here I analyze the qualities of ʻāina within an ʻŌiwi context to explore how it shapes knowledge and our sense of being. For example, the impact of a school's morning protocol goes beyond simply gathering students to start the day—it is a reconfiguration of haumāna and kumu around an ʻŌiwi consciousness where ʻāina, spatial awareness, and inclusion are central to learning.

"We Begin Our Day with Protocol"

Three of the four schools involved in this inquiry conducted a form of morning protocol or ceremony to begin their school day. Whether they referred to this gathering as "piko," "wehe," or "wehena"—this spatially anchored activity transcends placemaking into a Hawaiian conception of time and acknowledges an individual's genealogical ties to place. Through morning protocol, these schools intentionally identify where they are located within larger regions and learn about the storied landscapes and associated mele or chants of their surroundings so that they can honor the places and people of an area. One principal explained:

> We do a morning oli, Ua Ao Hawaiʻi, [we] do Hawaiʻi Ponoʻī then the Kumu Alakaʻi does a manaʻo for the day, then the students do another oli for the waters of Kane and that's the Kumu and the students, so we do that all together.

Ua Ao Hawaiʻi, literally meaning Hawaiʻi is enlightened or conscious, represents a clever play on the word ao since aʻo means to teach, training, or counsel. Ao means light, day, dawn, or to dawn or grow light. The coupling of ao, aʻo, and piko is symbolic in this instance. To the Hawaiian, piko refers to the navel cord, genital organs, and/or the crown of the head. Thus in the Hawaiian view, there are three piko, the top of the head, the center of the body (literally the navel area) and lastly, the genital area. As a spatial concept, however, the idea of conducting morning piko represents a physical space that transcends toward relational development. It is a space designated for the ancestor-descendant relationship to be continually nurtured over time. This can also be conceived of as lōkahi, or unity or accord.

Another educator described their morning piko as "a place, a union of moʻokūʻauhau, [where] everyone starts their day as one." The idea of beginning the day all together in a designated place "as one" is a highly inclusive act because students, faculty, and staff are invited to recall the great deeds of their own ancestors, or the ancestors of that area. Another educator explained, "We have wehena, it's a school-wide practice. We blow the pū and everyone gathers at eight o'clock in the morning and then it goes into first period, second period academics." Wehena at this school involves students, faculty, and staff gathering to sing, chant, and offer general school reminders or notices for that day. At another school, one educator noted that ". . . the neatest part of the whole experience [was] the way the day starts." At this school, located in the lower elevations of a watershed, students, faculty, and staff (including any campus visitors) gather outdoors for their morning wehe. An educator explained, "Everybody focuses through oli, there's the usual oli that are a part of the repertoire that you know, a couple of oli that were written for the school that the kids recall the history and moʻokūʻauhau . . . nobody [is] monkeying around, everybody [is] focused." Thus, these elements, when taken in their totality, can heighten the awareness of place and its spatial composition.

"ʻĀina Does Not Discriminate"

One of the most profound lessons about how ʻāina teaches came from Dr. Kahakalau:

> The ʻāina does not discriminate. There is no discrimination at all if you interact with the land. That stream, if you go in there and it's too fast, everybody, whether you're smart, skinny, whether you're beautiful, it doesn't matter, ʻāina, it's you

know, either the stream is too fast and everybody is gonna eat it, you fall down . . .

In reflecting on the concept of aloha ʻāina, Dr. Kahakalau observed how students receive positive feedback through reciprocal interaction that couples the Hawaiian value of aloha with ʻāina. Common thinking is that aloha ʻāina means "let's love the land," which is not a wrong idea. However, the value of aloha ʻāina is inclusive and reciprocal. Kahakalau explained, "The more important value is the aloha ʻāina coming this way [motioning toward herself] than going that way [motioning away from herself]."[4] In this way, for "those students who need aloha, the land can give it unconditionally." She explained that for many youth, the organic structure and order of ʻāina can offer clarity, purpose, and meaning to their personal lives in ways they may not receive from their family or community. Students can get positive feedback by working the land and seeing the results of their work based on simple environmental processes. Students have the opportunity to experience reciprocity through their hands-on work with the ʻāina, ma ka hana ka ʻike—indeed, through working one learns.

ʻĀina Teaches as a Living Medium

ʻĀina is a critical pedagogical element for Hawaiian-focused charter schools because they recognize how it teaches as a living medium. It has an immersive quality, as one kumu observed: "I can actually touch things, smell them, eat them, that's teaching right there." She continued,

> It's a living laboratory right here. You can walk right outside. It's okay, we're gonna go look at the noni right now, you know what I mean? We're

gonna smell the laua'e and pick some right now and make ho'okupu, and we're going to go pick our 'auamo.

Another kumu explained how 'āina, as an authentic medium, can serve learning in ways that can be more apparent when making connections between abstract ideas and practical application. "When students are out taking care of a stream, or opening 'auwai, learning about water quality, *cooperation* becomes important, *aloha* becomes important, *mālama* becomes important, so 'āina is to me the most authentic medium" [emphasis added]. Under these conditions, mundane tasks can take on heightened importance because abstract ideas or values (e.g., mālama) become apparent in a stream that students are clearing or measuring for water quality. In a similar example, this kumu noted that by applying the concept of kaona to a mundane task such as weeding, "we can teach ourselves how to be better people, how to interact with one another." Therefore, authentic teaching and learning of abstract ideas and values can occur "best when you're on the 'āina," compared with being "in a classroom [where] you kind of have to be intentional about teaching something like that."

'Āina Teaches as a Medium of Service

Building close relationships with their communities is a prominent kuleana held by all four schools involved in this inquiry. First, it is important for students to establish a relationship with 'āina. This is significant because a relationship-based education teaches students "how to work together, [and] the 'āina definitely does do that." Furthermore, that relationship extends beyond their own schools. These schools stated clearly that they held a kuleana to be active and of service in their communities. All the schools included in this inquiry offered kōkua to their surrounding communities or to a specific community of cultural practitioners. One school, for example, utilized its curriculum to cultivate aloha for its moku, which in turn nurtured the desire to care for the moku. One school administrator explained that the school relies on its kumu to establish and maintain close community relationships over time. This approach, beyond showing commitment to community and place, offers consistency with school projects from one year to the next. The principal explained that the relationships are for the long term: "So it's not that we going and Uncle needs help, and we help him" and then it's "okay Uncle, the school year pau, a hui hou, and we never see them again." Under this approach, the students may change as they advance through their grade levels, but the projects remain, the teachers remain, and "the relationship stays there, we kōkua."

Another outcome of being of service is that schools can support and fulfill a community's respective vision of place. By working side by side with community members, students begin to learn how to care for that area's 'āina and its resources. A former principal gave this example:

> With our curriculum, the idea is that you cannot foster that love and desire to take care of a place unless you've been there and worked it. The first and second grade learn about the Puna district; the mele, the stories of the Puna area. Our kumu is working with a practitioner in Puna so we can help clear mangrove from the loko to make it sustainable again. It's one of the few loko i'a that we have here. So, our haumāna learn about the moku, you work with the people in that moku and kōkua.

197

The key is to get involved and become engaged with the community. This way, students come to "know [the] community of practitioners" and, in the process, learn a practice and care for places so that they can eventually assume a greater sense of responsibility.

The Contribution of ʻĀina Education toward Indigenous Planning

> By taking home kalo to mālama, students make the ancestral connections they have with their older sibling Hāloa. They start to view their yard as ʻāina as opposed to simply a yard. There is a difference between the idea of yard versus ʻāina, what ʻāina can be now, how we treat it, and how we could be treating it. (Kumu, Oʻahu Island)

This article has traced systems of land use and Hawaiian-focused education to understand spatial power. I have highlighted the impact of ʻāina-based education by questioning how ʻāina teaches. The connections between genealogy, relationship, and responsibility are just a few of the recurring themes among our schools. More importantly, the contribution of ʻāina-based education toward Indigenous planning acknowledges our ʻŌiwi relationship to place and recognizes that the genealogy of ʻāina itself serves in the production of knowledge and deploys methods based on the utility of that knowledge.

Samadhi (2001) states that tradition and culture create links between principles and patterns that are expressed through organic or built form. Borrowing from this idea, Hawaiian placemaking means that our material culture and beliefs are important to our cultural place-based identity because of their form-giving elements. Hawaiian placemaking, as an organizing principle, is based on Kanaka Maoli epistemic foundations. The significance of place and its use in this respect are in part derived from the long-term occupation and spatial development by our ancestors over time.

The real challenge for Indigenous planning is relating these and other questions to urban development scales. Consider that today, 55 percent of the world's population lives in urban areas, and that figure is expected to increase to 68 percent by 2050 (United Nations Economic and Social Affairs, 2018). How can we source our own knowledge to construct urban policies that directly relate people to a living and dynamic landscape through policy design? Matunga (2013) suggests that as a tradition, Indigenous planning must position its own history to "better understand its contemporary shape with its own form and focus and as a planning approach with its own sets of methodologies" (p. 6). From his Maori homeland, Edwards (2013) offers us the concept of "ancestor lensing" (p. 20) as a framework that grounds and reframes questioning and analysis from the Maori worldview. Thus, the concept of kupuna lensing is important to widening planning's methodological approach. One kumu hints at this technique:

> I want to know the wind and rain names, and I want to know what aliʻi ruled, had rulership, or how it changed hands and what the people did. What was their economic basis . . . like Kualoa, was this a place of the aliʻi? That kind of [information] dictates how we treat it.

With an eye toward urban development, an approach to Indigenous planning in Hawaiʻi must: (a) re-establish the processes of relationship building, (b) utilize Oceanic models to inform planning and design solutions; and (c) reposition planning training to access Hawaiian language materials to link older sources to contemporary spatial solutions. Drawing from this inquiry then, the emphasis that schools place on tradition and culture creates spatial principles that currently struggle to emerge as patterns that can successfully link 'ike kupuna to 'āina. Each time haumāna kōkua communities or families to restore lo'i kalo or to reconstruct loko i'a, they are reinforcing Hawaiian spatial patterns that our kūpuna left for us to learn from. In this way we are unconsciously influenced by our kūpuna. Those principles and patterns create relational bonds between student and 'āina, student and 'ike kupuna, and student and community. Students working in specific localized places alongside knowledgeable Hawaiian practitioners or 'ohana, use 'āina and its bounty to transfer and reinforce community-based principles through ancestral land use patterns. 'Āina, in this respect, provides a longer sense of time; thus there is the opportunity to develop policies based on land uses that rely on long-term relationships rather than short-term profit. The more clearly we see ourselves and our ancestors in the built and natural environment, the more successful those principles and patterns are.

REFERENCES

Andrews, L. (2003). *A dictionary of the Hawaiian language.* Facsimile of the first edition, with an introduction by N. K. Silva & A. J. Schutz. Honolulu, HI: Island Heritage Publishing. (original work published 1865)

Beamer, K. (2014). *No mākou ka mana: Liberating the nation.* Honolulu, HI: Kamehameha Publishing.

Brown, L., & Strega, S. (2005). Introduction: Transgressive possibilities. In L. Brown & S. Strega (Eds.), *Research as resistance: Critical, Indigenous and anti-oppressive approaches* (pp. 1–18). Toronto, Canada: Canadian Scholars' Press/Women's Press.

Cooper, G., & Daws, G. (1990). *Land and power in Hawai'i: The democratic years.* Honolulu, HI: University of Hawai'i Press.

Downes, C. D. (1986). *Islands in transition: A quarter-century of planning and economic development in the state of Hawai'i, 1960–1985.* Honolulu, HI: Department of Planning and Economic Development. Retrieved from https://planning.hawaii.gov/wp-content/uploads/2014/03/1986-Report.pdf

Edwards, S., & Hunia, R. (2013). *Dialogues of mātauranga Māori: Re-membering.* Te Awamutu: Te Wānanga o Aotearoa.

Gruenewald, D. A. (2003). The best of both worlds: A critical pedagogy of place. *Educational Researcher, 32*(4), 3–12. Retrieved from http://edr.sagepub.com/content/32/4/3.abstract

Hawaiʻi Department of Education. (2017). *Official enrollment counts.* Honolulu. Retrieved from http://www.hawaiipublicschools.org/VisionForSuccess/SchoolDataAndReports/SchoolReports/Pages/home.aspx

Jacobs, J. M. (1996). *Edge of empire: Postcolonialism and the city.* London, England: Routledge.

Kahakalau, K. H. (2003). *Kanu o ka ʻāina—Natives of the land from generations back: A pedagogy of Hawaiian liberation* (Doctoral dissertation). Union Institute & University, Cincinnati, OH. Retrieved from ProQuest Dissertations Publishing, 2003. 3081054.

Kanaʻiaupuni, S. M., Ledward, B., & Malone, N. (2017). Mohala i ka wai: Cultural advantage as a framework for Indigenous culture-based education and student outcomes. *American Educational Research Journal, 54*(1S), 311S–339S. http://doi.org/10.3102/0002831216664779

Kelly, M. (1982). Some thoughts on education in traditional Hawaiian society. In College of Education, University of Hawaiʻi at Mānoa, & the Bernice Pauahi Bishop Museum, *To teach the children: Historical aspects of education in Hawaiʻi* (pp. 4–13). Honolulu, HI: Author.

Kovach, M. (2005). Emerging from the margins: Indigenous methodologies. In L. Brown & S. Strega (Eds.), *Research as resistance: Critical, Indigenous and anti-oppressive approaches* (pp. 19–36). Toronto, Canada: Canadian Scholars' Press/Women's Press.

Lucas, P. F. N. (2000). E ola mau kākou i ka ʻōlelo makuahine: Hawaiian language policy and the courts. *Hawaiian Journal of History, 34*, 1–28. Retrieved from https://evols.library.manoa.hawaii.edu/bitstream/10524/431/JL34007.pdf

Matunga, H. (2013). Theorizing indigenous planning. In R. Walker, T. Jojola, & D. Natcher (Eds.), *Reclaiming indigenous planning* (pp. 3–32). Montreal, Canada: McGill-Queen's University Press.

McGregor-Alegado, D. (1980). Hawaiians organizing in the 1970s. *Amerasia Journal,* 7(2), 29–55.

McGregor, D. P. (2007). Kahoʻolawe: Rebirth of the sacred. In *Nā kuaʻāina: Living Hawaiian culture* (pp. 249–285). Honolulu, HI: University of Hawaiʻi Press.

McGregor, D. P. (2010). Statehood: Catalyst of the twentieth-century Kanaka ʻŌiwi cultural renaissance and sovereignty movement. *Journal of Asian American Studies, 13*(3), 311–326.

Office of Hawaiian Affairs. (2017). *A Native Hawaiian focus on the Hawaiʻi public school system, SY 2015. Hoʻonaʻauao (Education) Fact Sheet, No. 1*. Honolulu, HI: Author.

Office of Planning, State of Hawaiʻi. (2015). *State land use system review: Draft report*. Honolulu, HI: Author. Retrieved from https://planning.hawaii.gov/wp-content/uploads/2015/05/SLU-Review-Report_FINAL-DRAFTv2_05-05-2015_POSTED_TO_WEB.pdf

Porter, L. (2010). Managing the sacred. In *Unlearning the colonial cultures of planning* (pp. 107–124). Farnham, England: Ashgate Publishing.

Pukui, M. K., & Elbert, S. H. (1986). *Hawaiian dictionary*. Honolulu, HI: University of Hawaiʻi Press.

Samadhi, T. N. (2001). The urban design of a Balinese town: Placemaking issues in the Balinese urban setting. *Habitat International, 25*(4), 559–575.

Sandercock, L. (2004). Commentary: Indigenous planning and the burden of colonialism. *Planning Theory & Practice, 5*(1), 118–124.

Smith, L. T. (1999). *Decolonizing methodologies: Research and indigenous peoples*. London, England: Zed Books.

Territorial Planning Board, Territory of Hawaiʻi. (1939). *First progress report: An historic inventory of the physical, social and economic and industrial resources of the Territory of Hawaii*. Microfilm Collection. University of Hawaiʻi. Hamilton Library. V11951.

Trask, H. (1987). The birth of the modern Hawaiian movement: Kalama Valley, Oʻahu. *Hawaiian Journal of History, 21*, 126–153. Retrieved from https://evols.library.manoa.hawaii.edu/bitstream/10524/144/2/JL21142.pdf

United Nations Economic and Social Affairs. (2018). 68% of the world population projected to live in urban areas by 2050. Retrieved from https//www.un.org/development/desa/en/news/population/2018-revision-of-world-urbanization-prospects.html

GLOSSARY

ahu – heap of stones

ahupua'a – land division, often running from mountain to sea

'ai – to eat, enjoy, an eating; the means of eating, the fruits of the land; that which feeds

'āina – that which feeds, land

aloha 'āina – love of the land or of one's country, patriotism

ali'i – chief

aloha – love, affection

'auamo – pole or stick used for carrying burdens across the shoulders

'auwai – ditch

ho'āla – to awaken, rise up

hula – form of dance accompanied by chant (oli) or song

i'a – fish or any marine animal

'ike – to see, know, perceive

'ike kupuna – ancestral knowledge

'ili – sections of the ahupua'a selected for individuals in return for produce and labor. Tribute from 'ili 'āina was received by the konohiki for the chief of the ahupua'a. Tribute from 'ili kūpono was given to the paramount chief of the island.

kahuna – general name of persons having a trade, an art, or who practice some profession

kalo – taro (Colocasia esculenta)

kanaka – man, person; Hawaiian (distinct from foreigner)

Kanaka Maoli – Native Hawaiian

Kanaka 'Ōiwi – Native people of the land

kaona – hidden meaning, as in Hawaiian poetry; concealed reference

kauhale – small cluster of houses (formerly comprising a Hawaiian home)

konohiki – chief who managed an ahupua'a

kōkua – help, aid, assistance

kuleana – responsibility, right; small parcel of land awarded to commoners during Māhele

kumu – teacher

kupuna – grandparent, ancestor

loʻi – irrigated terrace

loʻi kalo – irrigated fields of taro (Colocasia esculenta)

loko – pond

loko iʻa – fishpond

makaʻāinana – commoner, populace, people in general; citizen, subject

ma ka hana ka ʻike – wise saying meaning, by doing one learns

makahiki – year, age

mālama – to take care of, tend, attend, care for, preserve, protect, beware, save, maintain

moku – district

mokupuni – island

moʻo – succession, series

moʻo āina – narrow strip of land, smaller than an ʻili

moʻokūʻauhau – genealogy, genealogical accounts

moʻolelo – history, story, tradition, myth; discourse

noni – Indian mulberry (Morinda citrifolia)

ʻohā – taro corm growing from the older root; fig., offspring, youngsters

ʻohana – family, relative, kin, related; root word: ʻohā

ʻŌiwi – Native son; iwi: bones

ʻōlelo makuahine – mother tongue, Hawaiian language

oli – chant

piko – navel, navel string, umbilical cord

puaʻa – pig

pū – large triton conch or helmet shell (Charonia tritonis) as used for trumpets

wahi pana – wahi: place; pana: celebrated or legendary place

wehe – to open

ABOUT THE AUTHOR

Konia Freitas was born and raised in Hawai'i on the island of O'ahu. She is an associate specialist and currently serves as the department chair of Kamakakūokalani Center for Hawaiian Studies at the University of Hawai'i at Mānoa. Her academic interests include Indigenous planning, Hawaiian-focused education, and Indigenous research methodology. She has professional land use planning experience and holds a PhD in urban and regional planning. Her doctoral research examined the link between education and land among Hawaiian-focused public charter schools.

NOTES

1. 'Āina is usually translated to mean land. However, it is used here to mean 'ai, to eat, enjoy; an eating; the means of eating, that is, the fruits of the land (Andrews, 1865; Pukui & Elbert, 1986). It is important to examine 'āina-based education from the origin of the word itself to explore the pedagogical opportunity that this approach offers

2. The term spatial power is used here to mean the dominant economistic ordering of space and place.

3. Distinguishes the period of time when only Kānaka 'Ōiwi inhabited the islands.

4. Hawaiian language contains directional particles such as mai, aku, iho, and a'e. Mai directs the action toward the speaker, as in hele mai (to come toward the speaker), whereas aku directs the action away from the speaker, as in hele aku (to go away from the speaker).

Anarchist Charges and the Politics of Hawaiian Indigeneity and Sovereignty

J. KĒHAULANI KAUANUI

In 2009, I delivered a talk at the Kamakakūokalani Center for Hawaiian Studies for an event critically reflecting on the fiftieth year of statehood for Hawaiʻi. My talk focused on the distinctions between de-occupation, decolonization, and indigenous self-determination. I challenged the notion that occupation and colonialism are mutually exclusive, as is often asserted by Hawaiian Kingdom nationalists. And, in turn, I proposed that we take up the analytic of settler colonialism, while also drawing on normative frameworks of international law as a tactic to challenge US Empire, and stressed the spiritual and material importance of decolonial resistance. I noted my affiliation with the nationalist movement, dating back to 1990, as a diasporic Hawaiian woman.

CORRESPONDENCE MAY BE SENT TO:
J. Kēhaulani Kauanui
Wesleyan University 255 High Street
Middletown, Connecticut 06469
Email: jkauanui@wesleyan.edu

207

Hūlili: Multidisciplinary Research on Hawaiian Well-Being, Vol. 11, No. 1

A video of my talk made its way to YouTube, and in the comments section, David Carr posted critical comments focused on nationalism and anarchism.[1] From what I know about Carr, he is an educator as well as the curator of the Hawai'i 70s–80s Punk Museum online.[2] Here is an excerpt of his feedback:

> Post-modernists pass for radical these days. Indigeneity, tracing a geneology [sic] to precontact peoples is a racial claim to sovereignty. That's old fashioned 19th century politics. Thanks Heidegger and Foucault for helping to orchestrate this retreat from class. Academia is giving birth to these neo-anarchist bourgeois geniuses who never ever mention class, just as JKK did not for this entire speech. JKK represents the far right conservative wing of fake anarchism for our time. Sorry JKK, but anarchists don't promote ethnic nationalism, and no amount of confused pretzel logic can dress up your ideology as anti-nationalist. Why not just come clean and admit you are a liberal academic with a taste for postmodernism because it allows you to imagine yourself as a radical without having to actually engage in class war against capital?

Although I never identified myself as an anarchist in the talk, nor did my work on anarchism come up on the panel, I nonetheless want to respond to the charges Carr levied online since they offer an opportunity to distinguish the diversity of anarchist practices, clarify common misunderstandings about Hawaiian nationalism often held by non-Kanaka, and offer some initial thoughts on bringing together an indigenous sovereignty politic in relation to anarchist philosophy and activism.

Several comrades and colleagues who have read Carr's comments asked why I would even take time to respond to them. However, when one distills Carr's critique, he raises a set of questions that I have been asked by political radicals I respect, who have asked me in private how I reconcile my Hawaiian nationalist commitments with an anarchist political orientation. Moreover, Carr unfortunately is not an outlier among radical leftists as he represents a revolutionary class-struggle anarchist position.

Here I aim to grapple with anarchist political frameworks vis-à-vis assertions of Hawaiian indigeneity and sovereignty. Bringing together an indigenous sovereignty politic in relation to anarchist philosophy and praxis can be challenging in light of a statist kingdom nationalist movement on the one hand, and a US state-driven containment of Hawaiian claims within federal policy on Indian tribes on the other. This fraught terrain begs for a decolonial anarchist approach that challenges settler colonialism while also engaging international law as a tactic to challenge US occupation. By turning to the non-statist/non-Western form of indigenous Hawaiian "sovereignty," known as ea, for guiding cultural principles toward ethical relationships, I argue that anarchism need not be at odds with lāhui (Hawaiian peoplehood, often glossed as nation). Thus, this short essay is my initial attempt to examine ways the two may come together. Hence, in tending to Carr's "anarchist charges" against me (his accusations), I offer my own understanding of "anarchist charges" (responsibilities) in the context of Hawai'i.

I should first note the irony that Carr would hurl the label of "postmodern" as an insult at any indigenous-identified person, given the colonial imposition of modernity premised on the notion of "progress" from that which has been deemed primitive and savage. Postmodernism involves a reappraisal of modern assumptions about culture, identity, history, and language. As myriad scholars and activists have documented, coloniality manifested throughout the world and determined the socioeconomic, racial, and epistemological value systems of "modern" society. This is precisely why coloniality does not just disappear with political and historical decolonization (when the period of territorial domination of lands ends and countries gain independence); it is part of the logic of Western civilization (Wynter, 1995; Mignolo, 2011). Relatedly, Carr's understanding of the Hawaiian sovereignty claim as a form of "ethnic nationalism" is not uncommon, yet it is a misnomer. For one, citizenship within the Hawaiian kingdom was not limited to Kanaka Maoli. Moreover, ethnicity, race, and indigeneity are not the same as each other. Even in the case of those not advocating for Hawaiian independence, such as the many in support of a federally recognized Native-specific governing entity, they cannot be fairly understood to be "ethnic nationalists," since they are working within a US-Native trust model that is a policy for those who are indigenous and suffered the blow of US colonialism.

Also note how Carr claims that assertions of indigeneity—by way of the tracing of one's genealogy to precontact peoples—are a racial claim to sovereignty. Yet, as I documented extensively in my book, *Hawaiian Blood*, genealogy and race are not one and the same. The 50 percent blood quantum rule that Kanaka Maoli are subject to equates Hawaiian cultural identity with a quantifiable amount of blood. This classificatory technology of the state emerged as a way to undermine Hawaiian sovereignty and reduce Kanaka Maoli to a racial minority, reinforcing a system of white racial privilege bound to property ownership. This correlation of

ancestry and race imposed by the US government on Kanaka Maoli has had far-reaching legal and cultural effects. In any case, indigeneity and race are divergent from each other, and also from ethnicity and nationality. While all are arguably socially constructed, these categories of social difference are all distinct.

It is not uncommon for anarchists who maintain (out) dated doctrinaire notions to dismiss assertions of indigeneity as a problematic form of identity politics and/or retrograde ethnic nationalism. Those attached to enduring constructions of what is known as early "big-A Anarchism" tend to assert the primacy of class struggle and workers' movements. In contrast, many contemporary "small-a" anarchists have been compelled to grapple with the realities of anarchist practices increasingly deployed by on-the-ground struggles—such as Idle No More, Black Lives Matter, and the resistance to the Dakota Access Pipeline. These anarchist engagements have entailed a reckoning with the evolving intersectionality of classic anarchist preoccupations with capitalism and the state. This is not to create a binary of the "old" big-A Anarchism with a "new" small-a anarchism, since intersectional thinking has a long history tracing back to the late nineteenth and early twentieth century, especially (but not exclusively) with regard to gender and sexual oppression.[3] But anarchism from the mid-twentieth century to the contemporary period has taken up more expansive cultural questions that are often rejected by those who are wedded to singularly class-based politics, elevating class to foundational status.

In his book, *Unruly Equality: U.S. Anarchism in the Twentieth Century*, Andrew Cornell (2016) offers the first comprehensive intellectual and social history of American anarchist thought and activism across the twentieth century. He challenges the prevailing historiography that suggests anarchism disappeared after the Red Scare following the Bolshevik Russian Revolution of 1917. Alternately, Cornell argues that far from fading away, anarchists dealt with major events such as the rise of Communism, the New Deal, atomic warfare, the black freedom struggle, and a succession of artistic avant-gardes stretching from 1915 to 1975 (p. 26). Cornell notes that classical anarchism reached its highest point of influence in the decade before World War I and ended with its lowest point of influence at the onset of World War II. The foundation for the contemporary anarchist movement began in the 1940s with the formulation of radical pacifism during World War II. Although Cornell identified three major strategic tendencies within classical anarchism—insurrectionary, syndicalist, and bohemian—anarchists did not form unified political parties with concrete policy platforms, and instead belonged to a series of informally connected anarchist labor unions, literary groups, newspapers, and other organizations loosely grouping anarchists by cultural background, language, and strategic preference, but generally subscribing to the same "anarchist praxis." His central argument addresses the shift in the focus of American anarchism from "classical anarchism," which was focused around the organization of workers, to one of social anarchy, which foregrounded political activism around ecology, feminism, and opposition to cultural alienation—addressing the intersectional hierarchies of class, race, gender, and sexuality in relation to the state (p. 12).

This history is crucial to understanding the divergences within the anarchist tradition that have shaped debates as to what constitutes anarchism today.[4] Carr represents a class-struggle anarchist position. His tirade reveals resentment of how the late nineteenth and early twentieth century anarchist movement expanded from the narrow, traditional focus on class struggle to a broader, more diverse organizing against all forms of social domination and hierarchy. Notably, during the shift documented by Cornell, the global movement of decolonization in the 1950s and 60s challenged American anarchists as to how they might take anticolonial stances without aiding and abetting in a similar power structure taking the place of any overthrown state system. As Colin Ward (2004, p. 33) notes, anarchists often hold hostility toward territorial politics.

But today, even social anarchists, like the editorial collective[5] of "An Anarchist FAQ" (2009), assert a categorical rejection of nationalism. They address two directly related queries: "Are anarchists against nationalism?" and "Are anarchists opposed to national liberation struggles?" In response to the first, they answer, "Yes, anarchists are opposed to nationalism in all its forms." To defend this position, they first define what they think anarchists mean by nationalism and the importance of distinguishing between **nationality** (which they define as "cultural affinity") and **nationalism** (which they assert is "confined to the state and government itself"). They continue, "nationalism, at root, is destructive and reactionary, whereas cultural difference and affinity is a source of community, social diversity and vitality."[6] They go on to assert that nationalism "creates the theoretical justification for authoritarianism. . . . In addition, nationalism hides class differences within the 'nation' by arguing that all people must unite around their supposedly common interests (as members of the same 'nation'), when in fact that have nothing in common due to the existence of hierarchies and classes." Here we see their assumption that "nation" is linked to "state."

I have encountered anarchists who have strong reactions against any forms of nationalism because they see it as inextricably tied to aspirations for state power and always already linked to separatism, patriotism, xenophobia, or ethnic chauvinism—rather than autonomy. With regard to the quest to form a new state as an end goal to national liberation, this has never been a supposition indigenous peoples could make, especially given the fact that today's international law, which purports to be secular, still affirms the sovereignty of states over peoples. Here, "peoples" is a distinct concept that is often synonymous to "nations" as a way to describe collective polities of those related by kinship.

In his work on "postcolonial anarchism," Roger White, a member of Anarchist People of Color, has written of anarchists' hostility to nationalism. He explains:

> The rejection of nationalism by many North American anarchists is often an expression of a colonial mindset that requires all of the peoples of the world fighting for liberation to define their social selves in relation to the class war. In this war there are two classes—the workers and the ruling class.... Other anarchists who don't subscribe to industrial age class war dogma simply would like to see anarchists cut their ties to the left completely. This severance would presumably free them of all of the political baggage that solidarity with revolutionary nationalists and indigenous autonomist struggles attract. The two above interpretations of the international role and responsibility of the anarchist movement with respect to the fight against neo-colonialism and imperialism are not the ideas of an anti-state fringe. They represent the two strongest tendencies in the North American scene. (White, n.d., p. 3)

Here White's snapshot of the tensions inherent in anarchist apprehension of indigenous struggles gets at the polarization in Carr's dismissal of my political position on Hawaiian sovereignty as a bourgeois ethnic nationalist movement that he assumes neglects class struggle.

In the Hawaiian context, the formation of the Kingdom as a state must entail an acknowledgment of the role of Western imperialism. Kamehameha established the monarchy in 1810, after forging a battle to unify the islands starting in 1795. This was arguably a response to nearly two decades of foreign encroachment. These decisions were already taking place within a field of imperialism, and this increasing pressure on Hawai'i likely played a large role, as efforts to create legal sources for Hawaiian authority intensified. By 1843, the Kingdom gained international recognition when Britain, France, and the United States acknowledged its sovereignty. But that is only part of the story.

In the 2009 film, *Hawai'i: A Voice for Sovereignty*, Kanaka scholar and activist Kaleikoa Kaeo commented on the Kingdom's motto—*Ua mau ke ea o ka 'āina i ka pono*—the life of the land is perpetuated in justice. Kaeo explains that for Hawaiians, sovereignty does not come from kings, constitutions, or guns: instead, "sovereignty comes from the land.... the land itself is our sovereignty." The motto of the kingdom was declared by Kamehameha III at an 1843 ceremony after the Paulet Affair, whereby English Admiral Richard Darton Thomas ended a short-lived British occupation—through a diplomatic resolution—and affirmed the United Kingdom's recognition of Hawaiian sovereignty.[7] But, although the monarch promulgated the motto, we can see how it has the potential to undermine notions of Western state power with a nonproprietary relationship to the land as the foundation. The motto includes the word ea—the

211

power and life force of interconnectedness between deities, ancestral forces, humans, and all elements of the natural world (Goodyear-Kaʻōpua, 2013). Ea contrasts with the Westphalian system of states and so articulates sovereignty according to a land-based system rather than a state-centered system. Thus, acknowledgment of Hawaiian indigeneity also allows for the more general consideration of non-Western models of sovereignty and how they may inform our politics and social practices.

There are other points of reference that may relate to anarchist sensibilities in terms of the how the common people lived on the land. Reverence for the land (ʻāina, that which feeds) is front and center; the mountains, streams, winds, animals, and trees are not anonymous inanimate objects—they are living entities with names and may be the kinolau (embodied manifestation) of deities, while others are ʻaumākua (ancestral). To be sure, precolonial Hawaiian society was stratified along the lines of genealogical rank, a chiefly hierarchy. But for the question of anarchism and resonances with pre-monarchal Kanaka governing practices, we might look to the ahupuaʻa system. Each island, or mokupuni, was ruled by a mōʻī (paramount chief) and divided into large sections, or moku-o-loko. These moku were further divided into ʻokana or kalana—districts—and each district was comprised of many ahupuaʻa (wedge-shaped sections of land). The mōʻī allocated ahupuaʻa to lesser chiefs who entrusted the land's administration to their local land stewards, the konohiki. In turn, they managed land access for makaʻāinana (the common people) who labored for the chiefs and fulfilled tributary. The ahupuaʻa usually followed natural geographical boundaries, such as ridgelines and rivers, and ran from mountain to sea. Thus, ahupuaʻa included all the materials required for sustenance for members of the society who had shared access. As grassroots Kanaka Maoli activist Andre Perez noted in an interview I conducted with him for the anarchist radio program, Horizontal Power Hour:

> In those valleys were the villages and the people who lived, and they had their own decentralized power over their valleys, their water, their land, their resources, their politics—and collectively they made up the nation. . . . Even with over 120 years of US occupation, colonization, forced assimilation . . . we've never lost the sense of the ahupuaʻa . . . the [concept] is still very much paramount now in local politics, government politics. . . . The ahupuaʻa . . . was a very efficient way to manage the resources in a way that was . . . sustainable (Perez & Kauanui, 2013).

Although the makaʻāinana worked in relationship to the konohiki—who were accountable to the paramount chief of said island—the way in which Kanaka Maoli viewed land offers insight into Hawaiian epistemological frames that are relevant today for indigenous revitalization of the lāhui. One of these tenets is that of aloha ʻāina, reverence for the land, which is core to Hawaiian values and premised on ecological and spiritual balance, as well as responsibility. It is also important to note that the makaʻāinana can and did challenge chiefly authority, and the ties between the common people and the chiefs were premised on cultural ethics of reciprocity.

There are many projects in Hawaiʻi that serve as rich examples of decolonialist undertakings—including traditional voyaging practices, hula, and taro cultivation, to name just a few—ones that are restorative and revamp ways for ethical living for the well-being for the lāhui and others. For some, this mode resembles a form of prefigurative politics "Hawaiian style"—but is perhaps more aptly described as "indigenous resurgence."[8]

With regard to the current nationalist movement in Hawai'i, we must not rely on the US state and its subsidiary, nor wait for the resurrection of the Hawaiian Kingdom. Pursuing ea is critical, given the complex political realities we encounter as Kanaka Maoli in the face of aggressive attacks on our nation and lands. Meanwhile, it is crucial to resist this ongoing theft and all attempts by the fiftieth state and the US federal government to alter our existing political status. In other words, we must

not forfeit our national rights under international law or otherwise surrender. Asserting our national rights is a necessary *tactic* by which to challenge US domination. The concept of lāhui may be a sticking point for many anarchists who bristle over the abidance to any notion of distinct peoplehood. But this is about our survival *as a people*—a decolonial project that does not hinge on the restoration of any state. This is not "confused pretzel logic" as Carr claims; this is about insisting on an indigenous distinction in the face of ongoing settler colonial domination and military occupation. This is about envisioning sustainable sovereign futures.

REFERENCES

Alfred, G. T. (2009, March 23). Resurgence of traditional ways of being. Public lecture at the Heard Museum in Phoenix, presented by the Arizona State University Library Channel Classic Presentation, December 12, 2013. Retrieved from https://www.youtube.com/watch?v=3ABP5QhetYs

Anarchist FAQ Editorial Collective. (2009). An anarchist FAQ. Retrieved from https://theanarchistlibrary.org/library/the-anarchist-faq-editorial-collective-an-anarchist-faq

Cornell, A. (2016). *Unruly equality: U.S. anarchism in the twentieth century.* Oakland, CA: University of California Press.

Ferguson, K. E. (2013). *Emma Goldman: Political thinking in the streets,* Lanham, MD: Rowman & Littlefield Publishers.

Goodyear-Ka'ōpua, N. (2013). *The seeds we planted: Portraits of a Native Hawaiian charter school.* Minneapolis, MN: University of Minnesota Press.

Kaleikoa, K. (2009). In C. Bauknight (Director). *Hawai'i: A voice for sovereignty* [Motion picture]. United States: Vivendi Entertainment.

Kauanui, J. K. (2008). *Hawaiian Blood: Colonialism and the Politics of Sovereignty and Indigeneity.* Durham, NC: Duke University Press.

Mignolo, W. D. (2011). *The darker side of Western modernity: Global futures, decolonial options.* Durham, NC: Duke University Press.

Perez, A. (Interviewee), & J. K. Kauanui (Host). (2013, January 22). Episode 53: Mapuche resistance and Hawaiian self-determination. In The Dream Committee (Producer), *Horizontal power hour.* Middletown, CT: WESU, 88.1 FM. Retrieved from https://archive.org/details/Episode53 MapucheResistanceAndHawaiianSelf-determination_229

Price, W. (2016). In defense of revolutionary class-struggle anarchism. Retrieved from https://www.anarkismo.net/article/29243?userlanguage=de&save_prefs=true

Ward, C. (2004). *Anarchism: A very short introduction.* Oxford, England: Oxford University Press.

White, R. (n.d.). Post colonial anarchism: Essays on race, repression and culture in communities of color 1999–2004. Retrieved from https://theanarchistlibrary.org/library/roger-white-post-colonial-anarchism.pdf

Wynter, S. (1995). 1492: A new world view. In V. L. Hyatt & R. Nettleford (Eds.), *Race, discourse, and the origin of the Americas: A new world view* (pp. 5–57). Washington, DC: Smithsonian Institution Press.

ACKNOWLEDGMENTS

This essay originated as a conference paper titled, "Radical Rapprochement: Anarchism, Indigeneity, and Sovereignty," which was presented on a panel titled, "Hawaiian Anarchist Praxis: Radically Reimagining Resurgence, Decolonization, and Rapprochement," at the 2016 annual meeting of the Native American and Indigenous Studies Association in Honolulu at the University of Hawai'i at Mānoa. I would like to extend my thanks and appreciation to two friends who provided valuable feedback on the work prior to my presenting it at the conference: Rana Barakat and Cynthia Franklin. I also offer mahalo to the two anonymous readers who reviewed this piece for *Hūlili* and offered insightful feedback for me to revise and improve the work.

ABOUT THE AUTHOR

J. Kēhaulani Kauanui is a professor of American studies at Wesleyan University. Her first book is *Hawaiian Blood: Colonialism and the Politics of Sovereignty and Indigeneity* (Duke University Press, 2008), and her second book is *Paradoxes of Hawaiian Sovereignty: Land, Sex, and the Colonial Politics of State Nationalism* (Duke University Press, 2018). She is also the editor of *Speaking of Indigenous Politics: Conversations with Activists, Scholars, and Tribal Leaders* (University of Minnesota Press, 2018). Kauanui currently serves as a coproducer for an anarchist politics show called "Anarchy on Air," a majority-POC show coproduced with a group of Wesleyan students, which builds on her earlier work on another collaborative anarchist program called "Horizontal Power Hour." Kauanui is one of the six original cofounders of the Native American and Indigenous Studies Association (NAISA), established in 2008.

NOTES

1. https://www.youtube.com/watch?v=5kmmjHABfh4. Carr is also known as "Iganzabissassa"; https://www.youtube.com/user/iganzabissassa

2. Carr's moniker is "Comrade Motopu": http://comrademotopu.com/hawaiirelatedtop.htm

3. See, for example, Kathy E. Ferguson, *Emma Goldman: Political thinking in the streets.*

4. For example, in spring 2016 Wayne Price produced an article called, "In defense of revolutionary class-struggle anarchism," where he challenges Laurence Davis's defense of Uri Gordon's and David Graeber's views from his criticisms. In Davis's piece, "Anarchism and the future of revolution," he documents two conflicting trends within the contemporary anarchist movement: the "exodus" mode and the revolutionary "class-struggle" position. The latter is rooted in the anarcho-communist and anarcho-syndicalist class struggle traditions, and "premised on the belief that a vast movement of the oppressed must rise up and smash the capitalist state." The other stream is associated with "a 'revolutionary exodus' strategy focused less (at least initially) on direct confrontation with the state and more on the construction of alternate institutions and social relationships that will ultimately render [the state] and the capitalismarket redundant."

5. Iain McKay, Gary Elkin, Dave Neal, Ed Boraas.

215

6. Emphasis in original. They go on to assert that nationalism "creates the theoretical justification for authoritarianism. . . . In addition, nationalism hides class differences within the 'nation' by arguing that all people must unite around their supposedly common interests (as members of the same 'nation'), when in fact they have nothing in common due to the existence of hierarchies and classes."

7. The saying comes from the result of a conflict that began in February 1843 when Lord George Paulet on HMS *Carysfort* unilaterally established the Provisional Cession of the "Sandwich Islands." On July 26 Admiral Richard Darton Thomas sailed into Honolulu harbor on his flagship HMS *Dublin*. He became Local Representative of the British Commission (the government of the Provisional Cession) by outranking Paulet. His intention was to end the occupation, and on July 31, he handed the islands back to King Kamehameha III who said the words, "*Ua mau ke ea o ka ʻāina i ka pono*" in a speech during a ceremony to mark his restoration.

8. For an understanding of "indigenous resurgence," see Gerald Taiaiake Alfred, "Resurgence of traditional ways of being."

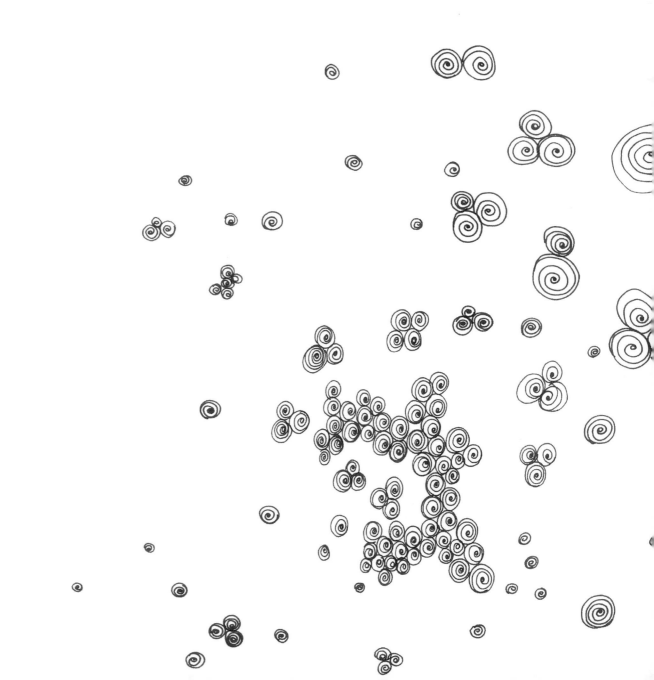

The Story of James Medeiros

CHASE BARNES

Only semisober, I was leaving a nightclub in Waikīkī one night when a haole marine walked up and pushed me. At first I didn't understand why he pushed me, but then he yelled that I was trying to talk to his girlfriend, and that she "doesn't like niggers." At that moment, a person I had befriended just a couple of hours earlier walked up and punched the guy in the face. The guy fell down the stairs and has been in a coma ever since. My new friend's name was James, but everyone called him "Baby James."

Baby James was an average-sized man, but he was much smaller than the people he hung around. Half Hawaiian, half Puerto Rican, and just a little crazy, he carried a distinct scar on the right side of his eye from one the many scraps he had been in. This man was the first person to befriend me here in Hawai'i and to teach me about some of the struggles "real locals" face in the islands.

CORRESPONDENCE MAY BE SENT TO:
Chase Barnes
Email: barnes6@hawaii.edu

Hūlili: Multidisciplinary Research on Hawaiian Well-Being, Vol. 11, No. 1
Copyright © 2019 by Kamehameha Schools

I had moved to Honolulu on August 16, 2012, on separation leave three months before my time in the military was officially over. Moving to Hawaiʻi was highly recommended by my military superiors, as well as other branches of the government, as a safety precaution and as a way to isolate myself from the people I worked with and against during my six years in the military. Although I had visited Oʻahu a couple of times as a child and during deployments, I knew almost nothing about the culture, land, and struggle for independence. All I knew was that it is an extremely expensive place to live, and that there are a lot of beautiful women here.

After finding a place to live in Waikīkī two weeks after moving to Hawaiʻi, I decided to visit a nightclub. The line at Zanzabar was really long, but I kept noticing locals walking to the front, cutting in line, and getting in for free. I walked down the block and saw a group of Polynesian guys making fun of dudes walking by them, sometimes flirting with their girlfriends. Most of the dudes were too scared to say anything back. When I walked past, the Polynesian guys immediately started making black jokes, so I started cracking fat jokes on them, purposely mistaking them for other races, like Puerto Rican, Micronesian, Japanese, etc. One of them told me I had some balls and said I should walk away before I get "falsed." I had no idea what that word meant, so I asked them. They just laughed as they walked to the front of the line of Zanzabar, telling me to follow them. The bouncer, Samson, stopped me at the door, and Baby James told him I was with them. Since I got in for free, I bought them all a shot as a token of my appreciation. I've been with that crew of nightclub bouncers ever since.

I didn't think much of that night. I didn't know that the marine who got punched was in a coma, or that Baby James got arrested. I didn't think much about it. All

I knew was that someone had called me a nigger, and that one of James's friends had told me that I should come to the Playbar the next day because drinks were one dollar. So the next night I got to the Playbar around 2:00 a.m., and everyone was pretty drunk already. One of the guys from the night before laughed and yelled out, "Hey! That's the guy who called me a fat Puerto Rican." He walked up to me and introduced himself, Willy Boy Tamasoa, but he said to just call him "B" or "Brandon," like everyone else does.

B told me James went to jail the night before, after punching the other guy out. All these stories about James and his family came pouring out:

> "You know James works here and at Zanzabar, right?"
>
> "News to me," I said, not really caring much.
>
> "James's dad is one of the original beachboys," Brandon said.
>
> "What's that?" I replied.
>
> Everyone laughed.

Brandon referred to his friends as "sole," "aiga," and other terms I had never heard of. At the end of the night, they recommended that I come out to drink the next night, and I soon realized that they wanted me around only for free drinks.

Two months passed, and by that time, because I was hanging with James, I was getting into all the clubs for free and had his friends buying me drinks. James's guard card had been suspended because of the nightclub incident, so he could no longer work at Playbar, and since I was around so much, they had me replace him as security.

Baby James was still at the club every night, drinking and telling stories as if he were Joe Pesci from Goodfellas. His dad would always come in and get him from the club. Father James was always soft-spoken and polite, asking permission to go inside the club and get his son. Everyone gave him respect, but it was a different kind, as if they were scared of him. I guess father James had been some type of gangster in his heyday, but he just appeared as an old, fragile man to me.

During our drunken nights at the club, Baby James would always tell me, "You know, me and you are the same, and yet so different." I never really knew what he was talking about.

One night outside the club, James's dad collapsed and had to be rushed to the hospital. We didn't see James too much for a while, because he was taking care of his dad. When his father got better, James returned, but he was much quieter, and he was no longer telling stories and trying to talk to girls who wanted nothing to do with him. Our friends and I started with the racist jokes again, and James stood up, yelling at us, telling us we shouldn't criticize or make fun of each other's culture. He said we've been unfairly comparing each other's cultures with the culture of haole, or white culture, which steals from us and turns us against each other. He said making fun of another person's culture because it's different is like self-admission of how superior whites are to your own group. I thought to myself, "What a buzzkill." But James was right.

A Death in the Family

I was sitting in class one day when I got a call from a friend, telling me that Brandon had passed away. I was shocked, and James took it really hard. Brandon was one of James's closest friends, and I could hear the pain in James's voice when he described how Brandon would not wake up when his mother was calling his name. To make matters worse, James was planning to throw a party for Brandon the very next day at our club. Brandon's birthday was a couple of days later, and we were supposed to be celebrating.

No one ever talked about what caused Brandon's sudden death, as most of us didn't want to know and refused to gossip, out of respect. At the same time, James's father had gotten much worse. He was staying in the hospital, and James began selling drugs to make extra money. I don't think he was very good at it, because other Waikīkī drug dealers would complain about him to me but never to him, out of respect for his dad. James said he would sell only to white people, as if that made things better.

> BABY JAMES WOULD ALWAYS TELL ME, "YOU KNOW, ME AND YOU ARE THE SAME, AND YET SO DIFFERENT."

Within a couple of months, his dad died in the hospital, and James slipped into a depression. To cope with his depression, he began using the drugs he was supposed to sell. It took almost no time for him to drop weight and to age in appearance. Cops often mistook him for a homeless person. He came into the club on Labor Day, and we all just watched him. It was a sad sight to see. My boss said, "We have to do something." So we got him into rehab, and they back-paid his rent, and I agreed to pay two months of rent after rehab.

James was forgiven of all his drug debts, and after rehab he came back strong. But there was just one problem: He could not get a job. And without his dad's check coming in, James couldn't afford to pay his rent. Because of this, we were worried that he would go back to selling drugs, then slip into using them again. His sister was trying to convince him to move to Vegas and live with her. When I suggested that he should take up her offer, he looked at me as if I had stabbed him in the back.

He said, "Chase! Brah! I can't do that! Leave my fuckin home?! All these years of you living here, and you don't see that's what they want us to do?! We Hawaiians leave. There's no land for us to claim, you know? Big Sis is selfish, only thinking of herself and not the community, leaving for da ninth island. Dat ain't me, brah! That's the difference between me and you, us over here and y'all over there. We fight for independence; y'all fight for equality, and during that fight for equality, y'all end up anywhere you believe will give you a fair chance at life. You traded one inequality for another. We all poor here, and we'll just keep getting poorer as the cost of rent goes up. But hey, look, there's a pretty beach we can go to, until they say we can't; there's a restaurant we love to eat at, until it's bought out and turned into a shitty four-star that none of us can afford. I'm grateful, but you shouldn't have paid my rent. There is more to life than material things. This land is my home, and I'm not going nowhere."

A New Life

In his proud stubbornness, Baby James ended up moving to Waiʻanae Boat Harbor. I didn't know what that was until I had to do a group presentation for a political science class on homelessness in Hawaiʻi. I learned a lot about the homelessness epidemic here, and when I saw James shooting pool in the back of a bar in Waikīkī, I asked him about life at Waiʻanae Boat Harbor.

He told me there are many families there, and lots of kids. He told me that everyone helps out. "We self-govern, to the point where people can get kicked out of the community. We do not consider ourselves homeless. We don't beg for money, and we don't do drugs." I thought to myself, "Yeah, right." But James did look like he had gained weight. He started showing up more and hanging out with me and the boys, but when we offered him a drink, he would politely refuse. James had quietly quit drinking. He just showed up to see his friends and occasionally talk to girls who wanted nothing to do with him.

It wasn't until my political science class, and a seven-hour plane ride to Osaka, that I realized what Baby James had indirectly taught me about personal struggles, inner demons, family, social status, and the discrimination that Hawaiian people and other people of color face in Hawaiʻi. And for that, I will always be grateful to him.

"You traded one inequality for another."

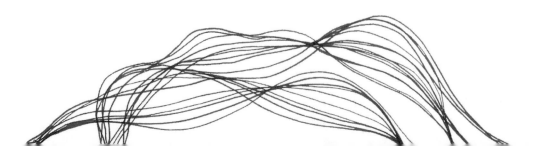

Sovereign Embodiment: Native Hawaiians and Expressions of Diasporic Kuleana

KĒHAULANI VAUGHN

This article highlights the Treaty of Friendship and Mutual Recognition between Ka Lāhui Hawaiʻi and the Juaneño Band of Mission Indians, Acjachemen Nation, ratified in 1992. Engaging in sociopolitical forms of recognition, such as treaty making, which acknowledge other Indigenous people and the traditional tribal territories on which they reside, diasporic Native Hawaiians living in California can also be understood as embodying a praxis of kuleana. Maintaining reciprocal relationships with land and people is an essential quality of being Indigenous. However, as displacement is a specific modality of settler colonialism, around 50 percent of Native Hawaiians now live outside of their homeland, with the largest populations of the displaced residing in California. This work reveals that trans-Indigenous recognitions actively regenerate social and political futures for Indigenous communities and are thus invaluable in combatting settler colonial institutions that continue to displace both California Indians and Native Hawaiians from their own lands and resources.

CORRESPONDENCE MAY BE SENT TO:
Kēhaulani Vaughn
Pacific Island Studies Initiative, University of Utah
201 President's Circle, Park Building Room 204
Salt Lake City, Utah 84112
Email: kehaulani.vaughn@utah.edu

Hūlili: Multidisciplinary Research on Hawaiian Well-Being, Vol. 11, No. 1

In April of 1992, Ka Lāhui Hawai'i and the Juaneño Band of Mission Indians, Acjachemen Nation, entered into treaty negotiations on the campus of the University of California–Irvine. Gathering in the traditional territory of the Acjachemen[1] and the Tongva, Ka Lāhui Hawai'i met with several Native nations to negotiate and sign treaties of mutual recognition. Carolyn Kuali'i, a Native Hawaiian undergraduate student at the University of California–Irvine, organized the event, which included cultural exchanges of song, dance, and gifts (Margolin, 1992). Kuali'i was born and raised in Southern California and is a citizen of Ka Lāhui Hawai'i. She was one of the primary planners of the treaty with the Acjachemen.[2] During this period, Ka Lāhui Hawai'i was engaged in diplomatic relations with many Native nations, domestically and internationally, in an effort to strengthen Native Hawaiian self-governance.[3]

The ratification of the Treaty of Friendship and Mutual Recognition between Ka Lāhui Hawai'i and the Acjachemen is a central consideration of this article. This treaty is an example of a nation-to-nation relationship outside of colonial governance and provides an alternative to federal recognition policies and structures. The treaty not only affirmed self-determination practices for the two Native nations, but also provided an example for Native Hawaiians living in California of a process that affirmed the lāhui at home. Hawaiians living in the diaspora who were involved in the treaty process embodied Native Hawaiian philosophies of kuleana and 'āina, what I call sovereign embodiment. They engaged in kuleana as praxis: acknowledging both the land and their hosts.[4] These understandings include working and assisting with other genealogical caretakers of lands where Hawaiians now reside and possibly will be buried. In doing so, trans-Indigenous recognitions, as exemplified in the treaty analyzed in this paper,

are invaluable both in combating settler colonialism and in actively regenerating social and political futures for Indigenous communities.[5] In the following paper I provide analysis of the treaty between Ka Lāhui Hawai'i and the Acjachemen, and through this example I argue that resistance to settler colonialism is a responsibility for both Kanaka 'Ōiwi in Hawai'i, as well as those in the diaspora.

Currently, close to half of the Native Hawaiian population resides outside of Hawai'i (Office of Hawaiian Affairs, 2013). California is home to the largest population of Native Hawaiians living outside of their homeland (Lepule & Kwoh, 2014). Those who have been displaced are often seen as "no longer Native," due to the centrality of 'āina, or land, to the identity of Native Hawaiians and other Indigenous communities.[6] Much of the scholarship within Hawaiian studies has yet to include populations in the diaspora. This gap within the field reproduces ideas of authenticity that contribute to a logic of Native dismemberment. Although 'āina is of central importance in Hawaiian epistemology, I argue that one's indigeneity and kuleana are embodied off island.

Indigeneity encompasses creation stories and details existences from specific places. It exemplifies genealogical responsibilities to land and resources for the next generations. For Native Hawaiians, these responsibilities represent specific kuleana tied to place and family. Taking these central notions of Indigeneity into consideration, including the Hawaiian concept of kuleana, how might Native/Indigenous people who are diasporic— particularly Native Hawaiians—become more integral in our Native nations while situating their stories within Hawaiian and Native/Indigenous studies?[7] Additionally, how might Native Hawaiians living outside Hawai'i fulfill a specific kuleana that acknowledges their family and responsibilities to the greater lāhui? Furthermore, how are these actions a continuance of Native Hawaiian protocol and epistemologies that center ʻāina and kuleana and further demonstrate a sovereign embodiment? Following the work of Native Hawaiian scholar Noelani Goodyear-Kaʻōpua, which charted the values that frame Hawaiian studies, this article humbly accounts for and integrates the growing Native Hawaiian community that lives within the diaspora into Hawaiian studies and the active call for ea.[8]

One of the central questions within the discipline of Hawaiian studies, and for scholars of Hawaiian studies, is: Who are Kanaka Maoli? As Native Hawaiian scholar Jonathan Kamakawiwoʻole Osorio stated, "ʻO ia ka nīnau maoli (That is the real question). Who the hell are we? If our own activism and scholarship do not continually seek the answers to that question, then it is activism and scholarship for someone else" (as cited in Goodyear-Kaʻōpua, 2016, p. 6). As Osorio points out, defining who we are and expanding our previous notions of ourselves should be central to research inquiries within Hawaiian studies. Furthermore, how do we understand and define the community in light of the dynamic shifts and changes in Hawaiʻi and the diaspora? Defining identity through the logics of authenticity—which often is restricted to Native Hawaiians living *in* Hawaiʻi—produces a diminishing Native community and lāhui. In this way, Native Hawaiians residing in California and elsewhere are often perceived as less culturally authentic. By perpetuating these logics, Native Hawaiians themselves reinforce and legitimize Native erasure, a modality of settler colonialism.

This article seeks methods to expand definitions of Indigeneity that are grounded in self-determination and survivance. This article adds to the growing body of Native/Indigenous scholarship[9] and contributes to the central questions about culture, nation, and identity raised by Osorio, Goodyear-Kaʻōpua, and others. My work expands Native Hawaiian methodologies grounded in ʻāina to encompass Native Hawaiians in the diaspora.

Aho: Theoretical Framework

Goodyear-Kaʻōpua (2016) describes the core values guiding Native Hawaiian methodologies and the principal goals of Hawaiian studies. The four values she defines as aho, or cords, are as follows: (1) lāhui: collective identity and self-definition; (2) ea: sovereignty and leadership; (3) kuleana: positionality and obligations; and (4) pono: harmonious relationships, justice, and healing (p. 2). Grounded in these values and definitions, my research adds to the growing body of research in Hawaiian studies that enriches our definitions of who we have been and who we continue to be. As a Native Hawaiian living in the diaspora, I engage with the aho that Goodyear-Kaʻōpua articulates. Additionally, I ask, how can lived experiences on the ʻāina inform lived experiences and research in the diaspora? Furthermore, how can my research regenerate ways that allow us to be pono, or in balance with the ʻāina while in the diaspora?

As noted by Goodyear-Kaʻōpua, it is important to find practices and protocols that can be productive for the building and maintenance of the lāhui. In this vein, she draws from her own lineages while engaging with other ʻŌiwi scholarship, and more broadly with other intellectual lineages and traditions. She calls this practice being "selectively promiscuous" (2016, p. 9). Thus, I also work closely with other Native studies thinkers and scholars who center Indigeneity to inform my research and to engage with Native Hawaiian life in the diaspora *and* the people who now host us.

By highlighting a relationship between Ka Lāhui Hawaiʻi, a group of Native Hawaiians in the diaspora, and a federally unrecognized tribe formalized through a ratified treaty, I illustrate how Native Hawaiian values grounded in ʻāina are still central to those who reside outside of the homeland. Furthermore, it provides a model for those who are diasporic to engage in a recognition of ʻāina and its genealogical caretakers as embodied sovereigns. By being selectively promiscuous, this article demonstrates how a treaty reinforces both a genealogical responsibility to land and to Native nationhood. Moreover, by highlighting tribal voices, this methodology can be understood as a specific kuleana grounded within our own understanding of ʻāina and protocol. Therefore, this work will not focus on the rationale for the treaty between Ka Lāhui Hawaiʻi and the Acjachemen, although it will provide some background. Instead, this work centers Native voices and the contemporary meanings of the treaty for the tribe. By engaging in these relationships, Hawaiians embody an understanding of ʻāina and kuleana, which simultaneously works against the state logics of recognition. These acts of sovereign embodiment honor kupuna, or ancestral knowledge, and serve the greater lāhui.

Like our homeland, there is and always will be a genealogical responsibility to care for and protect the land and resources. In this respect, California is no different than Hawaiʻi, meaning that Kanaka Maoli who live outside of Hawaiʻi should assist the people who have similar responsibilities to land. With a greater influx of Native people being displaced from their homelands due to settler colonialism, understanding who is Native and who is settler is a central question to any particular locale. Although Native Hawaiians are an Indigenous people and have a genealogical connection and responsibility to land, we are Indigenous only to Hawaiʻi. Native Hawaiian scholar Haunani-Kay Trask, in her seminal work, reminds us of the prevalence of Native erasure in Hawaiʻi and in American society overall. She states, "As on the continent, so in our island home. Settlers and their children recast the American tale of nationhood; Hawaiʻi, like the continent, is naturalized as but another telling illustration of the uniqueness of America's 'nation of immigrants'" (Trask, 2000a, p. 2). Therefore, Native Hawaiians living in the diaspora need to actively work against settler colonialism and its logics and structures that displace and marginalize Native people, with particular attention to the Native people of the land where they now reside. Furthermore, positive collaborations between Native nations affirm Native self-governance and work against the assertion of individual rights to land and resources within nation-state structures. For these reasons, we should align our struggles of self-determination and build larger social movements that center understandings and responsibilities to ʻāina as a collective.

Juaneño Band of Mission Indians, Acjachemen Nation

To understand the full significance of the treaty between Ka Lāhui Hawaiʻi and the Acjachemen, a brief history of the Juaneño Band of Mission Indians, Acjachemen Nation, is necessary. The Acjachemen have several creation stories.[10] Like other Indigenous groups, they believe they come directly from the land. Like Native Hawaiian creation stories, Juaneño creation stories dictate an inherent genealogical responsibility to protect and live responsibly with land and resources. However, this way of life was ultimately disrupted and severely affected by the mission system.

While there were foreigners who came to California and traveled along the coast, none of them had a significant impact on the Native people until the founding of the missions. The mission period in California began in 1769 with the establishment of Mission San Diego. Junípero Serra, a Spanish missionary, used Indian slave labor to build the Mission of San Juan Capistrano in 1775, from which the name Juaneño originates.[11] Located in the contemporary urban area of Orange County, the Juaneño have become severely outnumbered in their own land. Although they have consistently resisted Native erasure through the maintenance of culture and the protection of sacred sites, the Juaneño, along with other California Indians, have experienced multiple formations of colonialism. These include specific colonial histories and relationships with Spain, Mexico, and the United States.

Despite the public discourse of missions "civilizing" and being advantageous to the Natives, missions became the first prisons in California and the first institutions where sexual violence and genocide were naturalized as disciplining tactics targeting Native communities (Sepulveda, 2018). Poor food rations, coupled with the large number of people incarcerated at the missions, created high rates of disease, which also caused deaths. The missionaries forced Natives in the missions to adopt Christianity by outlawing Native spiritual traditions that were embedded in relationships with land. Although the mainstream history of the mission period is glorified—evident through the prevalence of mission-style architecture, the fourth-grade public school curriculum in California,[12] and the canonization of Junípero Serra—the mission period had devastating effects for California Indians, including the outlawing of their language and culture, and the death of many (Miranda, 2013).

In 1846, the United States and Mexico went to war, and with the signing of the Treaty of Guadalupe-Hidalgo in 1848, California became a part of the United States. Due to the discovery of gold in northern California that same year, the population of settlers increased dramatically. With the large numbers of settlers arriving during the gold rush, a high percentage of California Indians were hunted and killed by settlers. The first governor of California, Peter Burnett, through the Act of the Government and Protection of Indians, legalized the kidnapping of California Indian children and made them indentured servants to white guardians. This act established a slave trade of California Indians and was followed by policies that legally authorized the state government to pay settlers for the killing of Indians—payments that were later reimbursed by the federal government (Johnston-Dodds, 2002). This made the genocide of California Indians an endorsed policy at the state and federal levels.

Devastated by introduced diseases and genocide, the California Indian population plummeted. Some tried to conceal their identities by adopting Spanish surnames and mixing in with the Spanish and Mexican population that still remained in California (Miranda, 2013). This was a strategy for survival. However, generations later, these survival strategies have become obstacles for the current generation in proving lineal descent to the Native communities from which they originate. Proving ancestry is required by federal governmental agencies, including the Office of Federal Acknowledgment, the agency which manages federal recognition procedures and stipulates proof of ancestry as a requirement for any federal recognition application.

In 1852, the United States signed eighteen treaties with California Indian nations. Unbeknownst to the Native nations who agreed to these treaties, the treaties remained unratified by Congress (Johnston-Dodds, 2002). The purpose of these treaties was to designate land for reservations; but since the treaties were not ratified, most California Indian reservations were not created until the turn of the century. However, a reservation was never created for the Juaneño Band of Mission Indians, Acjachemen Nation, nor for other nearby coastal tribes.[13] Currently, none of the California Indian tribes in Los Angeles or Orange County are federally recognized. While not having a land base, most of the Acjachemen reside in Los Angeles, Riverside, San Diego, and Orange counties (Coffman, 2011). Some tribal members have been able to remain in San Juan Capistrano, which is the tribe's cultural center.[14] Although two bands of the Juaneño have applied to be federally recognized, the federal government has denied them recognition. The rationale for this denial is that the federal government considers the Juaneño to no longer exist as a contemporary Native American tribe (US Department of the Interior, Indian Affairs, 2011). However, the band of Acjachemen that ratified the treaty with Ka Lāhui Hawai'i has never applied for federal recognition.[15] Notwithstanding this designation, the Juaneño Band of Mission Indians, Acjachemen Nation, continues to assert their sovereignty through actions such as sacred site protection and representation within the United Nations Permanent Forum on Indigenous Issues. They also continue to practice cultural and spiritual beliefs and to believe that they have an inherent responsibility to care for and protect their homeland.[16]

Ka Lāhui Hawai'i

Ka Lāhui Hawai'i was formed in 1987 through grassroots efforts as a Native initiative for self-governance (Wong-Wilson, 2005, p. 146). During the period of the treaty signing, Ka Lāhui Hawai'i was one of the largest and strongest Native Hawaiian sovereignty groups in existence. It offered classes and workshops on self-determination, sovereignty, and political education, both domestically and internationally.[17] Amanda Mae Kahealani Pacheco characterizes Ka Lāhui Hawai'i as "arguably one of the most mobilized and public native Hawaiian sovereignty organizations. Some of its key members have also held positions in the Office of Hawaiian Affairs, as well as the Center for Native Hawaiian Studies at the University of Hawai'i" (Pacheco, 2009, p. 353). While there were many Native Hawaiian sovereignty organizations, Pacheco notes that Ka Lāhui Hawai'i had a diverse citizenry that represented different constituencies such as academics, cultural practitioners, and state officials.

A constitution structured Ka Lāhui Hawai'i's government, and the original constitutional convention was held in 1987 (Wong-Wilson, 2005, p. 146). Ka Lāhui's constitution, otherwise known as Ho'okupu A Ka Lāhui Hawai'i, outlines a unicameral structure of governance that was approved through consensus by both its citizens and honorary members.[18] This was created with the intention of providing equal power and representation among people from nonurban and rural areas, and from less-populated islands. It also allowed for islands to engage in island-specific discussions and decision-making. However, Ka Lāhui Hawai'i's governance structure initially included no representation for diasporic Hawaiians.

In my interview with Mililani Trask, I raised the question of diasporic Native Hawaiians and political representation within Ka Lāhui Hawai'i. She said that originally Hawaiians residing off-island did not have specific representation or voting. But then she explained, "By working through nationhood we found the solution and it was a traditional solution" (personal communication, July 2015). The traditional solution was that Native Hawaiians residing off-island would be understood as yet another island named Moku Honu—Turtle Island.[19] She states, "In Ka Lāhui we had all the islands represented and then we had another caucus specifically for those Hawaiians who were involved in the diaspora" (personal communication, July 2015). Although Ka Lāhui Hawai'i eventually incorporated diasporic Native Hawaiians in the nation-building process, this was not done at the onset of the creation of Ka Lāhui Hawai'i.[20]

Ka Lāhui Hawai'i's political work spanned Hawai'i, the continental United States, and the international arena. This included working on Indigenous rights within the United Nations and treaty making among nations, including Native and non-Indigenous nations. Within Ka Lāhui Hawai'i's "Four Political Arenas of Sovereignty," it notes:

> Regardless of whether Nations/States (U.S.) recognize indigenous nations whose lands they have colonized, Native Nations can and must solidify diplomatic relations between themselves and other Nations/States. Indigenous nations face common threats and issues in the international arena. Native nations need to forge unified positions in the global arena for the protection of their lands, territories and human rights. (Government of Ka Lāhui Hawai'i, 1994, p. 12)

The section further asked, "How can we benefit from or help other native nations who are dealing with similar health, housing, education, etc. problems and issues?" (p. 12). Part of the belief was that Native nations could help each other when dealing with similar issues of education, health, and the general welfare of their people.

In its efforts to strengthen diplomatic relations between Native nations, Ka Lāhui Hawai'i thus signed and ratified a significant number of treaties. Describing this achievement, the Master Plan stated, "To date, Ka Lāhui Hawai'i has negotiated and ratified 17 treaties with 85 indigenous nations on the American Continent" (Ka Lāhui Hawai'i Constitution, 1994, p. 11). Therefore, Ka Lāhui Hawai'i, as well as other Native nations, was engaged in treaty making as a continued expression of sovereignty to strengthen Native nations. Articulating the importance of treaty making among Native nations, Trask says:

> We did find it was time to use our opportunities to begin to make treaties with other Indigenous peoples. Also, we noticed there was a strong bias. People wanted to look at treaties between Hawai'i and the United States and Hawai'i and Japan, but just as important or perhaps more important were modern treaties that were made with non-colonizers. So, this is the reason why we did what we did. It was part of a broader effort and not only Hawai'i, but in New Zealand and the Pacific. So that was why we did this. It was really to strengthen their [Native] nation and Ka Lāhui Hawai'i. And it was done in the anticipation that we have to work collectively on critical issues towards Indigenous peoples in a globalized world. (personal communication, July 2015)

233

Hence, Ka Lāhui Hawai'i's political agenda included the building of a network of Native nations that was expressed in treaty making. The Treaty of Friendship and Mutual Recognition between the Juaneño Band of Mission Indians, Acjachemen Nation and Ka Lāhui Hawai'i is just one of the many treaties Ka Lāhui Hawai'i ratified during this period.

As the Kingdom of Hawai'i was recognized through international treaties in the 1800s, it can be asserted that Ka Lāhui Hawai'i is a government that is in continuance of practices of Native nationhood. Ka Lāhui Hawai'i proclaimed that treaties ratified between the Hawaiian government and its signatories occurring prior to the illegal takeover by the United States in 1893 would be recognized and honored (Ka Lāhui Hawai'i Constitution, 1994, p. 11). Haunani-Kay Trask described the self-determining practices of Ka Lāhui Hawai'i as "an alternative polity that was in opposition to federal and state entities" (Trask, 2000b, p. 382). Therefore, Ka Lāhui Hawai'i acted as a sovereign government that operated in continuation of the Kingdom of Hawai'i.

While Ka Lāhui Hawai'i built new diplomatic relations between Native nations, it likewise advocated for federal recognition with the United States. However, federal recognition was not considered the ultimate expression of Hawaiian sovereignty for Ka Lāhui Hawai'i, as evidenced by interviews and treaty making with other nations. Mililani Trask elaborates, "There were limitations under the US system that could never be addressed under US domestic law" (Wong-Wilson, 2005, p. 148). Rather, Ka Lāhui Hawai'i advocated for a nation-to-nation status to "place the Hawaiian land base on the United Nations list of non-self-governing territories, since the land base still lies within the territory of the United States" (Dudley & Agard, 1993, p. 136). Clarifying the intended relationships between Ka Lāhui Hawai'i, the United States, and the United Nations, Mililani Trask says,

> A lot of people looked at Ka Lāhui and said we were selling out, we wanted to be under the US system. This was not quite accurate because what we were saying was that the first priority was not a political relationship with the United States. The first priority was to protect the land, to protect the people; education, health, and cultural preservation. The first priority was to create a Hawaiian nation to facilitate self-determination at home. The political strategy for dealing with the United States was the second priority. Under the United States, indigenous people can achieve only limited rights, but we could obtain land for our people's needs. And, we could at least get a share of our revenues to develop health, education, and culture. Those were Ka Lāhui's priorities for the eight years I served as kia'āina of the nation. (Wong-Wilson, 2005, p. 148)

Trask illustrates that although federal recognition was part of Ka Lāhui Hawai'i's strategic plan, it was not the main goal. Rather, the development of Ka Lāhui Hawai'i was to implement a culturally appropriate government to address Native Hawaiians' ongoing concerns. It can even be argued that Ka Lāhui Hawai'i is also a federally unrecognized Native Hawaiian nation. Overall, Ka Lāhui Hawai'i was committed to honoring the prior commitments and relationships of the Kingdom of Hawai'i while creating new diplomatic relations that epitomized Ka Lāhui Hawai'i as an international actor.

Historic Treaty Signing

News from Native California, a quarterly magazine published by Heyday Books, included an article in summer 1992 that documented the treaty between the Juaneño Band of Mission Indians, Acjachemen Nation and Ka Lāhui Hawaiʻi (Margolin, 1992, p. 33).[21] The article explains that the treaty signing was an important occasion with significance for the Native people of California. Describing the contemporary lives of the Native people of the Los Angeles area,[22] the article notes that "the federal government has never given recognition or acknowledgment as sovereign Indian nations . . . and anthropologists generally ignore the living descendants, having declared the culture all but extinguished" (Margolin, 1992, p. 33). The fallacy of the tribes' extinction further reifies the importance of being recognized as living people within a contemporary tribal nation by another Indigenous people.

Describing the significance of the ratification of the treaty, the article states, "By signing these treaties the native people of southern California went beyond resisting a government that tries to erode tribal rights, and took it upon themselves to expand those rights as befits nations that are independent not only in name but in spirit as well" (Margolin, 1992, p. 33). Margolin recognized that the political significance of the treaty surpassed the limited sovereignty granted by the federal government, which places Indigenous nations into domestic dependent nationhood (Deloria, 1985, p. 114). Instead, the two groups acted as international sovereigns and recognized each other through the ratification of a treaty.

In addition to the gift exchanges, which included song and dance on the University of California–Irvine campus to commemorate the occasion, the two groups, as ocean/water people, gathered at Dana Point beach, where they also shared in ceremony.[23] The article highlights the spiritual significance of the occasion as such:

> As the ceremony on the beach was being held, suddenly and gloriously a humpback whale emerged from the ocean and spouted. This whale, native both to the coast of California and the coast of Hawaiʻi, seemed by its presence to become part of the treaties as well. "All my relations" a voice muttered as the whale paid its regards and slipped back into the sea. (Margolin, 1992, p. 33)

Margolin, along with several people I interviewed, described the gathering on the beach with the appearance of the whale, and the cultural and spiritual confirmation that it provided.[24] This marked the occasion not only as political, but also as spiritual; often times for Native people, the spiritual intersects with the political.

Acjachemen Views of the Treaty

As several Acjachemen I interviewed noted the historic occasion of the treaty signing and its spiritual significance, this article also highlights contemporary views of the treaty, including its alternatives to federal recognition that are theorized and lived within Acjachemen communities. For example, Juaneño tribal member Angela Mooney-D'Arcy describes the treaty as surpassing colonial governments and institutions.[25] She says that the treaty represents

> an ongoing commitment to upholding our traditional relationships with one another and to that extent outside of, and prior to, and will extend after the settler colonial government is gone. It's

an expression of sovereignty. To me it's not relevant if it's with an unrecognized Nation because our engagement with each other is an expression of sovereignty. If we're serious about recognizing sovereignty, then settler colonial recognition or non-recognition should not be relevant. (personal communication, April 2017)

D'Arcy describes the inherent sovereignty that exists within Native nations regardless of federal recognition and maintains that the treaty is a testament to sovereignty that will endure beyond the current settler colonial government structure. Therefore, being federally recognized or having an unrecognized status has no relevance in regard to the inherent sovereignty expressed by the treaty.

Wyatt Belardes has similar views regarding the treaty as an expression of sovereignty.[26] He says:

> We are self-determining who we are and we are not asking the government to be a part of it. So, we are decolonizing [ourselves] because we are basically doing something that the government doesn't want. We are actively showing them this is what we are going to do and don't care if they like it or not. We are the original people of this land and we don't need [the government] to decide who we are. (personal communication, October 2016)

Belardes describes a direct action that exceeds the "asking for permission" entailed in seeking recognition from the federal government. He believes the treaty operates as an expression of sovereignty for both Native nations. In addition, Belardes sees a correlation between the Acjachemen people and Native Hawaiians, as both

communities are fighting to protect the land and its resources, and both are actively working against a government that has dissimilar values. He states:

> There is a whole ocean between us, but we are fighting the same battles and we are fighting to protect Mother Earth. Although we are two worlds apart, we are still going through the same struggles and both fighting, as our ancestors would have too. We are two governments fighting against the government that is supposed to be ruling over us. (personal communication, October 2016)

Belardes believes that relations between the two groups as ocean people existed prior to the treaty and that the treaty is a recent expression of this ongoing relationship.

When I asked another Acjachemen tribal member and Native studies scholar, Charles Sepulveda, what the treaty meant for them, he stated, "The treaty, as an act of resistance, is based on the love of ourselves as survivors that have continued responsibility to place. The treaty is a symbol of enduring sovereignty and the ability of an unrecognized nation to continue as international actors" (personal communication, April 2015). Sepulveda refers to the treaty as an act of resistance that is based on love—a love that is centered in having a continued genealogical responsibility to their place and to their people.

Additionally, Sepulveda believes that the treaty is an example of the continued relationships between distinct Native nations who enter into one another's territory:

> The treaty is an example of what the tribe is doing, or has done, that can allow us to see concrete things that we can do to work with other

people. We can't exist without having a relationship with other people. Having the Hawaiians recognize us as living people is an example of how other communities of color should interact with us. People don't have to be settlers, they can be guests. The Hawaiians acted as guests. Their actions can help provide hope. We can't control what other people do, but this is an example of how Indigenous peoples should enter into each other's lands and territories. (personal communication, April 2015)

Sepulveda describes a kuleana praxis that acknowledges the Native genealogical caretakers of the land where they reside by those who are representing their own Native nations and therefore expressing a sovereign embodiment. He recognizes that his tribe cannot exist without relations with others. He believes that engaging in an Indigenous protocol of acknowledgment can be a model for the way others can conduct themselves outside of their homelands. The degree to which people engage in this protocol distinguishes them as either settlers or as guests. This does not undo the native/settler binary; rather, it adds the layer of guests as determined by the Native group itself.

For the Juaneño, the Treaty of Friendship and Mutual Recognition with Ka Lāhui Hawai'i provides a form of Indigenous recognition, whereas federal recognition has been continuously denied. The treaty and its corresponding relationship also offer the potential of allies and new cooperatives for the maintenance of culture and sacred sites. This is especially significant in southern California, given the revisionist history of the mission period that romanticizes a Spanish past and writes of the Juaneño and other Native communities as extinct.

Weaving Aho

As more people move to southern California, it is vital to center Native life and build relationships among Indigenous communities that directly honor the people of the land. This includes Native Hawaiians living in California and in the broader diaspora. Trans-Indigenous recognitions, as exemplified by treaty making, demonstrate intentions that surpass a sole community's survival and create a larger shared community of Indigenous survivance in California and Hawai'i. Therefore, alongside other Native Hawaiian scholars, I argue that we should not only embody a praxis of kuleana, but also acknowledge the Native Hawaiian values of ea, pono, and lāhui that are central for Hawaiian studies and for a healthy Hawaiian nation—including those in the diaspora.

Elaborating on the Native Hawaiian value of ea, for instance, Goodyear-Kaʻōpua states that ea represents

> a political independence and is often translated as "sovereignty." It also carries the meanings "life," "breath," and "emergence," among other things. A shared characteristic in each of these translations is that ea is an active state of being. Like breathing, ea cannot be achieved or possessed; it requires constant action day after day, generation after generation. (Goodyear-Kaʻōpua, 2016, p. 9)

In other words, Native Hawaiians living in the diaspora are a part of the call to actively work toward ea. This work can begin with an acknowledgment of land and Indigenous hosts, which is a direct part of Native Hawaiian culture and protocol. Native Hawaiian scholar Manulani Aluli-Meyer discusses the significance of protocol for Native Hawaiians and states, "Given the nature of protocol, or the rituals for how one enters the ocean and forest, or even our neighbor's yard, is it any wonder that Hawaiians have something to say about intention?" (Meyer, 2003, p. 53). Indigenous protocols are a direct expression of intention. Protocols are reminders of the way Indigenous people believe they should and want to live in the world. Moreover, diasporic Native Hawaiians need to understand our role and function while outside of the homeland, and this would require recognition of the genealogical caretakers of the land wherever they reside. This recognition is a direct expression of ea. Grounding actions within this understanding empowers Native Hawaiians in the diaspora to see that their actions toward ea constitute a sovereign embodiment. Thus, engaging in a praxis of kuleana that acknowledges responsibilities to land held by other Native communities is a recognition of our interdependence and is one of the many expressions of ea.

Along with protocol and the interdependence acknowledged through its demonstration, self-defining our groups and the rights to do so is also a direct expression of ea. As Native Hawaiian teacher and community activist 'Īmai Winchester explains:

> Ea, I think, is the full realization that our purpose here is greater than owning material wealth, that our purpose needs to be aligned with aloha, with pono, with mālama 'āina, with finding some sort of balance in our interactions between ourselves and nature, between ourselves and one another.... The push toward sovereignty and independence is as much about interdependence and the realization of it. The emphasis that we place on individual success is going to start to become overshadowed by the need for interdependent cooperation (as cited in Goodyear-Ka'ōpua, 2016, p. 11).

In this way, Winchester articulates ea as interdependence with land and as cooperation between people. Instead of pursuing access to individual rights, Native Hawaiians in the diaspora need to engage in a form of interdependence, which is crucial to ea. With this understanding, we can actively work against the logics of individual rights, which are the backbone of settler individualism. Failing to do so, we advance the logics and structures of Native erasure and fail to engage in protocol and praxis that are integral to the maintenance of Native Hawaiian culture and the betterment of the lāhui.

Trans-Indigenous recognitions, including the treaty making between Ka Lāhui Hawai'i and the Juaneño Band of Mission Indians, Acjachemen Nation, demonstrate how we can align our aho, or cords, together to have greater ropes of resistance (Goodyear-Ka'ōpua, 2016, p. 6). As Maori scholar Linda Tuhiwai Smith stated:

> What is more important than what alternatives indigenous peoples offer the world is what alternatives indigenous people offer each other. To be able to share, to have something worth sharing, gives dignity to the giver. To accept a gift and to reciprocate gives dignity to the receiver. To create something new through that process of sharing is to recreate the old, to reconnect relationships and to recreate our humanness. (Smith, 1999, p. 105)

Trans-Indigenous recognitions provide the process that allows us to honor our ancestors by working with another community in our shared sense of responsibility to ensure our survival not only as an individual group, but also as a larger community that wants to ensure life for the next generations. Although these relationships are not new[27] or without conflict, Native Hawaiian scholar David Chang notes that, "These acts of identifying likeness serve as important reminders to us that we are engaged in a very old conversation when we talk about the notion of global indigeneity" (Chang, 2016, p. 248). Therefore, the continuance of this work reaffirms who we are as Indigenous people and provides better clarification to the question posed by Osorio at the beginning of this article, asking, "Who the hell are we?" (as cited in Goodyear-Kaʻōpua, 2016, p. 6).

From Mauna Kea to Oak Flats, Shasta River, and Standing Rock, Indigenous people continue to form trans-Indigenous recognitions for their collective survivance and in resistance to settler states. These recognitions embody acts of Indigenous refusal and resurgence. Additionally, these actions reaffirm individual self-determining Native communities while building larger trans-Indigenous communities and can provide models for decolonization. First Nations scholar Leanne Simpson reminds us that although these examples of Indigenous resurgence may last only for short periods of time, they can give us "a glimpse of a decolonized contemporary reality; it is a mirroring of what we can become" (Simpson, 2011, p. 98). Native Hawaiians and the Acjachemen involved in the treaty collaborated to build collective strategies for survivance. These relationships exemplify Indigenous self-governance and inherent responsibilities to land that may never be acknowledged by colonial structures of federal recognition. For Native Hawaiians, this praxis can reaffirm the core values that reinforce the life and land of the lāhui.

Responding to Goodyear-Kaʻōpua's call to add to the growing body of work that comprises Native Hawaiian studies, I humbly offer my own reflections as a Kanaka ʻŌiwi who is living and working in the diaspora. As Goodyear-Kaʻōpua notes, "Like our ʻāina we are a dynamic and changing people, and thus Hawaiian studies

practitioners continue to explore what it means to be ʻŌiwi because the answers are never complete. This tension—between powerfully asserting who we are against forces that work toward our extinction and holding open space to acknowledge that who we are is not a closed question—animates Hawaiian studies scholarship" (Goodyear-Kaʻōpua, 2016, p. 6).

Thus, for Hawaiians in the diaspora, the concern with maintaining ourselves as Kanaka ʻŌiwi is entwined with the political responsibility of maintaining a cultural grounding that is intimately tied to our survivance. The treaty between Ka Lāhui Hawaiʻi and the Juaneño Band of Mission Indians not only demonstrates the importance of continuing self-determining practices outside of Hawaiʻi, but also provides a model for diasporic Hawaiians to reaffirm ourselves by recognizing our Indigenous hosts. The Treaty of Friendship and Mutual Recognition between the Acjachemen and Ka Lāhui Hawaiʻi is just one example, and there are many others waiting to be documented or (re)told. As settler colonialism continues to displace Natives from their homelands, this is also an active call for diasporic Indigenous people to recognize their local Native host(s). This recognition is one way to honor kūpuna knowledge and directly disrupt logics and systems that are meant to continually erase Indigenous people.[28] Honoring this responsibility is to engage in acts of sovereign embodiment. Reminding us of this responsibility, Carolyn Kualiʻi, one of the main architects of the treaty, says, "All Hawaiians should be mindful of where they are. All have a kuleana to be respectful, especially those who are visitors to somewhere else" (personal communication, March 2015). For Kanaka ʻŌiwi this involves a larger conception of identity that recognizes that since we are made up of our kūpuna, our ancestors, our indigeneity is always embodied, wherever we go.

REFERENCES

Chang, D. A. (2016). *The world and all the things upon it: Native Hawaiian geographies of exploration.* Minneapolis, MN: University of Minnesota Press.

Coffman C. (2011). *The Juaneño-Acjachema: Exploring identity and the reproduction of culture.* Dubuque, IA: Kendall Hunt Publishing.

Deloria, V., Jr. (1985). *Behind the trail of broken treaties: An Indian declaration of independence.* Austin, TX: University of Texas Press.

Dudley, M. K., & Agard, K. K. (1993). *A call for Hawaiian sovereignty.* Waipahu, HI: Nā Kāne o ka Malo Press.

Goodyear-Kaʻōpua, N. (2016). Reproducing the ropes of resistance: Hawaiian studies methodologies. In K.-A. R. K. N. Oliveira & E. K. Wright (Eds.). *Kanaka ʻŌiwi methodologies: Moʻolelo and metaphor* (pp. 1–29). Honolulu, HI: Hawaiʻinuiākea School of Hawaiian Knowledge, University of Hawaiʻi Press.

Government of Ka Lāhui Hawaiʻi. (1994). *Ka Lāhui Hawaiʻi platform on the four arenas of sovereignty.* Hilo, Hawaiʻi: Author. Used with the permission and written consent of Mililani Trask.

Johnston-Dodds, K. (2002). *Early California laws and policies related to California Indians: Prepared at the request of Senator John L. Burton, president pro tempore.* Sacramento, CA: California Research Bureau, California State Library. Retrieved from http://tuleyome.org/wp-content/uploads/2016/05/Early-California-Laws_Johnston-Dodds.pdf

Ka Lāhui Hawaiʻi Constitution. (1994). *Hoʻokupu a Ka Lāhui Hawaiʻi, the Ka Lāhui master plan.* Hilo, HI: Author. Used with the permission and written consent of Mililani Trask.

Lepule, T., & Kwoh, S. (2014). *A community of contrasts: Native Hawaiian and Pacific Islanders in the United States of America, 2014.* Los Angeles, CA: Empowering Pacific Islander Communities.

Margolin, M. (1992). Hawaiian connections. *News from Native California, 6*(3), 33.

Meyer, M. A. *Hoʻoulu: Our time of becoming.* Honolulu, HI: ʻAi Pōhaku Press.

Miranda, D. A. (2013). *Bad Indians: A tribal memoir.* Berkeley, CA: Heyday Books.

Office of Hawaiian Affairs (2013). Native Hawaiian population by region in the United States: 1990, 2000, 2010. [table 1.19]. *Native Hawaiian Data Book*. Honolulu, HI: Author. Retrieved from http://www.ohadatabook.com/T01-19-13.pdf

Pacheco, A. M. K. (2009). Past, present, and politics: A look at the Hawaiian sovereignty movement. *Intersections, 10*(1), 341–387. Retrieved from https://depts.washington.edu/chid/intersections_Winter_2009/Amanda_Mae_Kahealani_Pacheco_The_Hawaiian_Sovereignty_Movement.pdf

Sepulveda, C. (2018). Our sacred waters: Theorizing *kuuyam* as a decolonial possibility. *Decolonization: Indigeneity, Education & Society, 7*(1), 40–58.

Simpson, L. B. (2011). *Dancing on our turtle's back: Stories of Nishnaabeg re-creation, resurgence and a new emergence*. Winnipeg, Canada: Arbeiter Ring Publishing.

Smith, L. T. (1999). *Decolonizing methodologies: Research and indigenous peoples*. London, England: Zed Books.

Trask, H. (2000a). Settlers of color and "immigrant" hegemony: "Locals" in Hawai'i. *Amerasia Journal, 26*(2), 1–24.

Trask, H. (2000b). The case for Hawaiian sovereignty and Ka Lāhui Hawai'i. *Policy Sciences, 33*(3), 375–385.

US Department of the Interior, Indian Affairs (2011). Final determination against acknowledgment of the Juaneño Band of Mission Indians. Washington, DC: Author. Retrieved from https://www.bia.gov/sites/bia.gov/files/assets/as-ia/ofa/petition/084B_juajbb_CA/084b_fd.pdf

Wong-Wilson, N. N. (2005). A conversation with Mililani Trask. *The Contemporary Pacific, 17*(1), 142–156. Retrieved from https://scholarspace.manoa.hawaii.edu/bitstream/10125/13839/1/v17n1-142-156-dialogue.pdf

ABOUT THE AUTHOR

Kēhaulani Vaughn is an assistant professor of education, culture, and society and the Pacific Island Studies Initiative at the University of Utah. Vaughn received her doctorate in ethnic studies from the University of California–Riverside and graduate degrees in Asian American studies and education from UCLA, with a graduate concentration in American Indian studies. Her research explores trans-Indigenous recognitions between Native Hawaiians living in California and federally unrecognized California Indian tribes. In addition to her research, she is deeply invested in community engagement and is a founding board member of Empowering Pacific Islander Communities (EPIC) and the Saturday Tongan Education Program (STEP) at the Claremont Colleges.

NOTES

1. Acjachemen can be spelled multiple ways, including Acjachemem. I choose to use Acjachemen because it was the spelling used in the treaty.

2. Kualiʻi built numerous relationships in California Indian Country. In my interview with her, she described her work to connect Native Hawaiians and California Indian Country as part of her kuleana. Although she acknowledges that she is not the first or only one to do so, she knows that her work has built lasting relationships.

3. Ka Lāhui Hawaiʻi signed several treaties with other Indigenous nations. These nations include but are not limited to the Confederation of the Tlingit Nation of Canada, the Kwakiutl Band, and the Black Hills Sioux.

4. The term "host" is used throughout this article to identify the Native people of a specific place. The term "guests" refers to all other people besides the Indigenous people of the area. My interviewees utilized these terms, and I honor their nomenclature.

5. Indian, Native, and Indigenous are used interchangeably throughout this article.

6. ʻĀina means land, but also means that which feeds. This feeding can be both physical and spiritual nourishment.

7. Native Hawaiian kūpuna have been traveling for generations. Like other Pacific Islanders, Native Hawaiians view the oceans as highways connecting islands to one another. Some

consider Turtle Island (i.e., North America) part of the history of travel between Indigenous communities. However, Native Hawaiians and other Indigenous communities are disproportionately being pushed out of their homelands due to settler colonialism and are unable to return due to various modalities of Native erasure.

8.   Ea has complex meanings in the Hawaiian language, as will be highlighted later in this article. Here it is used to refer to sovereignty and self-determination.

9.   Native studies, from my perspective, is an inclusive field that includes Native American studies, Hawaiian studies, etc.

10. One origin story, which they have in common with the nearby Luiseño people, discusses a time when there were several periods of only darkness and light until figures came into being. I choose not to publish the Acjachemen creation story to honor the fact that it is sacred.

11. Importantly, Junípero Serra was canonized by the Catholic Church in September 2015 despite numerous protests by many Indigenous communities, with the most notable objections coming from California Indian tribes. The Mission of San Juan Capistrano was abandoned by the Franciscans due to an Indian attack at the Mission in San Diego. However, in 1776 they re-established the mission and, in 1778, rebuilt it where it is currently located.

12. The current fourth-grade history curriculum in California has a section on the mission period. Most fourth-graders visit a nearby mission and are usually assigned to construct and build a replica of that mission. The history taught of this period is usually one of California Indians "becoming" civilized through the aid of Franciscan monks and the missions. Seldom is there any discussion of the negative effects on California Indians.

13. These tribes include the Chumash of Malibu, the Tongva of Los Angeles, and the San Luis Rey Luiseños.

14. San Juan Capistrano is the location of Mission San Juan Capistrano, the tribal office, and the Blas Aguilar Adobe Museum and Acjachemen Cultural Center. Thus, San Juan Capistrano continues to function as the cultural, political, and spiritual gathering place for the Acjachemen Nation, with annual events such as Swallows Day, the Swallows Day Parade, and Mission Days.

15. Some of the tribal members I interviewed discussed the factions that were produced via the process of federal recognition by the Juaneño bands that applied in the 1990s–2000s.

16. This can be seen through the Juaneño members' opposition to a toll road being built directly through a historic village and sacred site area. They also continue to engage in culture and ceremony.

17. During this time, there were eight thousand Native Hawaiian citizens of Ka Lāhui Hawai'i out of a membership of over twenty-three thousand. Non-natives could join Ka Lāhui Hawai'i and were encouraged to participate in debates and conventions, but they could not vote or hold office because the central goal was to achieve self-determination for Native Hawaiians.

18. The unicameral structure of governance moves away from a one-person, one-vote model and allows for each of the islands to have political leadership and representation with an equal number of votes, regardless of population size.

19. Native Americans often reference North America as Turtle Island, a name stemming from an Ojibwe creation story of the continent. Thus, naming the diasporic Native Hawaiian caucus as Moku Honu refers to and recognizes the Native people of Turtle Island as much as it invokes Native Hawaiian protocols for place, community, and reciprocity.

20. Despite Ka Lāhui Hawai'i's eventual adoption of a process for representation and voting for Native Hawaiian citizens residing in the diaspora, this does not equate to a full incorporation of diasporic Hawaiians. Those in the diaspora had to advocate for this, and I discourage a romanticized view of this inclusion.

21. Martin Margolin is the founder and longtime executive director of Heyday Books.

22. The article describes the Tongva of Los Angeles and the nearby Acjachemen of Orange County.

23. This ceremony included the drinking of Native Hawaiian 'awa and traditional song and dance next to the ocean, which was described by several participants as spiritual. The drinking of 'awa marks the ceremonial nature of the occasion and is usually done with accompanying protocol. 'Awa is a ceremonial drink found throughout the Pacific. Now consumed for social consumption, it was previously restricted to ceremonial occasions.

24. In individual interviews with L. Frank Manriquez and Carolyn Kuali'i, both discussed seeing the whale on the beach and its significance.

25. Angela Mooney-D'Arcy is a Native legal scholar heavily involved in protecting cultural sites. She currently teaches at the University of California–Riverside in the Ethnic Studies department.

26.   Wyatt Belardes is a Juaneño youth leader and grandson of the late David Belardes, who was tribal chief at the time of the treaty signing with Ka Lāhui Hawaiʻi.

27.   Native Hawaiian scholar David Chang notes that there were various encounters and relations between Indians and Hawaiians starting from the early eighteenth century.

28.   Since we have an increasing number of Native Hawaiians living in the diaspora, we also have an increasing number of people being buried outside of the homeland. Kupuna knowledge includes honoring and respecting iwi kūpuna—ancestral remains. Honoring and respecting iwi kūpuna who are planted/buried outside of the homeland requires building relationships with the genealogical caretakers of the land.

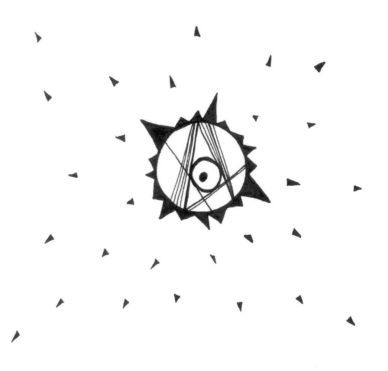

Solidarity Speaks: Aotearoa Citizen Alleges War Crimes in Hawai'i

MERA PENEHIRA

Although I have been a frequent and grateful visitor to the ancestral islands of Hawai'i over the last two decades, it wasn't until early 2015 that I became fully cognizant that these were lands and waters under an illegal occupation by the US government since the Spanish-American War. The 1851 treaty between the Hawaiian Kingdom and the British Crown, as well as our connection as peoples of the Pacific, culminates a significant relationship between Aotearoa (New Zealand) citizens and Hawai'i. As a wahine Māori and citizen of Aotearoa, I felt compelled to make a stand in solidarity with our tuakana of Hawai'i in calling for an end to the continued illegal occupation of these ancestral lands. This article presents a media release and the official complaint I filed with the attorney general of Aotearoa alleging war crimes by the illegal occupiers of Hawai'i, the US government. It concludes with the woefully inadequate response from the government of Aotearoa.

CORRESPONDENCE MAY BE SENT TO:
Mera Penehira
School of Indigenous Graduate Studies
Te Whare Wānanga o Awanuiārangi
Email: Mera.penehira@wananga.ac.nz

Hūlili: Multidisciplinary Research on Hawaiian Well-Being, Vol. 11, No. 1
Copyright © 2019 by Kamehameha Schools

Background and Introduction

There is heightened momentum in the political struggle and activism being undertaken by Native and Indigenous academics in our academic institutions and communities (Smith, 2007; Pihama, 2005; Penehira, 2011). In Hawaiʻi, a "growing body of historical work by a new generation of Native Hawaiian scholars" prompted a well-known historian to change the subtitle of his book from *The Story of America's Annexation of the Nation of Hawaiʻi* to *The History of the American Occupation of Hawaiʻi*. Coffman wrote, "In the history of Hawaiʻi, the might of the United States does not make it right" (Coffman, 2016, p. xvi).

Many Native and Indigenous academics assert that it is not acceptable simply to theorize, research, and write about the issues of colonization, historical trauma, and the atrocities being conducted on our lands and in our waters. A kaupapa Māori approach demands theory, research, *and* action (G. H. Smith, 2000; L. T. Smith, 1999; Pihama, 2005). We must make and take opportunities to stand alongside our whānau, hapū, iwi, and communities (Mikaere, 2003; Mutu, 2011). We follow a long line of activists, protestors, and protectors who have demonstrated the pressing need for this work to continue and have shown us how to conduct ourselves with power, strength, and dignity. Ka whawhai tonu tātou! Ake! Ake! Ake! We will continue the struggle! Always! Always! Always!

Te Whare Pora Hou is a Māori and Pacific women's political advocacy collective in Aotearoa. The following is a copy of the media communication released by Te Whare Pora Hou on July 28, 2015.

Media Release

Allegations of War Crimes against New Zealand Citizen in Hawaiʻi

"Dr Mera Lee-Penehira, from the University of Auckland, has this week lodged a criminal complaint with Attorney General Christopher Finlayson QC, under the International Crimes and International Criminal Court Act 2000.

"The U.S. unilaterally seized the islands of Hawaiʻi back in 1898 for military interests during the Spanish-American War, and has remained there as an illegal occupier ever since. This is about acknowledging and righting the wrongdoings of the U.S. in Hawaiʻi," says Dr Lee-Penehira.
A recent visit from leading political scientist Dr Keanu Sai of the University of Hawaiʻi, who met with tribal and political leaders, has brought to the fore the illegal occupation of Hawaiʻi, and

the implications for New Zealand. He states that, "In 2001, the Permanent Court of Arbitration at The Hague, acknowledged that, in the nineteenth century the Hawaiian Kingdom existed as an independent State recognized as such by the United States of America, the United Kingdom and various other States. By virtue of the 1851 treaty between the Hawaiian Kingdom and the British Crown, as well as our connection as peoples of the Pacific, New Zealand citizens have a special relationship with Hawai'i."

Dr Lee-Penehira has been to Hawai'i on a number of occasions in recent years, and last month visited Mauna a Wākea, a sacred site at the centre of contention between the U.S. government and Native Hawaiians. The planned construction of the world's largest telescope, the TMT project, on this sacred site, has received much media attention of late and many New Zealand citizens are concerned about this issue.

Marama Davidson, member of Maori and Pacific women's political advocacy group Te Whare Pora Hou, states, "Protectors of Mauna a Wākea have been occupying the sacred ancestral mountain on the island of Hawai'i for over 120 days now, to prevent the construction of this telescope. We stand in solidarity with the protectors in efforts to stop this destruction. This is a direct attack on the physical, spiritual and cultural integrity of the maunga, and the wellbeing of both the environment and people."

In lodging the complaint Dr Lee-Penehira is invoking her right as a New Zealand citizen under the 1851 treaty. "We need to challenge everything the U.S. government does in Hawai'i, because on the basis of law, it is quite simply wrong. The historical documentation is clear, that the Hawaiian Kingdom continues to exist under an illegal occupation by the U.S. and that the laws of occupation must be complied with. As a victim of war crimes committed in Hawai'i, this cannot be allowed to continue to take place with impunity."

The alleged war crimes at the centre of the complaint include both unlawful taxation by the State of Hawai'i, and the destruction of property by the State of Hawai'i for allowing the construction of telescopes on the summit of Mauna a Wākea.

Ms Davidson supports the complaint, saying, "These allegations of war crimes committed in Hawai'i are very serious, and if true will have a profound effect on all New Zealanders as well as the Trans Pacific Partnership negotiations that are ironically taking place this week in Hawai'i. It is now incumbent on New Zealand authorities to either prove that the Hawaiian Kingdom does not exist under international law and that there is no Hawaiian-British treaty, or initiate a criminal investigation into the allegations of war crimes committed against a New Zealand citizen."

War Crimes Complaint

The following is a copy of the criminal complaint I filed with the attorney general of Aotearoa/New Zealand, alleging war crimes committed in the islands of Hawai'i against me as a New Zealand citizen. I am grateful for the expert advice and assistance provided by political scientist Dr. Keanu Sai in compiling the complaint. This letter was submitted on July 24, 2015, and highlights the continued illegal occupation of Hawai'i by the United States.

Hon Christopher Finlayson QC
Attorney General
Crown Law Office
Level 3
Justice Centre
19 Aitken Street
Wellington, 6011
New Zealand

Re: Criminal Complaint under Section 8(b) and 11(2)(b) of the *International Crimes and International Criminal Court Act* 2000 arising from war crimes committed in the Hawaiian Islands against Dr Mera Lee-Penehira, a New Zealand citizen

Dear Hon Christopher Finlayson QC:

I am a New Zealand citizen who is invoking my right under the 1851 Treaty of Friendship, Commerce and Navigation between the Hawaiian Kingdom and the British Crown, which has not been cancelled or voided,[1] during my three visits of the Hawaiian Islands from 16–28 May 2014, 13–19 April 2015, and 29 May to 6 June 2015. Attached is a copy of my passport. Article VIII provides:

---

1. David Keanu Sai, War Crimes Report: International Armed Conflict and the Commission of War Crimes in the Hawaiian Islands, para. 1.9 & 9.9, Appendix III (July 18, 2015).

"British subjects in the Hawaiian Islands shall be at liberty to buy from and to sell to whom they like, without being restrained or prejudiced by any monopoly, contract, or exclusive privilege of sale or purchase whatever; and absolute freedom shall be allowed in all cases, to the buyer and seller, to bargain and fix the price of any goods, wares, or merchandise, imported into, or exported from, the Hawaiian Islands, as they shall see good; observing the laws and established customs of those Islands. The same privileges shall be enjoyed in the dominions of Her Britannic Majesty, by Hawaiian subjects, under the same conditions.

The subjects of either of the contracting parties, in the territories of the other, shall receive and enjoy full and perfect protection for their persons and property, and shall have free and open access to the courts of justice in the said countries, respectively, for the prosecution and defense of their just rights; and they shall be at liberty to employ in all causes, the advocates, attorneys, or agents, of whatever description, whom they may think proper; and they shall enjoy in this respect, the same rights and privileges as native subjects."

Unbeknownst to me that Hawai'i has been under an illegal and prolonged occupation by the United States of America since the Spanish-American War, the war crime of pillaging was committed against me through revenues collected by the so-called government of the State of Hawai'i under the guise of taxation. Therefore, I am filing this complaint in accordance with New Zealand law and the *International Crimes and International Criminal Court Act* 2000. *Te Karere TVNZ* news provided coverage of Hawai'i's illegal occupation by the United States of America on 19 July 2015, when they interviewed Dr Keanu Sai, a Hawai'i political scientist who is a recognized expert in the legal and political history of Hawai'i, and myself.[2] I am also a faculty of education at the University of Auckland. I've also requested Dr Sai to draft a *War Crimes Report: International Armed Conflict and the Commission of War Crimes in Hawaiian Islands,* which covers the broader context of Hawai'i's occupation. Therefore, I will be incorporating, as though fully set forth in this complaint, the information and evidence provided in his report. I would also like to add that this information was brought to the attention of Minister Te Ururoa Flavell, who graciously met with Dr Sai and me at the Hotel Novotel Auckland Airport on the evening of 15 July 2015.

This complaint is filed with the Office of the Attorney General, because your office has the capacity of exercising passive personality jurisdiction under Section 7A(2A)(c)(i) of the *Crimes Act*

---

2.   Te Karere TVNZ, "Academic places spotlight on Hawaiian Sovereignty," July 19, 2015, available at https://www.youtube.com/watch?v=7JoErl1xrmM

1961 since the following requirements have been met regarding crimes committed abroad where the victim is a New Zealand citizen. *First*, I am a New Zealand citizen; *second*, the war crime of pillaging is punishable under both New Zealand law and international humanitarian law, being the law applicable to the Hawaiian Islands since they are belligerently occupied by the United States; *third*, the offense allows for extradition under the 1970 United States/New Zealand Extradition Treaty and Section 15 of the *Extradition Act* 1999 because war crimes are not "of a political character," and therefore request for extradition is not based on "political opinions"; and, *fourth*, the alleged perpetrators have not been convicted or acquitted of the crimes committed against me. Accordingly, the New Zealand authorities are under a duty and obligation to exercise passive personality jurisdiction in prosecuting this case in accordance with Section 11(2)(b), *International Crimes and International Criminal Court Act* 2000, as hereinafter explained.

By this complaint I am expressly declaring that I have suffered grave harm and respectfully demand that your office initiate an immediate investigation into the private organization called the State of Hawai'i[3] for the war crime of pillaging under the guise of taxation in accordance with 11(2)(b) of the *International Crimes and International Criminal Court Act* 2000 and fraud. The so-called taxes were collected under what the State of Hawai'i calls a General Excise Tax (GET) at 4.712% while on the island of O'ahu that includes a 0.546% "County Tax" and 4.166% on the other islands,[4] and a Transient Accommodations Tax, also called a Hotel Room Tax, at 9.25%.[5] The County Tax is deposited with the City and County of Honolulu, Island of O'ahu.

When a car is rented at the State of Hawai'i's Honolulu International Airport, there is a State of Hawai'i GET at 4.712%, a Highway Surcharge at $3.00 a day, a Vehicle Registration fee between $0.35 and $1.45 a day, and an Airport Concession Recovery Tax at 11.1%. Except for the GET, the revenues collected for rental cars are deposited with the State of Hawai'i Department of Transportation—Highway and Airport Divisions. Although the GET is levied on businesses for doing business in Hawai'i, the State of Hawai'i allows these businesses to pass those extra taxes on to the consumer of all goods in Hawai'i.[6]

Since 2000, I traveled to Hawai'i on three occasions in my capacity as a researcher and faculty member at the University of Auckland as well as in my private capacity.

3.   See Dr Sai's Report, para. 12.1–12.7.
4.   *Department of Taxation, State of Hawai'i, Annual Report 2013–2014*, p. 3 (Nov. 25, 2014).
5.   Id., p. 9.
6.   Honolulu Civil Beat, "Hawai'i General Excise and Use Tax," available at http://www.civilbeat.com/topics/hawaii-general-excise-and-use-tax/

- 29 May to 6 June 2015: Research Trip (Meetings to discuss Maori and Indigenous Doctoral programme and its potential relevance in Hawai'i, visiting friends). Accommodation (University of Auckland funded) at Outrigger Reef Hotel Waikīkī for duration; airfares x 2 return to Hawai'i Island; 3 day rental car; usual food and dining purchases for duration; minor gift purchases including clothing, paddle bits and pieces, books and child sweet treats, estimated expenditure of U.S. $5,000.

- 13–19 April 2015: Research Trip (Meetings with various academics and community people to discuss and scope potential research projects). Accommodation (University of Auckland funded) at Outrigger Beach Resort Waikīkī for duration; usual food and dining purchases for duration; minor gift purchases including clothing, paddle bits and pieces, books and child sweet treats, estimated expenditure of U.S. $6,500.

- 16–28 May 2014: Conference Trip "World Indigenous Peoples Conference on Education (WIPCE) 2014." Accommodation (University of Auckland funded) at Aston Waikīkī Hotel for duration; Conference registration WIPCE Honolulu; usual food and dining purchases for duration; minor gift purchases including clothing, new paddle and bits and pieces, and books, estimated expenditure of U.S. $7,000.

Attached to this complaint are credit card purchases while I was in Hawai'i, which include bookings/invoices showing amounts and with my name, as well as a copy of the State of Hawai'i Annual Report of Taxation (2013–2014), which is evidence of the crime of pillaging at a colossal scale.[7] I am also providing evidence of criminal fraud committed against my partner and me when we acquired a marriage license from the State of Hawai'i. We paid for a marriage ceremony held at Waimānalo Beach, Island of O'ahu, and a party on June 2, 2015. The following day, after paying $60.00 to the State of Hawai'i Department of Health, we received a marriage certificate, a copy of which I am attaching to this complaint. Being that the organization of the State of Hawai'i is not a government de jure nor de facto, but rather an Armed Force as defined under the laws and customs of war, its collection of $60.00 is also considered pillaging and its marriage certificate fraudulent. Because of this fraud my partner and I are applying for a marriage license from the New Zealand government.

———————▶

7.   Id., para. 12.12–12.13.

253

Additionally, I am reporting the war crimes of destruction of property by the State of Hawai'i for allowing the construction of telescopes on the summit of Mauna Kea, which includes the proposed construction of the TMT telescope. I am attaching a cease and desist letter, dated April 16, 2015, provided to TMT International Observatory, LLC, by attorney Dexter Ka'iama, Esq., which fully elucidates the circumstances of the war crime. In this reporting, I am not claiming to be a victim, but merely reporting the war crime of destruction of property to the proper authorities because under New Zealand law and being a member of the International Criminal Court's Rome Statute, the Attorney General has the authority to prosecute war crimes committed abroad under universal jurisdiction.

Because I am unable to "have free and open access to the courts of justice [of the Hawaiian Kingdom] . . . for the prosecution and defense of [my] just rights" (Art. VIII, Hawaiian/British Treaty) because of the Armed Force—State of Hawai'i's effective control of Hawaiian territory, I am filing this complaint with my country's government. Therefore, I am requesting prosecution of the following named individuals responsible for the pillaging of my personal property and criminal fraud that has rendered my marriage license worthless. I am also seeking restitution. The individuals include, but are not limited to, former State of Hawai'i Governor Neil Abercrombie, present State of Hawai'i Governor David Ige, former and present Lieutenant Governor Shan Tsutsui, Director of Taxation Frederick D. Pablo, Acting Deputy Director of Taxation Ted S. Shirashi, Director of Transportation Ford Fuchigami, and City and County of Honolulu Mayor Kirk Caldwell.

I represent all citizens of New Zealand who live in Hawai'i, travelled through Hawai'i, or have done business in Hawai'i, because we all have suffered the same, if not, similar harm done by the Armed Force—State of Hawai'i. However, should my government provide clear and conclusive evidence that the Hawaiian Kingdom does not exist under international law and that the 1851 Hawaiian/British Treaty has been voided, please disregard this complaint and accept my apologies for the misunderstanding. But if it is unable to provide clear and conclusive evidence to the contrary, I should expect the Attorney General and the respected office you represent to expeditiously commence criminal proceedings in this matter.

Should you require further information or elaborations on the materials submitted, please do not hesitate to contact me by email at [removed for privacy].

Sincerely,

Dr Mera Lee-Penehira

Ake! Ake! Ake! The Ongoing Struggle!

The Crown Law Office responded to my letter in August 2015. Although the response was woefully inadequate, we celebrated the achievement of having engaged the crown in a conversation at this level concerning the illegal occupation of Hawai'i by the United States government!

In short, the crown's one-page response declined to initiate a criminal investigation, stating that the Hawaiian Kingdom ceased to exist and that its 1851 Hawaiian-British Treaty was voided on August 12, 1898. However, the office provided no evidence to substantiate that conclusion, other than directing me to a government website. Moreover, they stated, "To the extent the allegations of unlawful conduct are based upon the assertion that Hawai'i is under an illegal occupation by the United States of America, the underlying claim is incorrect."

In my correspondence back to the crown, I advised them that such a response completely ignored the information provided in the report (146 pages) of political scientist Dr. Keanu Sai, which accompanied my complaint. I further advised the crown that as a citizen of Aotearoa/New Zealand, I found their response to this serious matter very unsatisfactory.

My interaction with the Crown Law Office remains an important and unfinished struggle of particular significance. We cannot let our governments get away with anemic responses to serious allegations of war crimes and crimes against our ancestral lands. The degradation of sacred sites such as Mauna a Wākea cannot be allowed to continue. The pollution of the waters of Waikīkī—and indeed all of the islands—cannot be allowed to continue. Our strength as Native and Indigenous protectors of these lands and waters lies in our solidarity. Mouri whenua, mouri moana, mouri ora, mouri tangata! The life force of our lands and waters is indeed the life force and energy of ourselves!

REFERENCES

Coffman, T. (2016). *Nation within: The history of the American occupation of Hawai'i*. Durham, NC: Duke University Press.

Mikaere, A. (2003). *The balance destroyed: Consequences for Māori women of the colonisation of tikanga Māori*. Auckland, Aotearoa: University of Auckland, The International Research Institute for Māori and Indigenous Education.

Mutu, M. (2011). *The state of Māori rights*. Wellington, Aotearoa: Huia Publishers.

Penehira, M. (2011). *Mouri tū, Mouri moko, Mouri ora! Wellbeing strategies and Māori women with hepatitis C*. (Doctoral dissertation). University of Waikato, Aotearoa.

Pihama, L. (2005). Mana wahine theory: Creating space for Māori women's theories. In P. Leistyna (Ed.), *Cultural studies: From theory to action* (pp. 360–374). Malden, MA: Blackwell Publishing.

Smith, G. H. (2000). Protecting and respecting Indigenous knowledge. In M. Battiste (Ed.), *Reclaiming Indigenous voice and vision* (pp. 209–224). British Columbia, Canada: University of British Columbia Press.

Smith, L. T. (1999). *Decolonising methodologies: Research and indigenous peoples*. London, England: Zed Books.

Smith, L. T. (2007). The native and the neoliberal down under: Neoliberalism and "endangered authenticities." In M. de la Cadena & O. Starn (Eds.), *Indigenous experience today* (pp. 333–352). Oxford, England: Berg.

ABOUT THE AUTHOR

Associate professor Mera Penehira descends from the iwi of Ngāti Raukawa, Rangitāne, and Ngaiterangi. Mera is a mother, academic, and active(ist) in her community. She completed her master's in educational psychology at the University of Auckland. Her doctoral research centered on Māori women's health and traditional healing practices, in particular moko, traditional Māori skin carving. Mera has a passion for Native and Indigenous women's well-being, the ocean, wa'a, and how these intersect. Mera is the International Indigenous Doctoral Programme coordinator in the School of Indigenous Graduate Studies at Te Whare Wānanga o Awanuiārangi, Aotearoa. She works with students in Hawai'i, Washington state, and Aotearoa.

Her Fiery Eyes of Indignation

WAYNE RICKS

It was August 1985. I first met Auntie Pi'ikea while working at Uncle Mua's house in Mā'ili.[1] I was building a hidden closet for Uncle Mua. He didn't tell me what it was for, but I could only guess it was for cocaine and money, since he was Wai'anae's big-time coke dealer. Carpenter skills like mine were in demand and, since I was a cocaine user, I fit in real good in the drug world. Auntie Pi'ikea slipped me a note telling me that she had work for me, and for me to call her.

CORRESPONDENCE MAY BE SENT TO:
Wayne Ricks
45-728 Ko Street, Kāne'ohe, Hawai'i 96744
Email: ricksj@hawaii.edu

Hūlili: Multidisciplinary Research on Hawaiian Well-Being, Vol. 11, No. 1

The next day I went to a pay phone, and I paged her beeper with the pay phone number. Two minutes later she called me and gave me instructions on how to get to her house up in Waiʻanae Valley. I drove up the valley, meandering all the way to the end of a dirt road to a small house, unfinished and unpainted. Auntie was there to greet me. She showed me around and explained what had happened. She had hired a carpenter to build her a small, one-bedroom house, and he took off with the money she paid him without finishing the job. She told me that kind of shit happens when you're working with addicts. She told me she checked me out, and Uncle Mua had vouched for me. He said I was dependable, mature, and trustworthy, and that I knew my shit when it came to construction.

SHE WAS FIERCELY PROUD AND DIDN'T WANT TO BE DEPENDENT ON ANYONE.

Auntie Piʻikea had a few projects she wanted completed in her tiny house so she could bring her two children home to stay. Her children had been staying at her brother's place temporarily while she finished construction on her home. I immediately began working on finishing her simple, no-frills house.

She had no running water, no bathroom, and no kitchen. She had temporary power from an extension cord from the neighbor's house. A friend had given her permission to build a dwelling on his property. She had no permits, just a dream of having a home of her own where she could live with her children—your basic American dream.

As I worked on her house, Auntie Piʻikea would confide in me as she got to know me. She explained that her father was a full-blooded Hawaiian, and he was on the waiting list for Hawaiian Homestead land. When he

died he was still waiting, and now that he was in the afterlife, she figured he was still waiting. The torch had been handed to her brother and her; they were still waiting for an award for a homestead. Her brother was married with three children and had a good-paying job as a heavy equipment operator. He was renting a house down behind Tamura Superette in Waiʻanae.

Auntie Piʻikea criticized her brother all the time, but I got the feeling it was because she hated the idea that she had to depend on him to house her kids. She was fiercely proud and didn't want to be dependent on anyone. She was a proud Hawaiian, and I could see that in her. She had high cheekbones, sunbaked brown skin, kinky black hair, and those fiery eyes of indignation with enough attitude to take on the whole world. She would pull no punches. She told it like it was, and she wouldn't take any shit from anyone. It didn't matter who you were, if she thought you were wrong, she would let you know. She was a hundred-and-ten-pound pit bull that would tear your limbs off if you wanted to scrap with her. She was absolutely tenacious.

During the week when welfare checks went out, Auntie Piʻikea's pager would beep off the hook. I'd hear her telling people to meet her at certain locations, and she would tell me she had to run errands and that she would be back. Yeah, Auntie Piʻikea was a drug dealer. We would get into conversations about why she dealt drugs. She told me she was on welfare, and she hated it. She didn't like being dependent on the government, but she had very little choice in the matter. The father of her children had split and didn't want anything to do with her or the kids. He was living somewhere, doing drugs, and wasting his life away. She was on her own, and it was difficult finding a job, especially for a single mom with two children. What jobs she did find would not help her out of the welfare trap. Any money she would earn would be just enough to pay for childcare, and then the government would take away her welfare, and then she would be in a deeper hole than she was now. She understood the vicious circle of the welfare game, and she hated it. She'd say, "Wayne, this welfare bullshit is fucked up. Those assholes don't want us to get ahead, they just want to keep us down."

Auntie Pi'ikea had specific rules to follow in dealing her drugs, and she was very strict about it. If you wanted drugs from her, you had to follow her rules or else you would end up sucking dirt and rocks. There was one rule she was adamant about: She would not take anyone's EBT card. If you came to her with food stamps to buy drugs, you'd get an earful. She would be livid and say, "You fucka, I told you no bring me food stamps! Dats for your kids. You betta feed them. I catch you no feeding dem, I going buss your ass!" By the time she was done with you, she would have torn you a new asshole.

Auntie Pi'ikea trusted me, and she was happy that I finished all her projects she needed done. She brought her children home, and they were so happy to be with their mom. Her house was not fancy. It was not even a functioning, standard, American-style home. But it was her home, and it was the best way she knew how to live.

Sometimes she asked if I would help her deliver stuff to town. Yeah, I started running drugs for Auntie Pi'ikea. She had me delivering to her māhū friends downtown. That was the first time I had interacted with māhū. They were friendly, respectful, and fun to hang out with. Auntie liked them because they were dependable and honest. They paid in full, and there was no bullshit. They were her best customers.

Eventually ice—crystal methamphetamine—was introduced and became the drug of choice for many local folks. In her entrepreneurial mode, Auntie Pi'ikea switched over to dealing ice. Here's the tricky thing about drugs: Some drugs affect you in ways you can handle, meaning you can function in society and keep your addiction a secret. Other drugs take you down hard. You end up doing things you never considered before, and you find yourself committing acts that would normally outrage you. Meth took Auntie down hard.

One day I showed up to pick up my deliveries, and I found Auntie Pi'ikea sitting in her barren house, sipping on some Crown Royal. Her eyes were black and sunken,

THAT WAS THE FIRST TIME I HAD INTERACTED WITH MĀHŪ. THEY WERE FRIENDLY, RESPECTFUL, AND FUN TO HANG OUT WITH.

indicating she had been up for days. She was slurring and babbling. She said, "Wayne, dey like kill me. I been up for days watching for dem. Dey wen kill my dogs. I found my dogs poisoned. I tink dey stay spraying poison through my walls. I like you seal up all da cracks in my house. I like you put raza wire around my roof so dey no can get up on da roof." I asked her, "Who's they?" She told me it was the government, trying to take her down. Auntie was experiencing delusional paranoia that comes with psychosis.

Back then, ice was the bomb. It came from the Korean yakuza. Ephedrine, the main ingredient, was readily available in Asia and was not a controlled substance at that time. A couple of hits, and you were literally up for days. As soon as you started to come down, another couple of hits, and you were back at it again, with all the pain gone away. Sleep deprivation is used as a form of torture, so you can only imagine what no sleep for days would do to your senses.

Auntie Pi'ikea told me there were no deliveries because she didn't re-up her supply. She had sent her kids back to her brother's house because she feared for their lives. Later, her kids told me they split because they couldn't handle not having a bathroom, and they had no privacy. They also said that their mom was acting weird, and they were scared for her. I too was scared for her, because I'd always seen her be so strong. I had grown close to her, and she was acting suicidal, so I stayed with her until she finally fell asleep. That night was the last time I saw her. Shortly after that I went to work for the Koreans. By that time I had gained a reputation that I could be trusted.

I admired Auntie Pi'ikea because she was a proud Hawaiian woman trying to make her way through a haole world. Right or wrong, dealing drugs was her way of trying to make a go of it. Along with dealing comes the money—and power—to control your environment. Auntie really needed that because she was lost in this world of America. She felt powerless without land that should have been hers in the first place, waiting on a ridiculously long list of homestead applicants. She was locked into the welfare trap, and while she vehemently opposed it, she needed it for her kids to survive. The long arm of colonialism has had far-reaching effects that continue to take their toll on the Hawaiian people.

I loved Auntie Pi'ikea.
And I will never forget her fiery eyes of indignation.

ABOUT THE AUTHOR

As a Vietnam veteran, Wayne Ricks was disillusioned after the war, and drugs became a huge part of his life as he self-medicated to escape his realities. He ended a forty-year run by serving time in a federal prison. After his release, he decided to continue his education to make something of himself. He didn't want his epitaph to read, "Here lies a wasted soul." He wrote this true story as evidence of how drugs had become intertwined in local lives, causing havoc and destruction for so many.

NOTE

1.   Aside from the author's name, the names used in this essay are pseudonyms to protect the identities of the people described.

Manuscript Guidelines

Hūlili welcomes manuscripts in English or ʻōlelo Hawaiʻi (Hawaiian language) from established and emerging scholars involved in research on Hawaiian well-being from diverse fields such as economics, education, family resources, government, health, history, natural resource management, psychology, religion, sociology, and so forth. We welcome manuscripts with an empirical focus as well as contributions at the cutting edge of theoretical debates and practice in these fields.

Submit manuscripts via email to hulilijournal@ksbe. edu, preferably as an MS Word document. Alternatively, manuscripts may be mailed to *Hūlili*, Kamehameha Publishing, Kamehameha Schools, 567 South King Street, Honolulu, Hawaiʻi 96813. Please send one hard copy along with an electronic file on CD. Any photos and charts should be submitted as 300 dpi tiff files.

Manuscripts typically must not be previously published or under consideration with another publication. The editorial board may make an exception for published materials that are central to the knowledge base of Hawaiian well-being and would otherwise have limited distribution.

While there is no page limit for articles, content should be concise and relevant.

Provide an abstract of approximately 120 words.

Provide a title page with the title of the article, author's name, author's affiliation, and suggested running head (less than fifty characters and spaces). The title page should also include the author's complete mailing address, email, and a brief bio.

Style consistent with the *Chicago Manual of Style* (17th Edition) for main text and the *Publication Manual of the American Psychological Association* (6th Edition) for references is preferred. Provide appropriate citations, including source citations, for all tables, charts, and figures. Figures and tables are to be numbered consecutively (with Arabic numerals) and should be cited in the text.

Include a complete and accurate reference list at the end of the manuscript. All references should be referred to in text by name and year.

Use endnotes only when necessary. Endnotes should be numbered consecutively using Arabic numerals and added at the end of the manuscript, after the references.

Use a Hawaiian typeface to display proper diacritical markings (ʻokina and kahakō) in all text, charts, endnotes, citations, and appendices.

Prior to submission, manuscripts should be checked for content, editorial style, and consistency in citations of references, tables, and figures. Manuscripts will be returned for revision at the discretion of the editors.

Authors submitting articles agree to allow Kamehameha Schools to publish the articles digitally as well as in print form. Kamehameha Schools fully honors the intellectual rights of all contributors.

KAMEHAMEHA SCHOOLS®